PRAISE FOR *LINUX MADE EASY* BY RICKFORD GRANT

"It's a comforting and super helpful read, and is a real confidence builder."
—FREE SOFTWARE MAGAZINE

"Rickford Grant captures an energy and enthusiasm for Xandros Linux (and Linux in general) that is clearly instructive, enlightening and enthusiastically energetic."
—KICKSTART NEWS

"As a teacher, Rickford has a natural talent for anticipating when and how a newbie will goof up. Rather than let you goof up, he gives you tips for avoiding the goof up in the first place."
—MAD PENGUIN

"A great way to get installed and get comfortable using Linux in everyday life."
—INFOWORLD

"Provides a useful safety net for readers who might be uncomfortable switching operating systems."
—NEWSFORGE

"Does a great job in a rather non-geeky way of showing how Linux is set up."
—MACCOMPANION

"For Windows users who want to explore Linux for everyday use, this is the most practical text I have seen."
—PC UPDATE

"What makes *Linux Made Easy* an especially valuable book is the friendly writing style combined with a large number of useful tips and tricks, many of which can be used on any distribution, not just Xandros."
—DISTROWATCH

"A fine choice if you're new to Linux."
—PC WORLD

"One of the most user friendly books on working with the Linux desktop around."
—READERS PREFERENCE

UBUNTU LINUX FOR NON-GEEKS

A Pain-Free, Project-Based, Get-Things-Done Guidebook

by Rickford Grant

**NO STARCH
PRESS**
San Francisco

Publisher: William Pollock
Associate Production Editor: Christina Samuell
Cover and Interior Design: Octopod Studios
Developmental Editor: David Brickner
Technical Reviewer: Carthik Sharma
Copyeditor: Megan Dunchak
Compositor: Riley Hoffman
Proofreader: Stephanie Provines
Indexer: Nancy Guenther

For information on book distributors or translations, please contact No Starch Press, Inc. directly:

No Starch Press, Inc.
555 De Haro Street, Suite 250, San Francisco, CA 94107
phone: 415.863.9900; fax: 415.863.9950; info@nostarch.com; www.nostarch.com

Library of Congress Cataloging-in-Publication Data

```
Grant, Rickford.
 Ubuntu Linux for non-geeks : a pain-free, project-based, get-things-done guidebook / Rickford Grant.
     p. cm.
 Includes index.
 ISBN 1-59327-118-2
1. Linux. 2. Operating systems (Computers)  I. Title.  QA76.76.O63.G7246 2006
005.4'32--dc22
                                                  2006015576
```

To Dr. James Howard Cremin, who, along with his family, gave me a place in which to find a sense of self during my early days of tumult and who managed to keep his cool when I blew out half the electricity in his house one Christmas morning. Sorry about that.

BRIEF CONTENTS

CONTENTS IN DETAIL

3
A NEW PLACE TO CALL HOME
Getting to Know the Desktop   **29**

4
MORE THAN WEBBED FEET
The Internet, Linux Style   **47**

5
ROUNDING OUT THE BIRD
Downloading, Installing, and Updating Programs the Easy Way   **65**

6
A TIDY NEST
File and Disk Handling in Ubuntu   **77**

7
DRESSING UP THE BIRD
Customizing the Look and Feel of Your System   97

8
SIMPLE KITTEN WAYS
Getting to Know the Linux Terminal and Command Line   121

10
GUTENBIRD
Setting Up and Using Your Printer and Scanner   169

11
FONT FEATHERED FRENZY
Adding New Fonts to Your System   183

12
POLYGLOT PENGUINS
Linux Speaks Your Language   195

13
PENGUINS BACK AT WORK
Getting Down to Business in Linux   205

14
BRUSH-WIELDING PENGUINS
Linux Does Art   219

16
PLUGGIN' IN THE PENGUIN
Ubuntu and Your iPod
265

17
COUCH PENGUINS
Video and DVD Playback in Ubuntu
281

18
DEFENDING THE NEST
Security
293

A
UBUNTU DESKTOP CDs FOR AMD64 AND
POWERPC USERS   303

B
CHECKING THE INTEGRITY OF DOWNLOADED ISOs   307

C
RESOURCES   313

INDEX   317

ACKNOWLEDGMENTS

There are a good number of people who deserve thanks for the help and support they provided either while or before this book was written, and there are still others whose help will come after the book is released. I would like to acknowledge all of them now.

Starting with my family, I'd like to thank Sumire, as always, for her support and encouragement throughout the project. The same thanks go to my mother, Dixie Angelina Burckel-Testa, who helped out with the initial proofreading of my earlier manuscripts and always lends a hand when she can. Thanks go out again to my auntie and uncle, Danica Lucia and David Zollars, for their continuous support and help (and for getting me into this book-writing business in the first place); and to round out the clan, thanks are due to my cousin and friend, Stephanie Garrabrant-Sierra, who tries to keep me on track whenever I am on the verge (or in the midst) of stumbling.

In the production of any book, editors are so very important, and I would like to thank my editor, David Brickner, who was, in addition to being full of good ideas for this book, a whole lot of fun to work with; Carthik Sharma, the technical editor, who kept everything I wrote by the book and pointed out a few easier ways of going about things (check out his blog, by the way, at http://ubuntu.wordpress.com); Megan Dunchak, who had the unenviable task of being the copyeditor for this what's-a-publisher's-template author—

and is cool enough to understand the value of a good D cell battery; and Riley Hoffman, who took a whole jumble of files, images, changes, and more changes and laid it all out, thus turning it into . . . well, a book.

Of course, as the folks at No Starch Press were the ones who actually published this book, a great deal of thanks goes their way. Each one of them has been so helpful in many ways: Christina Samuell, who managed this whole project (and me in the process . . . yikes!); Leigh Poehler for all sorts of things, including confidence building, guidance, and answers to a lot of absolutely inane questions; Patricia Witkin for all her work getting the message out to the people, being a great email buddy, and turning me on to Haruki Murakami; and last but not, as the saying goes, least, William Pollock for not only taking a chance on the completely unknown writer that I was, but also for turning me on to a great *pupuseria* in San Mateo. Of course, San Mateo, California is a bit far off for a quick lunch now that I am in New Jersey, but . . .

Speaking of New Jersey, it wouldn't be just of me to go on without mentioning a few of the people who have helped me out since my arrival here. I would like to thank my old friend David Lohrey, who in addition to being so happy to have me out here that he moved to Japan five months later, helped me get settled and acted as an ear while I was still going through culture shock; Jeff and Graciela Munsey, who helped make me feel at home here and so kindly came and looked after my beloved cat every day for two weeks while I was out of town; Grace Hsu (now a fellow black cat owner), for her help, thoughts, and timely commiseration; and Richard Roy, who helped make me feel a bit more at home in the Garden State and continues to keep an eye out for my survival in these parts.

Turning now to my friends and colleagues, let me thank Donald Hammang—cycle-pal, Windows expert, and keeper of the Great Saw; Sheldon Rudolph—lifelong friend, artist, composer, and my original compu-buddy from the Atari XL600 days; Steven Young—hiker, environmentalist, birder, ultimate gadget-geek, and the inspiration for *Linux Made Easy* (not to mention the person who first brought Ubuntu to my attention); and Tracy Nakajima—my Mac connection and de facto life advisor. Thank you all very much.

And although I am no longer in Japan, thanks are still due to the gang back there: my former colleagues Setsu Uesaka, Toshiko Takagi, James Porcaro, and Andrezej Kozlowski for their indirect and, at times, very direct help while I was writing this book; and Enryo Nagata, Masayasu Tsuchida, and Seiichi Mizuta for their time, help, vision, and continued kindness.

Special thanks are also due to those people who provided me with support or helped direct me in ways they probably do not even realize—Dick Petrie, Kimberly Jo Burk, Peter and Cate Corvin-Brittin, Charlene Gawa, Leopi (Levy) Sanderson-Edmunds, and Olynxa Levy.

Finally, a special thanks to my sweet little black cat and dear feline friend, Muju, who, despite vociferously protesting as I spent *her* time writing this book, continues to listen to whatever I have to say and keeps me sane when I'm feeling down. Meow.

INTRODUCTION

 My computing life began long ago in the Commodore/Atari days. No doubt inspired by Alan Alda's television commercials at the time, I purchased my first machine, an Atari XL600 with a cassette drive for storage and 16KB of RAM—more than I thought I would ever need. Most of my time on that machine, I must admit, was spent playing cartridge-based games and transcribing pages and pages of machine code from the now-defunct magazine *Antic* to create even more games. Eventually, my interest in computers increased, especially after seeing my first (and actually *the* first) Macintosh at the UCLA bookstore. The very in-your-face nature of the Mac's operating system caused me to become an operating system maniac. To date, I have worked with a lot of different operating systems, including Mac OS up to and including OS X, every Windows version from 3.1 to XP, and even IBM's much forgotten OS/2.

Though tempted to join the Linux fray, I continued to steer away from it for a long time because I could not help but see it, as so many others do, as a system for never-seen-the-light-of-day-faced, late-night Dr. Pepper–drinking,

Domino's-pizza-eating compu-geeks. However, when I moved to Japan and was suddenly surrounded by machines loaded with Japanese versions of Windows, I encountered numerous problems, such as language constraints. Since everything, including Help files, was written in Japanese, I ended up using only a fraction of the full potential of most software. Then there were those annoying Windows-type problems, such as the constant freezes and restarts and the gradual system slowdowns, which were eventually only remedied by reinstalling the system. Getting the software I needed to do the things I wanted to do also took its toll on my wallet, and I began to rethink my initial resistance to Linux. With Linux's multilingual support, system stability, and extensive and free software packages, there were plenty of incentives for me to get over my preconceived notions about the typical Linux user.

After a few failed attempts at getting Linux to work on the oddball, Frankenstein-like collection of junk that was my computer, I finally succeeded with a CD-based Knoppix distribution, which worked well enough to hook me in a little further. I moved on to Mandrake (now known as Mandriva) next, since that was claimed to be the most newbie-friendly version, and then tried out SuSE as well, which I found to be rather quirky. Eventually, I tried out Red Hat Linux and stuck to that because it just didn't give me any grief; and I, like most others, do not want any more grief than necessary.

I started off with my three desktop machines at work and home set up as dual-boot systems running both Linux and Windows, but I gradually found myself using only Linux. Although I had expected to encounter numerous limitations in Linux that would force me to return to Windows often, I instead found that I had actually increased my productivity. Other than lack of native support for Windows streaming media, I was actually able to do more due to the extensive software base that was now installed on my machine. Without having to fork out money that I could ill afford to spend, I was able to manipulate my digital images, rip songs from CDs, create vector drawings, create PDF files, and do a variety of other things that I wasn't able to do under Windows. It was only a matter of time before my dual-boot setups became full Linux-only setups. I ceased to be a Windows user.

Since those early Linux days, I have gone on to try out a number of other distributions including JAMD, Xandros, Damn Small Linux, and most recently Ubuntu. I am happy to report that things have continued to get easier and better, and those early frustrations I suffered trying to get things to work with this machine or that piece of hardware are becoming more and more a thing of the past. Best of all, with the advent of live CDs, which allow you to try Linux out before you actually install it, you don't even have to take a leap of faith to get started.

Who Is This Book For?

If you are standing in the aisle of your local bookstore reading this right now, you may well be wondering who this book is for. If you also happen to see my previous books, *Linux for Non-Geeks* and *Linux Made Easy* on the same shelf (or have at least heard about them), you might also be wondering what the differences among these books are. These questions are reasonable enough. To put it simply, there are two differences: the experience level of the target reader and the distribution covered in each book. *Linux for Non-Geeks*, based on Fedora Core 1, was my first book and was written with folks like my mother in mind—average computer users with some computer experience in the Windows or Mac worlds who had an interest in Linux but were afraid to give it a go. My second book, *Linux Made Easy*, was based on Xandros 3 and was written at a more basic level for those who just wanted a free and easy way out of the grasping tentacles of the Microsoft empire.

Ubuntu Linux for Non-Geeks, as you might imagine, is based on Ubuntu Linux, and like the original *Linux for Non-Geeks*, it targets readers who are interested in Linux but feel the need for a jumping-off point of sorts. Although there are some similarities with its predecessor, *Ubuntu Linux for Non-Geeks* is different in many ways. This is not only due to the inherent differences between the Debian-based Ubuntu and the RPM-based Fedora Core, but also due to the advances made by Linux as a whole. These advances have resulted in a system that is easier and more convenient to use than ever before.

If you are familiar with computers, but unfamiliar with Linux, or somewhat familiar with Linux but not with Ubuntu, you are essentially the reader for whom I have written this book. So to avoid any misunderstanding on your part (and at the risk of being redundant), I must re-emphasize that this is not a book for seasoned geeks or power users. It is instead an introductory guide that will provide new users with some hands-on experience in order to get them up, running, and comfortable with the Ubuntu distribution of Linux.

Version Compatibility

This book was prepared for use with Ubuntu 6.06 (Dapper Drake) Desktop edition. Included with this book is a full working copy of that system on one CD, which functions not only as an install CD, but also as a live CD. This means that you can run Ubuntu directly off the CD without so much as touching your hard disk. You can thus give Ubuntu a try before making any hardware commitments. And since we're talking hardware, it is also worth pointing out that running a live CD session gives you the chance to see if Ubuntu works with the hardware you've got.

If you like what you see and all the hardware seems to work, you can go ahead and install the full shebang on your computer . . . and using the same disk, no less (instructions included in Chapter 2).

NOTE *The world of computers is exceedingly dynamic, and as such, there may be changes in the software or the links to the files for projects in this book after the book is released. I'll post any such changes at www.edgy-penguins.org/ULFNG.*

Concept and Approach

As a language teacher, I have always enjoyed programming books, mathematics books, and old-fashioned foreign language–learning texts because of their straightforward, skill-based orientation, one in which each chapter builds upon the skills acquired in the previous chapter. I have tried to organize this book in that manner so that you will never be called upon to do something that you have not already learned. I also like such books because they not only teach you how to do something, but they also provide you with the chance to put those morsels of knowledge into practice with exercises. I have therefore included several exercises, or projects, in this book so that you will have opportunities to apply your knowledge. This book will serve as a reference text and will also provide a dynamic learning experience so you can learn by doing, as they say.

The projects throughout this book have a secondary purpose as well: By working through them, you will properly configure and round out your Ubuntu system so that it can do anything you want it to do. By the time you finish with this book, your system will have all the bases covered. If that is still not enough to satisfy you, you will be happy to know that you will have access to even more—an unbelievably greater amount more—via the online Ubuntu repositories, which you will learn how to use in Chapter 5. If your interest is already piqued, take a look at these chapter descriptions:

Chapter 1: Becoming a Penguinista—Welcome to the World of Linux
What's Linux? What's Ubuntu? What's a distribution? Can I . . .? Will my . . .? Chapter 1 holds the answers to these and many other questions you might have as it introduces you to the world of Linux and what it takes to get it up and running on your machine.

Chapter 2: Wading and Diving—Running and (If You Like) Installing Ubuntu
The Ubuntu Desktop CD that comes with this book works as both a live and an install CD. Chapter 2 tells you how to run a live Ubuntu session off the CD and, assuming you catch the Linux bug after doing that, how to install the full Ubuntu system on your hard disk as your sole operating system or in a dual-boot setup with Windows.

Chapter 3: A New Place to Call Home—Getting to Know the Desktop
Regardless of whether you are an émigré from the Windows or Mac worlds, the Desktop is something you are already quite familiar with. Chapter 3 will point out the differences between Ubuntu's GNOME desktop and the one on your previous operating system, and it will teach you a number of cool tricks you can use to customize the look and feel of things. A couple of nifty GNOME Easter eggs are also introduced.

Chapter 4: More Than Webbed Feet—The Internet, Linux Style
"Have computer, will cyber-travel" could well be the mantra of the Internet age, and that being the case, Chapter 4 is an indispensable part of your Ubuntu experience. In this chapter you will learn how to

connect to the Internet and set up wireless connections, and you will meet the various software entities that allow you to interact with the Web.

Chapter 5: Rounding Out the Bird—Downloading, Installing, and Updating Programs the Easy Way

Ubuntu comes bundled with most of the software you need, but there is still much more available out there, free and waiting on the Web. Chapter 5 teaches you how to easily download and install applications using Advanced Package Tool (APT) and Synaptic. System and application updating is also covered.

Chapter 6: A Tidy Nest—File and Disk Handling in Ubuntu

From creating folders to copying files to browsing your system and network, all things file management are covered in Chapter 6. You will also learn how to work with USB storage devices, burn data CDs and DVDs, deal with CD-RW disks and multisession CDs, and create space-saving compressed archives of file folders.

Chapter 7: Dressing Up the Bird—Customizing the Look and Feel of Your System

Tired of looking at the same old desktop? Feeling nostalgic for the desktop in your previous operating system? Chapter 7 tells you how you can beat the déjà vu blues by changing the look and feel of just about every visual element of your system.

Chapter 8: Simple Kitten Ways—Getting to Know the Linux Terminal and Command Line

Many people still shy away from Linux because they perceive it as a system in which everything still needs to be done by typing commands. That perception is, as the saying goes, a load of squashed avocados. Still, there is a lot of cool stuff that can be done via the command Terminal, and Chapter 8 will tell you all about it as it tames your fears and piques your interest in commands. Really.

Chapter 9: Dining on Tarballs, Binaries, Java, and Even RPMs—More Ways to Install Programs

Ever wanted to compile your own application? Or maybe you'd like to convert an RPM to a DEB package? Or perhaps you'd just like to know how to run a Java application? In Chapter 9 you will learn how to do all these things, and you will even find out how you can run some Windows applications from within Linux.

Chapter 10: Gutenbird—Setting Up and Using Your Printer and Scanner

Just about everyone with a computer has or needs a printer, and Chapter 10 tells you exactly how to get yours working with your new Linux system. Scanner usage and support are also discussed.

Chapter 11: Font Feathered Frenzy—Adding New Fonts to Your System

Whether you want to use the same fonts that your Windows-using friends are plugging into their documents or you just want to add a bit of flair to your own, Chapter 11 will tell you how to do it in Ubuntu.

Chapter 12: Polyglot Penguins—Linux Speaks Your Language

Need to jot off a note in Urdu? Write a book in Korean? Send a letter in Chinese to your friend in Chengdu? All of the basics you need to know to read and write in just about any language in the world are provided in Chapter 12.

Chapter 13: Penguins Back at Work—Getting Down to Business in Linux

Work can be a drag, especially when there are so many other things you could be doing. Still, wearing the ol' fingers to the bone is a part of life for just about everyone outside of a Jane Austen novel, so you'll be glad to know that Linux is a very capable system in this regard. Chapter 13 introduces you to the various productivity applications bundled with or available for your system.

Chapter 14: Brush-Wielding Penguins—Linux Does Art

Those of you with an artistic bent will find Chapter 14 especially useful. Working with your digital camera, modifying images, and building web albums are just some of the topic areas covered.

Chapter 15: Tux Rocks—Music à la Linux

Chapter 15 is the music lover's treasure trove. You will learn how to rip CDs, encode MP3 or Ogg Vorbis audio files, and even find out how to create your own mix-and-match audio CDs from those files. A number of audio ripping and playback applications are also covered.

Chapter 16: Pluggin' In the Penguin—Ubuntu and Your iPod

Need I say more? Have an iPod? Want to use it in Ubuntu? Chapter 16 tells you how.

Chapter 17: Couch Penguins—Video and DVD Playback in Ubuntu

Sitting in your dorm room trying to figure out how to play your DVD copy of *The Baxter* on your Ubuntu-ized computer? Just finished filming a video of your sibling talking while asleep and want to do some creative editing of the evidence? Chapter 17 covers these and other video-related topics.

Chapter 18: Defending the Nest—Security

Although Linux is about as safe and secure a system as you are likely to come across, some folks feel a bit more secure . . . well, feeling a bit more secure. Chapter 18 tells you how to add a few lines of defense to your system.

Appendix A: Ubuntu Desktop CDs for AMD64 and PowerPC Users

The CD bundled with this book is designed to work with i386 processors. It will also work with AMD64 processors, although not in 64-bit mode. Want to run Ubuntu with an AMD64 processor in 64-bit mode or on a PowerPC machine? It's easy enough to do. Appendix A shows you how to download Ubuntu Desktop CD images and burn them to disk.

Appendix B: Checking the Integrity of Downloaded ISOs

Once you've downloaded an ISO from the Internet, it's best to check its integrity. You want to successfully install Ubuntu, don't you? Appendix B shows you how to check the integrity of an ISO in Windows, Mac OS X, or Linux.

Appendix C: Resources

Are you crazy for Ubuntu and want to say so? Check out a forum. Do you have a hardware compatibility question? Some websites seem to have all the answers. Are you looking for free downloads or do you want to read up on the other Linux distributions? Appendix C is a great place to start.

How to Use This Book

It is possible, of course, to use this book as a mere reference text that you only consult when you have a problem to solve, but that would negate the basic concept behind its design. Instead, I recommend that you go through the entire book chapter by chapter, doing the projects along the way. This will give you a much broader understanding of how things are done (and of how you can get things done), and it will reduce the chance for anxiety, confusion, and worse yet, mistakes.

It is best to read this book and complete its projects when you are relaxed and have time to spare. Nothing makes things go wrong more than working in a rush. And keep in mind that Linux and the projects in this book are fun, not just work exercises. The whole point of the Linux world, in my opinion, is that it offers all kinds of fun. So go ahead and enjoy it.

About the Conventions Used in This Book

There are only a few minor points worth noting about the conventions I have used here. I have put in **bold** type the items within your system that you need to click or directly manipulate in any way, such as buttons, tabs, and menus. Where words or phrases are defined, they have been set in *italics*. Any text that I ask you to input will be indicated by `monospace` font. I have also opted to use the more graphically suggestive term *folder* instead of *directory*—no doubt the legacy of my many years as a Mac user.

About the Projects in This Book

The projects and other information in this book are primarily geared toward users who have installed Ubuntu using the CD that comes with this book. Most of the information also applies to Ubuntu live sessions run from the CD. You should note, however, that some projects and actions cannot be performed in live sessions, as they require write access to your hard disk, and this is not possible during live sessions.

1

BECOMING A PENGUINISTA

Welcome to the World of Linux

 Now we begin our project to get you up and running in the world of Linux. If you have already made the commitment and have Ubuntu installed on your machine, you are essentially ready to go. Others of you might have made the commitment psychologically, but have yet to act on that commitment. And some of you are probably reading these words in the aisle of a bookstore, wondering about Linux and about whether you should spend your money on this book or on a latté every morning for the next couple of weeks. For those in this last group, I can only say, "Get this book." Save the wear and tear on your stomach and nerves.

In any case, the first thing we need to do is get you up to snuff on what this Ubuntu thing is all about, why you might want to install and use it, and what you will need in order to do so. I expect you will have lots of questions along the way, and if you are like most people, a few doubts. I hope that by the time you finish this book and have your Linux system up and running, your doubts will be gone and your questions, for the most part, will be answered. Anyway, until you are ready to make the commitment, you can still follow along, because the CD that comes with this book contains, in addition to the Ubuntu installer, a live Ubuntu environment—meaning that you can have a taste of the Ubuntu Linux experience without having to even touch what you've got on your hard drive. You can kick back, put your worries in check, and go with the flow.

What Is Linux?

Your computer, despite being a collection of highly sophisticated parts, is really just . . . well, a collection of highly sophisticated parts. On its own, it can do nothing other than switch on and off and spin a disk or two. In order for it to do anything truly useful, it needs an operating system (OS) to guide it. The OS takes an essentially well-endowed but completely uneducated hunk of a machine and educates it, at least enough so that it will understand what you want it to do.

You already know of and have probably used at least one of the many operating systems that exist today. Windows, DOS, and the Mac OS are all such operating systems, and Linux is yet another. Linux is, however, different from these other operating systems, both in terms of its capabilities and its heritage. Linux was not created by a corporation or by some corporate wannabes out to make money. The Linux core, referred to as the *kernel*, was created by computer enthusiast Linus Torvalds, a Finn and a member of Finland's Swedish ethnic minority, who wanted to create a better Unix-like system that would work on home computers, particularly his.

Rather than keeping his creation to himself, Torvalds opened it up to the world, so to speak, and the Linux kernel, which communicates with the hardware, and makes it accessible to the other applications and support libraries created by compu-geeks around the globe who work to make Linux better and more powerful. It is this combination of applications built around the core of the Linux kernel that is the essence of all Linux distributions today.

Linux has acquired many fans and followers since its creation in 1991. Such devotees praise Linux for its many features, as well as for being robust, reliable, free, and open. Despite these positive characteristics, however, Linux is, on its own, just a text-based system. There is no pretty desktop, and there are no windows or charming little icons to make you feel safe and comfy once you are behind the keyboard. Powerful though it may be, Linux is still strictly a black-screen, command line–driven operating system. I guess you could think of it as DOS on steroids, though a Linux purist will surely cringe at the thought. Sorry.

Although you can use Linux by itself, accomplishing all your tasks by typing commands on a black screen (the most common way of doing things when Linux is used as a server), you don't have to. It is fair to say that with the advent of the Macintosh and its easy-to-use graphical user interface (GUI, pronounced *goo-ee*) in 1984, users of other operating systems began suffering something akin to GUI envy. They began clamoring for a GUI to call their own. The final result was Windows, which gave DOS a GUI and eased many command-wary users into the Microsoft world.

Similarly, many members of the Linux world felt the need and desire to go graphical. Various GUIs (called *window managers* and *desktop environments*) and a subsystem with which to handle them (somewhat confusingly referred to as the *X Window System*) were developed by the community at large to bring about the change. The graphical desktop environment, GNOME, that is included in your Ubuntu distribution is one example of the fruit of that development.

About the Penguin

You may have been wondering about the penguin in the chapter title, so I might as well explain that now. The penguin was chosen by Linus Torvalds as the Linux mascot, and what has come to be thought of as *the* Linux penguin was designed by Larry Ewing and is named Tux (see Figure 1-1). This explains not only the ornithological references and graphics throughout the book, but also why there are so many penguin icons in Linux distributions and so many programs that include *penguin* or *Tux*, such as TuxRacer, XPenguins, and Pingus. This, combined with the fact that Linux is a revolutionary OS, helps to explain why Linux users are sometimes referred to as *Penguinistas*.

Figure 1-1: Tux, the Linux mascot

Why Should I Use Linux?

People use Linux for different reasons. For many it is a matter of power, stability, multilingual capabilities, or even personal philosophy. However, for others, crass as it may sound, it is a matter of money. Just think for a moment about what it usually costs to get started with an operating system. Go to wherever it is you go to buy software, and take a walk down the aisles. Make a list in your head of all the things you want to buy and how much each costs: an office suite; a game or two; maybe a graphics program with which to make yourself look better in your digital photos; and a collection of all those firewall, antispam, antivirus, and anti-adware programs that you really need to protect yourself in the Windows world. Now do the math.

After you pick yourself up off the floor, you will understand that we are talking big bucks here. On the other hand, for the price of this book you will have all of the things you wanted and more in the Linux world. Despite the worries that many people have, making the move to Linux means not only savings for you, but also more computing versatility. You will not be hamstrung at some point along the way because you don't have this or that program when you need it most—you'll have it all from the get-go, or else be able to download it easily . . . and at no cost!

You might counter with the fact that there are a lot of freeware applications out there for other operating systems, but c'mon, let's face it—these are often rather limited in terms of their capabilities. The programs with a little more oomph are mostly shareware, and most shareware programs these days are limited in some way, or they only let you use them for a short time unless you are willing to pay for them. Sure, their costs are relatively low, but $25 here and $35 there eventually adds up to a considerable chunk of change. There is also the problem that some of these programs, unbeknownst to you, install backdoors, or keyloggers, or make your system a sudden garden of adware. Finally, at least in my experience, the majority of such programs are hardly worth the money asked. The only shareware programs I ever found worth buying were Lemke Software's GraphicConverter and Plasq's Comic Life, both for the Mac.

Is It All Just About Money?

While money is important to the average user, it is certainly not the only reason for taking the Linux plunge; there are a variety of other reasons as well. As I mentioned before, Linux is noted for its stability. Try running your present system for a month without restarting and see what happens. Linux has been known to run without a reboot for over a year without a hitch or decrease in performance. With its multilingual capabilities, Linux is also a perfect choice for language students or users in a multilingual environment.

In addition, Linux is infinitely customizable: You can get your system to look and act the way you want it to without being wizarded to death. And then there are the applications that come with most Linux distributions. In addition to their wide variety, most are well up to industry snuff, with some, such as Evolution and the GIMP, being sources of envy for those outside the Linux world.

Finally, with the advent of Microsoft's new Windows Vista system and its more demanding hardware requirements (especially if you want to take advantage of its most touted new features), you may find your present machine on the fast track to obsolescence. Turning it into a Linux machine will ensure it several more years of working life. Shame to put good hardware out to pasture so early, after all.

But Is Linux Really Ready for the Desktop?

Despite the advances Linux has made in recent years, this question still pops up quite often, and that's fair enough. But consider this: When you install a program on your present Windows system and get an error message saying that the program can't run because some DLL file is missing, or when you connect a piece of hardware and can't get it to run, no one asks if that operating system is ready for the desktop.

In my own experience, I have found no reason to doubt that Linux is ready. Sure, Linux has its occasional quirks, but so does every other operating system. Linux is ready and able. If my mother, hardly a computer wiz, can do the work she needs to do and can keep herself amused till the middle of the night using her Linux system (without blowing the whole thing up), then I think it's pretty safe to say that you'll do all right too.

What Is a Distribution?

An operating system consists of a lot of files that perform a lot of different functions. And because there is no Linux corporation to package and distribute the files that make up Linux, the task of getting Linux onto your computer in working order, along with the applications that you are likely to want, has fallen to a varied group of entities—companies, universities, user groups, and even private individuals. These entities create Linux system and application collections called *distributions*, or *distros*. You could bypass such distros and try to collect everything you'd need to set up a system all on your own, but you would undoubtedly lose your mind in the process. Most people, even the geekiest, opt for the distros.

The majority of these distros, whatever their ultimate target audience, basically consist of the same main elements: the core operating system (better known as the *Linux kernel*), some sort of installer program to get all the system parts and applications properly installed on your machine, the X Window System to provide graphical interface support, one or more graphical desktop environments, and a series of applications, such as word processors, audio players, and games, as well as all the files needed to make these things work.

There are, of course, a large number of distros. Some are geared toward specific audiences, such as businesses, educators, gamers, students, programmers, system administrators, and specific language users. What makes each distro different is the specific software that is bundled with the Linux kernel, as well as other convenience features like the package, or application, installation mechanism, and the installer for the system itself. Some distros are especially appropriate for home users due to their ease of installation. Ubuntu, a relative newcomer to the Linux world, is one of these, joining other distros that have long been popular in the ease-of-use arena, such as Mandrake, SUSE, and Fedora Core. There are also many other new distros, like Xandros and Linspire, that are specifically geared toward making the transition for Windows users easier. While many of these entities charge for their distros, most also provide them free for download.

What Is Ubuntu?

Ubuntu is a completely free, easy-to-use, and extremely popular Linux distribution that is geared toward the desktop user. It is one of the hottest Linux distros in the marketplace today. It is also one of the few Linux distros with what could be described as a social agenda behind it.

Ubuntu was the brainchild of South African millionaire entrepreneur Mark Shuttleworth, who is probably better known for being one of the first space tourists—the first African in space, to be exact. Shuttleworth invested over $10 million starting up the Ubuntu Foundation based on his belief in free software and in order to fix what he describes as "bug #1"—Microsoft's dominance of the desktop PC marketplace. As Shuttleworth states in his blog (available at https://wiki.ubuntu.com/MarkShuttleworth):

> I believe that free software brings us into a new era of technology, and holds the promise of universal access to the tools of the digital era. I drive Ubuntu because I would like to see that promise delivered as reality.

As you can see, it's a vision thing.

Befitting the nationality and goals of the man who brought it into being, the word *ubuntu* comes from the Zulu and Xhosa languages. *Ubuntu*, according to Wikipedia, is a concept meaning something along the lines of *humanity toward others* or *I am because we are*. If you're interested, the 2005 film *In My Country*, starring Juliette Binoche and Samuel L. Jackson, although not one of the greatest films ever produced, is on many levels a 100-minute examination of the concept of ubuntu.

Why Ubuntu Then?

With so many distros out there, you may wonder why you should opt for Ubuntu. Well, as they say, numbers don't lie, and Ubuntu's popularity is not without good cause. These traits are especially crowd pleasing:

Easy to install
It's fair to say that most Linux distributions these days are pretty easy to install (and definitely easier and faster to install than Windows). Ubuntu is right in line with these improvements, and the fact that you can install it with only a few mouse clicks while running the live CD means it is pretty much ready to go whenever you are.

Easy to use
Ubuntu is easy to use in that it is very Windows-like in operation, and yet it's more Linux-like than other Windows user–oriented distributions.

DEB based
Ubuntu is based on the *Debian* distribution, which means that it utilizes Debian's very convenient DEB package system for application handling and installation. The two preconfigured, graphical package installers that come with Ubuntu make installing applications even easier. There are so many packages available for Debian systems like Ubuntu that you are likely to find more software out there than you'll ever know what to do with.

Up to date
Some distros are updated at a snail's pace, while others strive to be so cutting edge that they are often plagued with bugs. Ubuntu, with its reasonable six-month release cycle, tries to stay as up-to-date as possible, while at the same time making sure that things are not released before they are ready for prime time. In this way, you are ensured of having an up-to-date yet less buggy distro at your disposal.

Dependable and robust
> I know these terms come across as mere hype, but after you smack Ubuntu around a bit, you come to understand what they mean. Knock things down and around, and they bounce right back—this is very important for beginners who often have a knack for screwing things up. Nothing turns a new user off more than a twitchy system that has to be velvet gloved all the time.

Desktop user–oriented
> A lot of Linux distributions, although quite capable in the desktop arena, cater more to geeks and developers, taking up valuable disk space with a lot of junk you'll probably never use. Ubuntu's purpose is to grab desktop market share from the Redmond folks, so the needs of the common end user are always in mind. The result is that Ubuntu's GNOME desktop environment is a very comfy place for the average desktop user to be.

Hardware Compatibility

Well, enough of this background babble; it's time to get things rolling. If you haven't installed Linux on your machine yet and are wondering whether you can, it is relatively safe to say that Ubuntu will run on most machines out there today. Of course, this statement comes with a major caveat: You just never know until you get up and running. There are so many minor parts to your machine that it is difficult to say whether each part will cooperate with your installation. Ignoring minor parts for the time being, there are video cards, sound chips, LAN cards, monitors, and so on, and they all need to be considered.

Diving In

If you are going to buy a new machine on which to run Ubuntu, then it is reasonable enough to do a bit of worrying and check things out first, but if you are going to install it on the machine you have, I recommend just diving in. After all, you don't really have to install anything the first time out. You have a live CD right here in this book, after all, so you can just pop that CD in your drive, boot up your machine, and, *biff, bam, zowie*, you'll be up and running (or not) in a minute or two. If everything seems to be going as it should . . . well, your worries are over, and you can go ahead and install the system when you're ready and willing. That is one of the Ubuntu advantages— not only do all the essentials fit on a single CD (compared to four or more for other distros), but that CD is both a live operating environment and the installer! You can't get much more convenient than that.

When Research Is Required

If things don't work out for you with the live CD, you can search the Web to see if you can identify what part of your hardware puzzle is causing your problems. (Or if you are looking to buy a machine on which to install Ubuntu, you can search for hardware that is supported by Linux.) Of course, before you can do this, you need to know what models of hardware you have. You should know at least what motherboard, central processing unit (CPU), monitor, and video card you have if you want to be able to find out anything of value. Identifying your CPU and monitor should be easy enough, but the motherboard and video card may require a bit more searching.

If you have no documentation that clearly states the make and model of these devices, you can find out most things you need to know from within Windows by going to the Windows Control Panel, double-clicking **System**, and then clicking the **Hardware** tab in that window. Once in the Hardware tab, click the **Device Manager** button, and see what you can find about your system components there. Sometimes the information there is rather limited, so you might instead want to try out a shareware application such as HWiNFO (www.hwinfo.com) or Sandra (www.sisoftware.net) to get more useful details, such as the specifications of your motherboard or the supported video modes for your present setup (see Sandra in Figure 1-2).

Figure 1-2: Finding out your hardware details from within Windows with Sandra

Both HWiNFO and Sandra should give you the information you need about your motherboard, but if they don't (or if you don't feel like bothering with them), you can always just open up the case of your computer and look at your board. You needn't worry about damaging anything because you don't need to touch anything—so don't. You may need a flashlight to find it, but the model name and number should be stamped on there somewhere, either in the middle of the board or around the edges. Mine, for example, says quite clearly in the middle of the board, *AOpen MX46-533V.* You should be looking for similar information.

Once you have all your information, you can do a variety of things to check out your hardware's compatibility with Ubuntu. You can simply do a Yahoo! or Google search by entering your motherboard's make and model plus the word *Linux.* This works for other hardware devices too.

You can also post a question to the Ubuntu User Forums (at www .ubuntuforums.org) or one of the other various Linux forums or mailing lists on the Web. A listing of some of these is provided in Appendix C at the end of this book. Just write that you are a newbie and want to know if anyone has had any experience using Ubuntu with the board (or other hardware) in question. You will probably get quite a few responses. Linux users are usually rather evangelical in terms of trying to draw in new Penguinistas.

Hardware Requirements

All worries about compatibility aside, there are some minimum hardware requirements that you will need to meet:

- A computer with an i386-based, AMD64, or PowerPC processor
- About 2 gigabytes (GB) of hard disk space, though having at least 10GB would be a bit more comfy
- Sufficient memory (RAM)

NOTE   *The CD that comes with this book is designed to work on machines with i386-based processors (basically, all the Pentium chips, including Celeron, Xeon, and the new Core Duo, as well as processors from AMD). Though this CD will install Ubuntu on an AMD Athlon 64, it will only run in 32-bit mode. To make full use of your Athlon 64 processor, you need to download the 64-bit version of Ubuntu. The included CD will not work on PowerPCs.*

As for RAM, the official specs tell you that you need a minimum of 128 megabytes (MB) to run Ubuntu. While you can no doubt get by with this, you'd get by much better with more. My basic rule of thumb, no matter what OS I am dealing with, is that you need the recommended (not the minimum) memory plus at least 128MB. Regardless of what the official specs say, put in more. You won't regret it.

Saying that the more memory you have, the better, may sound a bit simple, and perhaps even cavalier, but trust me on this one. When you have too little memory, no matter what system you are running, weird things happen: Applications seem to take years to open, or don't open at all; menus take forever to render their little icons; freezes and general system meltdowns just happen much more often.

To be realistic and exceedingly honest, I would say that 256MB is the absolute minimum you want to have. I personally would recommend that you have at least 384MB of RAM in order for things to move smoothly and comfortably. It is such a waste to have a pretty speedy CPU and not be able to appreciate it because its hands are tied by a lack of memory. It is sort of like trying to do jumping jacks in a broom closet. Sure, you could do it, but you would be all contorted, and you'd be smashing your hands into the walls every 1.4 seconds.

Fortunately, it is pretty hard to find a machine with only 128MB of RAM these days, but if you do happen to have such a beastie, you can at least take solace in the fact that memory is relatively cheap, so go for it.

Good News for Mac and AMD64 Users

It is again important to mention that the CD that comes with this book is designed to work on machines with i386-based processors, which pretty much covers the vast majority of PCs out there. If your machine has an AMD64, you will be glad to know that it will also work, albeit not in 64-bit mode. And if you're a Mac user with a PowerPC architecture machine? Sorry, but no go.

Fortunately there is good news for those of you who were a bit disappointed by the content of that previous paragraph. Ubuntu is available in native AMD64 and PowerPC versions. Check Appendix A for information on how to get them. The information provided there will also be of use to i386 users who happen to lose or damage the disk that comes with this book.

Speaking Ubuntu

It's worth noting that there are a lot of weird phrases you are bound to come across when dealing with Ubuntu, especially when searching for information on the Net. In particular, I am referring to four seemingly incongruous phrases: *Warty Warthog*, *Hoary Hedgehog*, *Breezy Badger*, and *Dapper Drake*. These are the unlikely code names of each of the releases of Ubuntu since its first appearance in 2004. The important one for you to remember is that of the current release (the one on the CD that comes with this book): *Dapper Drake*. In the future, when you upgrade to the next release, you will be upgrading to *Edgy Eft*. Hmmm.

You are also likely to come across a few other variations of the Ubuntu theme. These are Kubuntu, a KDE-based version of Ubuntu; Edubuntu, a special version of Ubuntu designed for use in the classroom; and Xubuntu, which is a lightweight version of Ubuntu based on the XFCE desktop.

Where Do I Go from Here?

Now that you know more about the world of Linux and Ubuntu, and you've got your disk in hand, it's time to get down to it. If you have already installed Ubuntu on your machine, just flip ahead to Chapter 3. If your machine is still Linuxless, though, it's time to take it out for a spin and see if you like it. So for now, strap yourself down in front of that computer, clip on your spurs, and go straight to the next chapter. It's time to become a Penguinista!

2

WADING AND DIVING

Running and (If You Like) Installing Ubuntu

As I have already mentioned, one of the great things about Ubuntu is that it comes on a live CD, which means that you can try it out before you install it . . . or never install it at all, if that's what you prefer. Better yet is the fact that, unlike earlier editions of Ubuntu, you don't need an additional installation CD if you do choose to install it—the Ubuntu Desktop CD functions as both a live and an install CD. And while in the good-better-best swing of things, the best point of all is that installation from the live CD is actually much, much easier than any other installation process you've ever dealt with.

In this chapter, I will be covering the basics of starting up and running Ubuntu from the live CD, and then, assuming you've caught the Linux bug, the painless steps to installing the system on your hard disk. Let's put this book to use and get Ubuntu up and running. . . .

Going in for a Dip

To get a taste of what Ubuntu is all about (and to check out your hardware to see if it's all comfy-cozy with Ubuntu), there is probably no better way to go than to run Ubuntu directly from the live CD. To do this, just place the Ubuntu Desktop CD in your disk drive and restart your machine. When the machine starts up again, it should boot up from the CD, and, after a bit of white text scrolls up the screen, you should see the first Ubuntu startup screen (Figure 2-1). If the screen does not appear, and your machine instead boots up into your usual operating system, then it is very likely that your machine's BIOS needs to be changed so as to allow you to boot from CD.

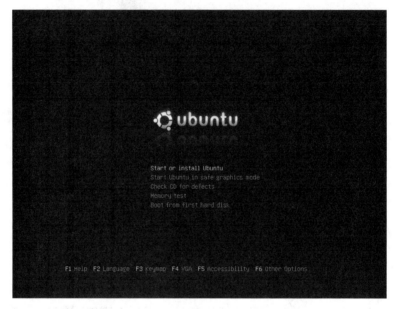

Figure 2-1: An Ubuntu live session startup screen

You can access your machine's BIOS by restarting and then pressing whatever key the onscreen startup instructions assign to accessing the BIOS setup. This is usually DELETE or F1, but not all machines are the same. If the onscreen information passes by so fast that you miss it, you can check your user's manual to see what the correct key is. Once you get into the BIOS setup, change the boot sequence so that your CD drive is first.

Once your machine does boot from the live CD, and you do see the Ubuntu live session startup screen shown in Figure 2-1, either press ENTER or just do nothing for about 30 seconds in order to continue. This will start up your Ubuntu in English with a US keyboard layout. Remember, your hard disk will go untouched, so rest easy—you're not going to touch, let alone hurt, anything.

If you would like your system to appear in a different language, press F2, select your language of choice using the cursor keys, and then press ENTER. You can change the default keyboard layout by pressing F3 and then following the same steps. Once you're done, press ENTER to start up the system.

Special input mechanisms required for typing in certain languages (i.e., Chinese, Japanese, and Korean) are not supported in live CD sessions.

From then on out, it is strictly autopilot time for you—all you have to do is wait. There will be some scrolling white text now and then, and an occasional period when things will go black for a few seconds, but eventually things will go totally graphical when the GNOME desktop environment begins its initialization process, and when that is done . . . well, you will be face to face with the Ubuntu desktop, meaning you're ready to roll—but I'll hold off on talking about that until Chapter 3.

Taking the Plunge—Installing Ubuntu

If you have already installed Ubuntu on your machine, are satisfied running it from the live CD, or still haven't made up your mind what to do, you can skip right over the rest of this chapter and go on to the next one to get started working with the Ubuntu desktop. If, however, you haven't installed Ubuntu yet and are ready and raring to do so, then you had better stay right where you are and read on.

Single- or Dual-Boot Setup?

If you don't already have Windows installed on your machine, you can skip right over this section. If, on the other hand, you do, then you are going to have to decide whether or not you want to keep it.

It is possible to have both Windows and Linux installed on the same machine and for them to happily coexist. This is known as a *dual-boot setup.* It has also become incredibly easy to set up such a system. I started out with a dual-boot setup; however, I eventually found that I used the Linux side of things exclusively. Having so much disk space being taken up by a Windows system I didn't use seemed a waste of prime real estate, so eventually I just dumped the whole thing and went for a straight Linux-only setup. My feeling is that unless there is some application that you really need that is not available on the Linux side (probably some game), then go for the Linux-only setup and just forget about Windows. Linux has most of what you will need anyway, and because the applications in the OpenOffice.org office suite can read and write Microsoft Office files, you'll still be able to collaborate with Windows users, if that is of concern to you.

You may be thinking that if you do as I suggest and dump your Windows system when you install Linux, you might have to reinstall Windows if you don't like Linux or if you can't get it installed properly. That would be a considerable waste of time and energy, to be sure. However, believe it or not, there are advantages to my suggestion even if your no-go scenario turns out to be the case.

You may have noticed that your Windows system, as you've used it over time, has gotten sort of gunked up—it is no longer the quick little kitten it used to be. Menus don't pop open as quickly as they used to, things take longer to start up than they did before, and you find yourself asking, "What the Sam Habberdack is that?!" all the time as mysterious things happen with increasing frequency.

This is just the nature of the beast, and a very good way of getting things back to normal is to reinstall the whole thing. So even if you do decide to come back to Windows later, you'll be doing yourself a favor, because it should run better than before. It's a little more work up front, but in the long run, you'll be a happier camper.

If, on the other hand, you opt for a dual-boot setup, from which you can run both Windows and Linux, you will have the best of both worlds. Starting up in either system is easy. When you start up your machine, you will be greeted by the GRand Unified Bootloader (GRUB) screen, from which you can choose to continue booting up Linux or choose Windows in its stead. After that, bootup proceeds as normal for the system you selected. This setup works fine, so you needn't worry.

So as you see, either way you decide to go, you can't really go wrong. Just be sure to back up your important files before starting the installation; proceed with common sense, patience, and a positive attitude; and you'll be fine. In short: Don't worry.

Getting Ready for Action

There is less you need to do to prepare for an Ubuntu installation than for many other Linux distributions. Once you've decided whether or not you want to go the dual-boot route, all you really need to have on hand is your single Ubuntu Desktop disk and, for guidance and security, this book. The only mental energy you'll probably need to expend is to come up with a username and user password, just as you do for most other operating systems.

Usernames and User Passwords

Your username is something that you will be using quite a bit. You will input it every time you boot up your system, so be sure it is something you can live with, especially in terms of typing. It can be just your first name, or your initials, or whatever you want it to be. It must, however, begin with a lowercase letter, followed by numbers and/or other lowercase letters. Mine, for example, is simply *rg*, but you could use something like *hope4u2pal*, though that would get rather tiring to type at login day after day. Think of your fingers when deciding upon your username.

You also need to come up with a user password, which you will also need to type every time you log in. You will need to use it when you install new software or change certain system settings, as well. It should be a minimum of eight characters in length and consist of numbers and letters (upper- and lowercase) for improved security. You can, of course, get by with fewer characters and only letters if you prefer. The installer will advise you if the password you enter is unacceptable, so don't worry too much. Be sure to write it down and keep the paper you've written it on in a safe place so you don't end up locking yourself out of your system.

If you have experience working with other Linux distributions, you may be surprised to learn that the root account is disabled by default in Ubuntu. There is, therefore, no installation step for inputting a root password. You can check the website for this book (www.edgypenguins.org/ULFNG) to learn ways of getting around this setup. You can also set up a root password later at any time after the system is installed, so if having a root account is of importance to you, don't worry.

Dual-Booters Take Note

If you are going to be creating a dual-boot setup, it is a good idea to first defragment your present Windows disk before moving on to installing Ubuntu. This will make the repartitioning phase of the installation process must faster and safer.

You can do this while still running Windows by double-clicking **My Computer**, right-clicking the icon for your hard disk, and selecting **Properties**. You can then defragment your hard disk (in Windows XP) by clicking the **Tools** tab in the Properties window and clicking the **Defragment Now** button. In Windows NT, you can do this by going to the **Start** menu and selecting **Control Panel ▶ Administrative Tools ▶ Computer Management ▶ Disk Defragmenter**, while in Windows 98 and some other versions, you can do the same by selecting **Programs ▶ System Tools ▶ Disk Defragmenter**.

Doing the Deed

Well, now that we've covered all that prelim stuff, let's get down to the actual Linux installation. Set this book on your lap so you can follow along, and then get ready for action. It's time to do the deed!

Fortunately for you, the installation process is extremely easy, as there are very few steps in which you actually have to do anything. Most of what you will be doing is clicking buttons on your screen. Nothing hard about that, eh?

Of course, when you look at the directions and descriptions listed here, it may look like a long and cumbersome process. It is not. It will be over more quickly than you can imagine. As a beginner frequently referring to this text, you might take a bit longer, of course, but don't worry. All in all, the whole process is faster and easier than that for Windows XP or Mac OS X. And keep in mind that with XP and OS X, you are installing the operating system with just a few bundled applications. In an Ubuntu installation, on the other hand, you are installing not only the operating system itself, but also most of the applications you will ever want or need to use. You will thus be getting a lot done in one fell swoop.

One more thing before we start. Some people approach installing a system with a good deal of trepidation. The process makes them nervous, as if the house is going to go up in smoke if they click the wrong thing somewhere along the line. Needless to say, there is no need for such concern. As long as you have backed up your data, you will be okay. If you screw up the installation the first time out, so what? Just start over again. No harm done, as you have nothing to harm. Just make sure that you give yourself more time than you need for the process. Don't start installing one hour before you have to be at work or before you have to meet your friend downtown. Rushing makes people do weird things. Make things easy on yourself by giving yourself plenty of time and, as I mentioned before, by backing up any data you would mourn the loss of.

If you're ready, here are the steps:

1. **Start 'er up**   If you haven't already done so, boot up your machine from the Ubuntu Desktop CD.

2. **Start the installation**   Double-click the **Install** icon on the Ubuntu live desktop to start the installation. This will bring up the first page of the installation wizard (Figure 2-2).

Figure 2-2: The opening installation wizard screen

3. **Welcome (choose language)**   Choose the language you want to use during and after the installation process, and then click the **Forward** button. No matter what language you choose, you will always have the option of booting up in English once the system is installed. You can also add support for other languages later.

4. **Where are you? (choose location)**   The Ubuntu installer will select the default location for the installation language you have chosen. If your location is different, select the one appropriate for you by clicking directly on the wizard map (Figure 2-3). Once your selection is made, click **Forward**.

Figure 2-3: Choosing your geographic location in the Ubuntu installation wizard

5. **Keyboard layout**   The default keyboard layout for the installation language you have chosen will appear in the next wizard screen. If your keyboard layout is different, make the appropriate choice from the list. If you're not sure you've made the right choice, you can double-check by typing a few words in the text box at the bottom of the window. Once you've done this, click **Forward**. If need be, you can add other keyboard layouts later, after the system is installed.

6. **Who are you?**   On the next page of the installation wizard, you are asked to provide your real name, your login name, and a password. The wizard will automatically generate a name for your computer based on your username (*rg-laptop* in my case), but you are free to change this to something else if you like (I changed mine to *UbuntuAcer-RG*). Once all of the fields are filled in, as mine are in Figure 2-4, click **Forward**.

7. **Select a disk**   If your machine has more than one hard disk, or if you have another storage device attached to one of your USB ports, you will be asked on which disk you wish to perform the installation. Select your main hard disk, and then click **Forward**. If you do not have any other disks attached to your machine, this screen will not appear.

Figure 2-4: Providing your username, password, and computer name in the installation wizard

8. **Prepare disk space**   What you are asked at this point depends on what you have on your machine. Assuming you have an operating system on the disk already, such as Windows, you will be asked whether you want to resize the master partition or erase the entire disk. If you want to create a dual-boot Windows/Ubuntu (or other Linux distro/Ubuntu) setup, choose the resize option. You can, if you like, resize the partition on which your present system exists by using the slider in the middle of the window (Figure 2-5). Once your selection is made, click **Forward**.

What happens next depends on the selection you've just made. If you chose to erase the entire disk, you will be immediately taken to the final page of the wizard, where you can begin the installation. If, however, you chose to resize the existing partition, the partitioner will begin the process of resizing that partition before delivering you to the final page of the wizard. The partitioning process can take a bit of time, so sit back, have a glass of Inca Cola, and watch a rerun of *Green Acres* while you wait.

9. **Ready to install**   The final page of the wizard (Figure 2-6) lists the details of your soon-to-be installed system and hard disk partition setup, along with a point-of-no-return warning. You've come this far, so you might as well go for it, even though there's no turning back. Click **Install**.

Figure 2-5: Disk-partitioning options

Figure 2-6: Ready to install—the final page of the installation wizard

The partitioner will then do whatever writing to disk it must in order to finish the partitioning process, after which the installation itself will seamlessly begin, without any additional input necessary from you or anyone else. The progress of the installation will be indicated in a window like that in Figure 2-7 so that you don't have to fret (and so you'll know how much more time you have left to veg in front of the TV).

Figure 2-7: Keeping track of the progress of the installation

10. **Installation complete** As you can see in Figure 2-8, you've now come to the end of the first phase of the installation. You are given the option of either continuing to use the live CD or restarting the machine and running Ubuntu directly from your hard disk. Well, you didn't go through all of this just to keep using the live CD, so let's go for the second option by clicking the **Restart now** button, removing the live CD from your drive when it is automatically ejected, and pressing ENTER when prompted on screen to do so. Your machine will then restart.

Figure 2-8: A final warning before taking the plunge

After that . . . well, that's basically it. You now have Ubuntu installed on your machine. Congratulations. After a few moments, you will see the login screen, so to find out what to do then, go on to the next chapter. See you there. Aloha.

3

A NEW PLACE TO CALL HOME

Getting to Know the Desktop

Now Ubuntu is up and running, and you are ready and raring to go. If you are running Ubuntu from your hard disk, you will first see the login screen that will appear each and every time you boot up (Figure 3-1). There's no need to keep the login screen waiting, so type your username, and press ENTER. After that, you will be prompted for your user password in the same screen, so type it, and press ENTER again. Within moments, you will be face to face with your desktop in Ubuntu.

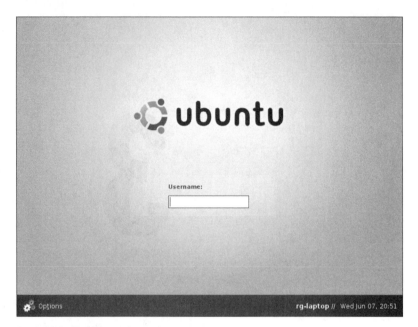

Figure 3-1: The Ubuntu login screen

Welcome to the GNOME Desktop

Ubuntu's implementation of the GNOME desktop is shown in Figure 3-2, and as you can see, it isn't all that different from what you might be used to in a Windows or Mac OS 9 environment, other than the fact that it has task-bars, or *panels*, at both the top and the bottom of the screen. There are also no desktop icons, except when running a live session from the Desktop CD, in which case you'll see a launcher to run the installation wizard (labeled Install) and a folder (labeled Examples), which contains a number of sample files. Among these is a video clip of Nelson Mandela discussing the meaning of ubuntu (the concept, not the distro). All in all, it is a very uncluttered place to be, and despite its superficial similarities to other OS desktop environments, things in the GNOME are different enough to be interesting.

The main elements of the GNOME desktop are the panels at the top and bottom of the screen and the icons that appear upon those panels. The desktop itself, although empty at startup, does see its share of action, but I'll come to that later. For now, I'll focus on the two panels.

The Top Panel

Of the two GNOME Panels on your desktop, the top panel is basically where all the action is. As you can see, there are three menus and two icons at the left end of the panel, and a few icons and a clock/calendar at the other end (Figure 3-3). So that you understand what each of the panel items does, I will now briefly describe each of them, moving from left to right, as seems to be the fashion these days.

Figure 3-2: The GNOME desktop in Ubuntu

The Menus

At the far left of the top panel, you will find a set of three menus. These provide access to most of what your system has to offer in terms of applications, locations, and utilities. These include:

Applications menu   The access point to the majority of your applications, a software manager, and some system tools.

Places menu   Your system navigator, from which you can hide all open windows so as to expose the desktop, access your home folder, browse your computer's filesystem and connected networks, and search for files on your hard disk.

System menu   The access point for your system preferences, software installer, and administration tools. This is also the place to go when you want to shut down or log out of your system.

Figure 3-3: The left and right sides of the top GNOME Panel

The Icons (Left)

Immediately to the right of the three menus are a set of two launchers. When these icons are clicked, they launch the following applications:

Firefox   Your web browser

Ximian Evolution   The very popular Linux email program, scheduler, and task manager

The Icons (Right)

At the right side of the top panel are a series of icons that perform a variety of functions. Some of these are indicators, while some are applets that allow you to perform certain functions. These consist of:

Update Notification Tool   Tells you when there are system or application updates and allows you to download and install the updates. Only appears when updates are available.

Battery (not shown)   Shows your current battery level. Only appears on laptops when charging or discharging the battery.

Network   Lets you see your network status and configure your network devices.

Wireless Signal Monitor   Shows the signal strength of your current wireless connection, if you have one, and allows you to switch from one wireless access point to another.

Volume Control   A volume controller. Duh.

Calendar/Clock   Date and time, date and time, date and time. Just as you suspected.

Quit   Brings you to the logout screen, from which you can logout, shut down, restart, or switch users.

The Bottom Panel

The bottom panel, as you can see in Figure 3-4, is a much simpler affair, containing only the four items I will now briefly describe.

Figure 3-4: The bottom GNOME Panel

Show Desktop   A button that minimizes all open windows and allows you to see your desktop when it is obscured from view.

Window List   A list of windows or applications you have open, which is very similar to what happens in the Windows taskbar.

Workspace Switcher An application that allows you to switch between virtual desktops. (I'll talk about this more in "Virtual Desktops" on page 42.)

Trash There is nothing mysterious about Trash . . . other than its rather Mac OS X–ish location on the panel.

Project 3A: Customizing the GNOME Panel

The GNOME Panel is not a static thing. You can add *launchers* (respectively known as *program shortcuts* or *aliases* to Windows and Mac users), utilities, and even amusements to make it do almost anything you want it to—within limits, of course. In the various stages of this project, you will customize your panel to get some hands-on experience working with it and to make things more convenient for you as you make your way through the rest of this book. You are, of course, free to change any of the customizations I ask you to make (though you won't have a say in the matter if you're working in live session from the desktop CD, as you won't be able to save your settings).

Each of the following subprojects is very simple. Most are only three-step, point-and-click procedures that you should be able to handle without any difficulty.

3A-1: Adding Utility Buttons to the Panel

The GNOME Panel allows you to add a number of utility applets. Each of these has some specific function, such as tracking your stocks, telling you the weather, or performing some particular system-related function. To start out, let's add a clearly useful utility to the top panel: the Force Quit button. The Force Quit button lets you quickly and easily deal with non-responding windows.

Yes, it does happen on occasion: A window suddenly refuses to do anything. Regardless of what you want it to do or what it is supposed to be doing, it just sits there as if it is on strike (maybe it is). With just one click of the Force Quit button, your cursor becomes a powerful surgical instrument that will kill the window you click. You definitely don't want to be without this button, so here's how to add it to the panel:

1. Right-click any open space on the top panel.
2. From the popup menu, select **Add to Panel**, after which the Add to Panel window will appear.
3. In that window, click **Force Quit** once to highlight it, as I've done in Figure 3-5. Click the **Add** button, and then click **Close** to finish the job.

To reinforce what you've just learned how to do, let's add another utility to the panel: the Run Application panel applet. Once you start installing applications in Ubuntu, you will find that some of those applications do not automatically install program launchers in your Applications menu. This means that you have to open a Terminal window and type a command every time you want to run such programs, which can get old rather fast. The Run Application panel applet is one way around this problem.

Figure 3-5: Adding launchers and utility applets to the GNOME Panel

To add the Run Application applet to the panel, just follow the same steps you used in adding the Force Quit button; but this time in step 3, highlight **Run Application** in the Add Launcher window instead of Force Quit.

NOTE   *If you later decide not to keep the Run Application panel applet on the panel, or if you just prefer keyboard shortcuts to pointing and clicking, it is worth noting that you can also bring up the applet by pressing ALT-F2.*

3A-2: Adding Amusing Applets to the Panel

The GNOME Panel not only allows you to add very functional utilities, but it allows you to add quite seemingly useless amusements as well. In this part of the project, we will be adding two such amusements: Geyes and a little fish called Wanda.

At first glance, Wanda does little more than bat her tail around and spurt out a bubble or two. However, if you click on her, a window pops up in which Wanda will spew out quotes and offbeat one-liners.

To get a glimpse of Wanda in action, limited though that action may be, the steps are essentially the same as those in Project 3A-1 on page 33, but I'll run through them one more time:

1. Right-click any open space on the top panel.
2. From the popup menu, select **Add to Panel**, after which the Add to Panel window will appear.
3. In that window, click **Fish** once to highlight it, click the **Add** button, and then click **Close**.

Wanda will now appear on your panel, so go ahead and give her a click to see what she has to say.

Now you can add Geyes, which is a pair of eyes that follows your mouse cursor around as it moves about your desktop. Follow the same procedure, but click **Geyes** instead of Fish in step 3.

3A-3: Adding a Program Launcher to the Panel

Now let's move on to something a bit more practical—adding program launchers to the panel. While it is very easy to run an application by navigating through the Application menu, there are no doubt some applications that you will be using frequently enough to want easy access to them. OpenOffice.org Writer is probably one of those.

Method 1

There are a number of different ways to add a launcher to the panel, but let's start with the most conventional. To add a panel launcher for OpenOffice.org Writer, follow these steps:

1. Right-click any open space within the top panel.
2. Select **Add to Panel** in the popup menu to bring up the Add to Panel window.
3. In that window, click the **Application Launcher** button.
4. A new screen will then appear, showing the contents of the Application menu (Figure 3-6). Click the small arrow next to **Office** to expand that menu, and then scroll down and click **OpenOffice.org Word Processor** to highlight it.
5. Click the **Add** button, and then click **Close** to complete the process.

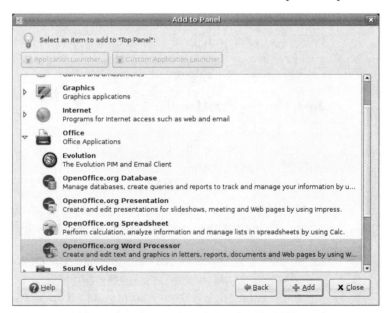

Figure 3-6: Adding an application launcher to the GNOME Panel

Method 2

There is another way to add program launchers to the panel, and it is actually a tad quicker. As an example, we'll add a launcher for the OpenOffice.org spreadsheet program, Calc. Here are the steps:

1. Go to the Applications menu, and navigate your way to (but do not click) **Office ▸ OpenOffice.org Spreadsheet**.

2. With your cursor over **OpenOffice.org Spreadsheet**, right-click.

3. In the popup menu that then appears, select (that's the usual ol' left-click this time) **Add this launcher to panel** (Figure 3-7). The Calc launcher will then appear in the panel.

Figure 3-7: Another way to add application launchers to the panel

Method 3

Now that you've learned two ways to add application launchers to the panel, I might as well let you in on a third, even easier method. Just open a menu, select the item you want to add to the panel, and then drag it there. Well, it can't get much easier than that, eh?

3A-4: Changing Panel Launcher Icons

With your two new program launchers now added to the panel, you may come to feel that it is rather difficult to distinguish one from the other. Fortunately, you can change the icon for any launcher quite easily. To learn how to do it, let's address our immediate concerns with the two OpenOffice.org launchers. Here's what we need to do:

1. Right-click the first program launcher you added (Writer), and select **Properties** from the popup menu.

2. In the Launcher Properties window, click the **OpenOffice.org** icon, which will bring up a Browse Icons window.

3. In that window, scroll down until you find **openofficeorg-20-writer.png**, and then click it once (Figure 3-8).

Figure 3-8: Selecting a new panel launcher icon

4. Click the **OK** button in that window, which will close it.

5. You will then be back at the Launcher Properties window, which should now look like that in Figure 3-9. If so, click **Close**.

Figure 3-9: A Launcher Properties window

Once you have completed the transformation, follow essentially the same steps for the Calc launcher, but this time around you should select **openofficeorg-20-calc.png** as the icon in step 3.

3A-5: Adding a Drawer to the Panel

One of the features I quite like about the GNOME Panel is the drawer. The *drawer* is a little drop-down panel that acts as the perfect location to place launchers that you do not want to place in your GNOME Panel because of space considerations. This is also a handy location to place launchers for applications that you must normally run by typing a command in a Terminal window or via the Launch Application window, such as those you compile yourself from source code or that are run via scripts. You'll learn how to do this in Chapter 9. Of course, you can put anything you want there, including frequently used files.

Adding a drawer to your panel is very easy, and is basically the same procedure that you used to add the Force Kill button to the panel. Here is all you need to do:

1. Right-click any open space on the top panel.
2. From the popup menu, select **Add to Panel**, after which the Add to Panel window will appear.
3. In that window, click **Drawer** once to highlight it, and then click the **Add** button. Close the window by, quite logically, clicking **Close**.

3A-6: Adding Program Launchers to the Drawer

The drawer you've just added is, of course, empty at this stage, so let's put it to good use by adding launchers for three useful, yet less glamorous, system utilities. These are System Monitor, which allows you to view your computer's running applications and processes, memory and CPU usage, and storage device usage; Terminal, in which you can type and execute commands (slightly geeky, I admit, but very useful); and Synaptic Package Manager, which you can use to download and install applications.

Here's what you need to do:

1. Right-click the **drawer** applet in the panel, and select **Add to Drawer** in the popup menu.
2. In the Add to Drawer window that then appears (and looks and behaves exactly the same as the Add to Panel window), click the **Application Launcher** button.
3. In the next screen, click the small arrow next to Administration, scroll down and click **Synaptic Package Manager** to select it, and then click **Add**. The Synaptic Package Manager launcher will now be loaded into the drawer.
4. Add a launcher for the System Monitor by scrolling down a bit, clicking **System Monitor**, and then clicking **Add**.
5. Scroll back up to the Accessories category, and click the small arrow next to it.
6. Scroll down to **Terminal**, click it, and then click the **Add** button. You can now close the Add to Drawer window.

The three launchers should now be loaded in the drawer, so click the drawer to sneak a peek. Yours should look the same as mine in Figure 3-10.

Figure 3-10: Launchers in
a GNOME Panel drawer

3A-7: Adding the Entire Contents of a Menu to the Panel

If you find that you use the applications in a particular submenu of your
Applications, Places, or System menus a lot, you can opt to add the entire
menu to the panel as either a menu or as a drawer in a manner similar to
the one you used in Project 3A-3's "Method 2" on page 36. To learn how
to do this, let's add the Games submenu to the panel as a menu, and the
Sound & Video submenu as a drawer. Here is what you need to do:

1. Add the Games menu to the panel by going to **Applications ▸ Games** and
   then right-clicking any of the launchers within that submenu.

2. In the popup menu that appears, select **Entire Menu ▸ Add this as menu
   to panel**.

3. Add the Sound & Video submenu to the panel as a drawer by going
   to **Applications ▸ Sound & Video** and then right-clicking any of the
   launchers you find there.

4. In the popup menu, select **Entire Menu ▸ Add this as drawer to panel**.

You should now have two new launchers on your panel with icons
matching those found in the Applications menu next to the relevant items.
Click each of these new panel entries to see how they work.

3A-8: Moving Things Around on the Panel

Well, now we've added all we are going to be adding to the panel. It may
seem a little messy up there right now, so let's do a bit of housekeeping by
moving things around. We will try to group things together somewhat
thematically so as to make them easier to deal with.

Fortunately, you can move panel launchers quite easily by right-clicking
the launcher in question, selecting Move from the popup menu, and then
dragging the launcher to the spot you want to place it. Once the launcher is
where you want it to be, click the launcher once, and it will stay there.

To get some practice with this moving business, let's move the launchers,
menus, and drawers you added by placing them in the following order, from
left to right: Applications, Places, System, Firefox, Mail, OpenOffice.org
Writer, OpenOffice.org Calc, Sound & Video, Games, Drawer. Place the

remaining launchers at the right end of the panel, to the left of the update notification tool, in the following left-to-right order: Geyes, Wanda, Force Quit. Finally, place the Run Application panel applet by itself, midway between the two clusters of launchers.

When you've made all your changes, your panel should look pretty much like mine in Figure 3-11.

Figure 3-11: The GNOME Panel with the new launchers

More Panel Fun

In addition to the basic customization you did in Project 3A on page 33, you can do a lot more to change the look and feel of your panel. Of course, you can remove any of your launchers, drawers, or menus by right-clicking the item in question and then selecting **Remove From Panel** in the popup menu, but there are still more options. Most of these are available by right-clicking any open space in the panel and then selecting **Properties**, which will bring up the Panel Properties window.

From this window you can change the position of the panel, alter its size, change its color, or make it transparent—very cool. You can also set the panel so that it will automatically disappear when you are not using it and have it reappear when you bring your mouse cursor into the area where the panel normally resides. Don't feel afraid to play around and give things a try—that's half the fun!

Project 3B: Manipulating Menus

Now that you have learned about some of the cool and useful things you can do with your panel, let's now move on to the topic of menus. A very nice feature of GNOME is that it allows you to edit its menus. You can add launchers, remove items, move items, and even change the icons that appear within the menus. All in all, you have a lot of control over things, but for this project, we'll limit our work to two of these areas: changing icons and moving menu items.

3B-1: Changing Icons Within Menus

As you no doubt recall, one of the problems with the OpenOffice.org Writer and Calc launchers we added to the panel was that they shared rather similar icons. If you go to **Applications ▶ Office**, you will see that the icons for the various OpenOffice.org modules, although not the same, are a bit similar.

One might also argue that those icons are also rather frumpy, which may violate your personal sense of aesthetics as much as it does mine. To remedy this state of affairs, just follow these steps:

1. Right-click the **Applications** menu, and select **Edit Menus** (or select **Applications ▸ Accessories ▸ Alacarte Menu Editor**).

2. In the Alacarte Menu Editor window that then appears, click **Office** in the left pane. The contents of that menu will then appear in the right pane.

3. In the right pane of the window, right-click **OpenOffice.org Word Processor**, and then select **Properties** in the popup menu. An Entry Editor window will then appear.

4. In that window, click the **Icon** button, and navigate to /usr/share/icons/hicolor/48x48/apps in the Icon Selector window that then appears.

5. To make it easier on yourself when adding icons for the other OpenOffice.org modules, drag the **apps** button at the top of the Browse window to the left pane of the same window (Figure 3-12). From now on, you will be able to navigate directly to this folder by double-clicking that icon in the left pane.

Figure 3-12: Adding a folder to your list of places

6. Scroll down to and click **openoffice.org-20-writer.png**, and then click **Open**.

7. The new icon should now appear in the Entry Editor window. If so, click **Close**, and you will be able to see the change in the Alacarte Menu Editor window.

8. Repeat the process for each of the other OpenOffice.org icons, being sure to select the appropriate icons for each of the OpenOffice.org modules (openoffice.org-20-math for the Formula module, for example). Once you're done, leave the Alacarte Menu Editor window open to continue work on Project 3B-2.

NOTE *There is no alternative icon for* OpenOffice.org From Template, *so you can skip that particular item.*

3B-2: Changing the Order of Icons Within Menus

While we still have everything open to the Office menu, let's deal with what I consider to be another problem: the order of the items in the menu. While it is natural enough to have the email client Evolution at the top of the menu, it doesn't make sense to have what is arguably the most commonly used OpenOffice.org module, Writer, way down there at the bottom of the menu.

Remedying this situation is easy. Just click the **OpenOffice.org Word Processor** icon in the right pane of the Alacarte Menu Editor window. Then click the up arrow on the right side of the window as many times as necessary until the Writer icon is right above the OpenOffice.org Database icon. Once you're done, your Menu Editor window should look something like mine in Figure 3-13.

Figure 3-13: Managing menus with the Alacarte Menu Editor

Virtual Desktops

It is now time to discuss a rather unique and convenient feature of Linux: *virtual desktops.* Rather than listen to me babble on and on about this virtual desktop business, it is probably best to learn by just giving it a try.

In your GNOME Panel, click the **Wanda**, **OpenOffice.org Writer**, and **Firefox** launchers. You will then have three windows open in your present desktop, or workspace. Now look at the Workspace Switcher to the right of the bottom panel. There should be four boxes, with the one on the left, your present workspace, in brown. Click one of the other grayed-out boxes, and all your open windows will suddenly disappear.

Actually, nothing has really disappeared—you are just viewing a new desktop. All your other windows are still open and running in the previous desktop. In this second desktop you can open something else: Go to the **Applications** menu, and select **Games ▶ AisleRiot Solitaire**. The AisleRiot Solitaire card game will soon appear.

You now have windows open in two different desktops, and you can switch back and forth between them. To do so, just go to the Workspace Switcher in your panel and click the first grayed box, which will take you to your original desktop. Once you've done that, the box for the workspace you were just in will gray, and you can then click that one to go back to your game desktop.

As you can imagine, this feature has some potential benefits for you, in addition to helping you avoid clutter. Just imagine that you are at work typing some long document in OpenOffice.org Writer. Eventually, you get tired and decide to goof off a bit by playing a game, such as Mines, for a while. To do this, you switch to another desktop where you open and play the game. A bit later, when you notice your boss making the rounds of the office, you simply switch back to the first desktop so that you look busy when he walks by and asks, "Keeping yourself busy, Boaz?"

Phew!

By the way, you can also switch between virtual desktops by simultaneously pressing and holding CTRL-ALT and then pressing your left and right cursor keys to move to your targeted desktop.

Moving Running Applications Between Virtual Desktops

So what happens if, let's say, you are running OpenOffice.org Writer in one workspace and the GIMP in another, but suddenly think that it would be handy to have them both running in the same workspace? Do you quit the GIMP and start it up again in the other desktop? Fortunately, things are much simpler than that, and there are actually two ways to get the job done.

The first of these ways is to right-click on the title bar of the window you want to move, and then select Move to Workspace Left or Move to Workspace Right. I find it less confusing to select Move to Another Workspace, and then select the workspace I want to move the window to by number: Workspace 1, Workspace 2, and so on.

Another way to move a window from one workspace to another is via the Workspace Switcher on the bottom panel. Within the four boxes of the Workspace Switcher, each representing a different workspace, tiny icons will appear for each of the windows you have open in a given workspace. The icons, as you can see in Figure 3-14, will even resemble the shape of the actual windows themselves. You can use these icons to move windows from one workspace to another using a basic drag-and-drop maneuver.

*Figure 3-14: The Workspace
Switcher shows icons of windows
you have open in each workspace.*

For example, let's say you want to move Firefox from workspace 2 to workspace 1. To do this, you would simply click the tiny icon within the second box of the Workspace Switcher, and drag it to the first box, after which the icon would appear there because the Firefox window itself would have moved there.

Finally, if you like to keep your hands more on your keyboard than on your mouse, you can also move a window from workspace to workspace by using hotkeys. With the window you want to move active (on top of the pile, so to speak), press and hold SHIFT-CTRL-ALT, and then use the left and right cursor keys to move the window to the desired desktop.

Wanda Revisited—GNOME Easter Eggs

Well, now that we've finished with our work in this chapter, it's time to goof around a bit by revisiting our precocious piscean pal, Wanda. Knowing what you now do about Wanda the Fish, you might find it odd for me to start talking about her again, but Wanda has a few more tricks beneath her fins. In fact, she is a good means by which to introduce two of GNOME's most famous Easter eggs. *Easter eggs*, in case you don't know, are hidden snippets of code that programmers seem to love to sneak into their programs. They are usually pretty useless things, but they can be found in all operating systems, numerous applications, and even on DVDs (to find out more about those, go to www.dvdeastereggs.com).

A good example of an Easter egg is my first encounter with one on my first Mac, an ancient Mac SE with a whopping 2MB of RAM. On that machine, you could bring up an image (or was it a slideshow?) of the Mac SE development team by pressing the seldom used debug key on the side of the machine and then typing G 41D89A. Pretty cool, I guess, but I would never ever have stumbled upon it had I not read about it in some magazine.

As my example shows, accessing these Easter eggs usually requires some unusual maneuvers, ones that you would never perform in the normal course of things. To see a Wanda-related Easter egg in action, click the **Run Application** button you just added to the panel, type `gegls from outer space` in the Command box, and then click **Run**. You will then see an odd little game of the Space Invaders genre, shown in Figure 3-15, in which Wanda defends our beloved planet from . . . well, gegls, I guess.

To try out the other Wanda Easter egg, open the Run Application panel applet again, but this time type `free the fish`, and then click **Run**. Wanda will now appear swimming around your desktop. If you then click directly on her, she will swim away and out of the picture . . . but she'll be back.

Figure 3-15: One of GNOME's Wanda-related Easter eggs

To put an end to Wanda's comings and goings, you will need to restart the GNOME Panel. There several rather inelegant ways of going about this, but for now we'll do it by opening the Run Application panel applet again, typing `killall gnome-panel`, and then clicking **Run**. Your panels will disappear for a second or two but will shortly reappear. Wanda, however, will be gone.

Shutting Down

Now that you know your desktop environment so well, you may feel like calling it a day and shutting down your machine. To do so, just go to the **System** menu and select **Log Out**. Your screen will darken, and then a small window (Figure 3-16) will appear with six choices to choose from: Log Out, Lock Screen, Switch User, Hibernate, Restart, and Shut Down (Hibernate is not an option when running a live session from the Desktop CD). Click **Shut Down**, and the shutdown process will begin. If, however, nothing seems to happen within a few seconds of clicking **OK**, press CTRL-ALT-BACKSPACE in unison, which will bring you to the login screen you saw at the beginning of the chapter (Figure 3-1). Once there, click **Shut Down** at the bottom of the screen. This will bring up a small window asking you if you are sure you want to shut down. Just click **OK**, and shutdown will commence.

Figure 3-16: GNOME's logout window

The actual shutdown will take a few seconds as the system closes its various services. When it is all done, the system should power down your computer as well, in which case you are done. On a few machines, however, the system cannot power down your machine. You will know if this is so in your case because all screen activity will come to an end. If you get to that point and nothing else happens for 15 seconds or so, then just power down the machine manually by pressing the power button. It is completely safe to do so at that point.

4

MORE THAN WEBBED FEET

The Internet, Linux Style

 These days, average home computer users spend more time surfing the Web and writing email messages than doing just about anything else. Even if you're not much of a surfer, there are still numerous other applications that aren't really Internet applications per se but that still make use of the Internet in some way, such as gathering song and album information when you rip audio CDs to create MP3 files. Having a computer that isn't hooked up to the Internet is like buying a new Maserati and then refusing to take it out of the garage.

Of course, how you connect to the Internet depends on your hardware and provider. There are a number of possibilities in this area, including high-speed local area networks (LANs), cable modems, and ADSL connections from phone companies. Most computers also have an internal 56Kb/s modem or can be connected to external dial-up modems for slower connections over regular phone lines. Depending on what you've got, setting things up on your system should prove a cinch in the case of LAN connections and any others that make use of your Ethernet port (such as cable modems), possibly a bit more work in the case of wireless connections, and sometimes a bit of a challenge when it comes to the ol' dial-up connections. In this chapter, you will learn how to set up these connections and learn a bit about what Linux has to offer in terms of the most commonly used Internet applications— your web browser and email client.

Setting Up a High-Speed Connection

If you have a high-speed Internet connection from your cable television company, or if you are connected to the Internet by a LAN at your office, you are really in luck, because these setups are probably the easiest to deal with. Most likely, all you have to do is connect the Ethernet cable from the wall (if you are using a LAN) or from your cable modem to the port of the network card on your machine. If you're using a wireless router, then the Ethernet cable will connect to the wide area network (WAN) port of your wireless router. After that, once you start up your machine, you should be ready to go without any further settings to fool with.

If you have a problem getting online, and you are trying to connect to via a LAN or cable modem, the problem could very likely be that your network card is not supported by Linux. This is relatively rare, but fortunately, easily remedied (by replacing it).

The problem could also be that your network or service provider does not automatically assign addresses via Dynamic Host Configuration Protocol (DHCP). *DHCP* is a means by which your Internet provider can automatically (dynamically) provide your system with the configuration information it needs in order to connect to the Internet. If your provider does not utilize DHCP, you will have to get the necessary information about settings from the network administrator or service provider and enter the settings yourself.

Setting Up a Cable or Ethernet Connection for Providers Not Utilizing DHCP

To input your cable or Ethernet settings yourself, first get the settings you need from your network administrator or Internet provider, and then perform the following steps:

1. From the **System** menu, select **Administration ▶ Networking**.

2. You will be prompted for your password at this point, so type it (that would simply be your user password), and click **Continue**.

3. The Network Settings window (shown in Figure 4-1) will soon appear, and when it does, select **Ethernet connection** by clicking it once, and then click the **Properties** button.

4. In the Interface Properties window that appears, make sure the box next to the words *Enable this connection* is checked, and then change the Configuration selection from DHCP to **Static IP address**.

Figure 4-1: The Network Settings window

5. The three text boxes shown in Figure 4-2 will become active, thus allow-ing you to enter the information provided to you by your Internet pro-vider or network administrator. Once you've entered the settings, click the **OK** button.

Figure 4-2: Manually inputting network
IP settings

6. Once you return to the Network Settings window, make sure **Ethernet connection** is still selected, and then click the **Activate** button.

7. Once the Ethernet connection item in the main pane says it is active, you can click the **OK** button and start surfing away to your heart's content.

NOTE   *If you are wondering what Internet protocol (IP) and domain name service (DNS) are all about, you can simply think of them in this way: the DNS translates the easy-to-remember URLs that you have come to know, such as www.yahoo.com, into numerical, or IP, addresses that the Internet can understand. The address http://www.yahoo.com thus becomes http://216.109.118.68. You can type the numerical version into your browser later to see for yourself.*

Setting Up a Wireless Connection

Laptops have made the computer a more versatile tool. With the right wireless hardware, you can now surf the Web just about anywhere you can catch a wave, so to speak. Whether you happen to be at your breakfast table, on your backyard deck, in the library of your university, or at your local Starbucks, Port City Java, or Dunkin' Donuts, you can now go online without having to physically hook up your computer to anything. Fortunately, the process of setting up wireless networking in Ubuntu is quite easy—little different than what you just read in "Setting Up a High-Speed Connection" on page 48. In fact, as I just mentioned, chances are that everything will just work from the get-go.

Hardware

If you lead a solely wired existence or are just inexperienced in this particular area, there are a few things worth knowing. To get started, you need to have the right hardware. If you just want to go wireless outside of the home, then all you need is a wireless network interface card (NIC). These are often built in to modern laptops, while for others they are usually add-ons in the form of cards that pop into the PCMCIA slot on the side of your computer (as seen on the right of Figure 4-3).

Figure 4-3: All you need for a WiFi setup—an access point and a network interface card

There are, however, also some NICs that plug into one of your machine's USB ports or, in the case of desktop models, one of its PCI slots. While support for NICs of this type has improved through the last couple of years, there are still gaps, and some can be rather tricky to deal with. If you're looking for a sure thing, Centrino IPW-2100 and IPW-2200 cards are definitely supported by Ubuntu. As for NICs of the built-in or PC card variety, you will find support much better, but even then you have to make sure, or at least hope, that the card you are using is Linux compatible. No matter what NIC you are wondering about, the easiest way to find out whether or not it will work is to just try it out. The Linux kernel now comes with several wireless drivers built in, and Ubuntu updates often provide new ones, so if you use a card that is compatible with one of those drivers, things will be smooth sailing. If things don't seem to work, check the Ubuntu forums to find a driver that is compatible or to see if anyone has experience with your particular card.

If you want to set up a wireless system in your home or office, then you will also need to get a wireless access point (WAP), shown on the left of Figure 4-3. Fortunately, Linux compatibility is not really much of an issue in this department, because the access point doesn't physically interface with your computer.

Unfortunately (for Linux users, anyway), there are a few WAPs that require you to use Internet Explorer to handle their setup chores. Because a Linux version of Internet Explorer does not exist, you will find yourself stuck unless you have a Mac or Windows machine somewhere else in the house to complete the job. Worse yet is the fact that some machines do not support browser-based settings at all. Instead, they require you to install special Windows software to do the job. When selecting hardware for your wireless setup, it is obviously best to stay clear of WAPs of this kind.

Activating Your Wireless Card

Setting up a Linux-compatible wireless PC card is actually relatively simple. First connect your WAP to your Internet source, and then turn on the WAP. Once it is up and running, plug your wireless NIC into the PCMCIA slot on your laptop, unless, of course, your NIC is built in, in which case you can forgo this step. Any LEDs on the external card will most likely light up at this time.

If your WAP was on when you booted up your computer, and your wireless card was in place during bootup, you probably don't need to do anything else to access the Internet. Otherwise, the only thing you will really have to do to get your card working is to configure it and then activate it. You can do this by performing the following steps:

1. Go to the **System** menu, and select **Administration ▸ Networking**. After typing your password when prompted to do so, the Network Settings window will appear.

2. In that window, click **Wireless connection** to select it, and then click the **Properties** button.

3. When the Interface Properties window appears, check the box next to the words *Enable this connection.* If you are in a location where more than one wireless signal is available, you can select the one to which you want to connect from the drop-down menu button next to the words *Network name (ESSID)*.

NOTE   *Some WAPs employ an added level of security in the form of Wired Equivalent Privacy (WEP) or, more recently (and more securely), a WEP key. If the WAP to which you are trying to connect requires such a key, you can type it in the box next to the words* WEP key. *If you don't know the key, then chances are you are not supposed to be making the connection in the first place.*

4. Go down to the Connection Settings section of that window, and select **DHCP**, since most public hotspots and home WAPs are designed to utilize DHCP. You can then click the **OK** button.

5. Back at the Network Settings window, click the **Activate** button (first making sure that **Wireless connection** is still selected).

6. When the Wireless Connection selection says it's active, click the **OK** button to complete the deal.

The network connection indicator at the right end of your top panel will now show a small green icon to its right, indicating that you now have a wireless connection. If you click that icon, you can see the Connection Properties window for that connection, which will show, among other things, the signal strength of your connection, as you can see in Figure 4-4.

Figure 4-4: Checking the signal strength of a wireless connection

Releasing and Renewing Your Wireless Connection

There will be times when you want to turn your wireless card off, such as when you use your laptop on an airplane, or when you just want to flush the IP address in your network settings (*release*) and update the settings with the IP address of a new network (*renew*), as you might when moving your laptop from one wireless hotspot to another without rebooting your computer.

This last point might seem a bit mysterious to you, so I will explain things briefly. When you boot up your computer, your wireless card (NIC) performs a scan of available networks (WAPs) in order to see which one it can connect to. Once it finds a network, it gathers an IP address from that network via DHCP in order to allow you to access the Internet. Utilizing release and renew allows you to change WAPs without having to reboot your computer or when your machine, for whatever reason, just can't seem to make the change on its own.

To turn off your wireless card or release the current IP address in your network settings, just follow the steps you used in "Activating Your Wireless Card" on page 51, but this time click the **Deactivate** button. To reactivate (or renew) the connection, just click the **Activate** button. All quite simple.

A Handier Way to Release, Renew, and Even Sniff

I try not to jump ahead of myself in this book, but this is one case where it is warranted. (Call it a preview of coming attractions if you like.) In Chapter 5 you will be learning how to add new software to your system via an application called Synaptic. One item that you as a wireless user may well find useful is a handy little application called WiFi Radar. WiFi Radar, shown in Figure 4-5, shows you what wireless networks are available to you and what the signal strength of each of those networks is. WiFi Radar also allows you to connect (or at least try to connect) to whatever networks it finds that are willing (knowingly or not) to have you. By using WiFi Radar's Connect and Disconnect buttons, you can also release and renew your network connections in a very simple fashion.

Figure 4-5: Checking available wireless
signals with WiFi Radar

All in all, WiFi Radar is a very handy tool, especially when you are on the road trying to freeload off a signal on which to send an email—not that I am advocating your doing such a thing, of course. Once you learn how to install software in Chapter 5, you can download and install WiFi Radar by doing a search for *wifi-radar* within Synaptic and then following the instructions for installing any application with that application.

Setting Up a Dial-Up Connection

Although much of the world is moving to high-speed Internet connections, many of you may still be using dial-up Internet connections, which means that you need to have a traditional dial-up modem to reach beyond your box to the outside world. In case you broadband surf-gods have forgotten, modems are those wonderful machines that whistle, chime, screech, and spit whenever you dial up your Internet provider. I suppose you could think of them as noisy telephones in need of a good burp.

The good news is that setting up your dial-up connection is a simple process that much resembles what I've covered thus far for other connection types. Now here comes the bad news—in the world of Linux, very few internal modems are supported. The main reason behind this compatibility problem is that most built-in modems are software dependent, and the software they depend on is part of, or designed for, Windows. Such modems are thus called *Winmodems.*

Of course, the Linux community has been working on ways to deal with these Winmodem beasts so that they will work with Linux systems. Though support for the wide variety of Winmodem models out there is still rather spotty, things are better than before, so you might just luck out. My advice is to hold off on the wondering and worrying and just give your modem a try to see if it works. If it does, then you're all set. If it doesn't, well, then you've got some options open to you, but at least you haven't done any damage to your system.

With all that intro-babble out of the way, let's get down to the steps for setting up your dial-up connection. First, get the setting information you need from your Internet provider. Most providers gear their operations to Windows and often Mac users, and very few offer Linux support, other than NeanderTech and a few others. Still, there is no technical reason for your Linux system not to work via their setup, so just nag and push them until they give you the information you want. After that, make sure your modem is connected to a live telephone connection—for example, the phone jack in your wall—and then do the following:

1. Go to the **System** menu, and select **Administration ▶ Networking**. After typing your password when prompted to do so, the Network Settings window will appear.

2. In that window, click **Modem connection** to select it, and then click the **Properties** button.

3. When the Interface properties window appears, check the box next to the words *Enable this connection.*

4. In the Internet Service Provider Data section of that window, type the dial-up connection phone number as given by your provider, and the dial prefix, if necessary, to dial out of your current phone system (some offices require that you first dial 9, for example, to make a call out of the office).

5. Type your username and password, as given by your provider, in the boxes in the Account data section of the window.

6. Click the **Modem** tab, and then select either **Tones** or **Pulses** in the Dial Type section of the window, depending on the type of dialing scheme you have for your telephone service. Most are tone dialers these days, so you can choose that if you're not sure. You can generally figure it out your-self by paying attention to the sounds made when you dial a call. If you hear a series of different tones—almost a melody that you can recognize—then you have tone dialing.

7. Select **Off** or **On** in the Volume section of that tab, depending on whether or not you want to hear your modem doing its dialing. While testing things out, it is a good idea to select **On** so that you can hear what is (or is not) happening.

8. In the same tab, now click the **Autodetect** button. The system should then perform a scan of your ports as it looks for a live modem. Once it finds one, it will specify the correct port in the box labeled *Modem port.* If it doesn't find one, well . . . that's not a particularly good omen in terms of the usability of your present modem, but you can still give it a try by picking a port on your own. Start out with /dev/modem, and if that doesn't work after going through steps 9 and 10, try out the others one by one before finally opting for more dramatic measures.

9. Once your modem port has been found (or you've chosen one on your own), click the **OK** button.

10. Back at the Network Settings window, make sure that Modem connection is still selected, and then click the **Activate** button.

Once the steps are completed and assuming your modem and system are in loving compatibility, you should then hear your modem begin its dialing, spitting, and churning sequence as it makes the connection with your provider. Once it does, you can go on and start your browsing, emailing, or whatever else it is you do online. When you are ready to end your Internet session, click the **Deactivate** button to bring it all to a close.

Of course, in the future when you wish to connect to the Internet, you will not have to go through all of those setup steps. All you will have to do is click the Activate button, which makes things all the easier.

What to Do if Your Modem Isn't Compatible

What I've just described is pretty much a best-case scenario. What happens, however, if your modem and Ubuntu do not see eye to eye? Well, there are a few options. My first, more radical suggestion, is to dump those extra movie channels from your cable service (nothing all that great on them anyway) and pay for cable Internet service instead. If that is not an option, then you have two ways to go. One is to try to geek around with your modem to see if you can get it to work. This is a slightly more complicated process, but there are instructions at https://wiki.ubuntu.com/DialupModemHowto. If you are faint of heart or a novice user, you may find what the process entails to be a bit more than you're willing to deal with.

The simpler, although costlier, way to get your modem to work is to change your modem. In this case, changing to a true hardware modem. *Hardware modems*, in case you are not familiar with the term, are modems that are not software dependent and thus work with whatever system you happen to use with them. You can think of them as telephones without a handset.

Such modems come in two forms: internal and external. As for the internals, the USRobotics models 56K V.92 Performance Pro Modem (internal slot) and 56 PC Card Modem (PC card slot, for laptops) are true hardware modems that are easily available and are said to work. You can check out the USRobotics site (www.usr.com) for more information on these models, though checking the Ubuntu forums for suggestions is always a good idea.

External Dial-Up Modems

Perhaps the safest of all solutions is to buy an external serial modem. An external modem sits in a box outside your computer, and it connects to the serial port in the back of the computer, which is usually the only connector with little prongs in it (see Figure 4-6). Because the modem doesn't use your operating system to operate, it does not tie up system resources while it's busy, which may result in a possible pickup in computer speed.

Figure 4-6: Serial port and connector

Most external serial modems should work with your system, or at least that is what most people will tell you. If you are worried and are looking for a sure thing, Zoom Telephonics (www.zoom.com) makes an external serial modem that is compatible with Linux, and they say so right on their website. The USRobotics 56K V.92 External Faxmodem is also said to work, though I haven't tried out this model myself.

If you find another model that you think will do the trick, before you commit to it by slapping down the cash, do a Yahoo! or Google search with that modem's make and model number, along with the word *linux*, and see what search results you get. Of course, you can also try out one of the Linux forums and ask about the modem make and model there. There are a lot of people in the same boat, so you are sure to get plenty of opinions and advice.

Firefox: Your Internet Browser

Now that you are connected to the Internet, you no doubt want to get down to some cyberspace discovery and exploration, and the most commonly used means of doing that is with a web browser. The default web browser in your Ubuntu system is Firefox, which is enjoying increasing popularity in not only the Linux world, but in the Windows and Mac worlds as well. Chances are you are already a Firefox user, but if you are not, then you needn't worry—things work more or less the same in all browsers. That being the case, you should be able to use Firefox's basic features without any instruction. Of course, there are some features that do distinguish Firefox from its competition, so I will mention those.

Controlling Browser Window Clutter with Tabs

Usually when you click a link on a web page, the new page opens in the same window. On some pages, links are coded so that the new page opens in a new, separate window, or maybe you occasionally opt for opening a link in a new window by right-clicking the link and then selecting the Open Link in New Window option. This can be very useful; however, once you have more than a few browser windows open, it gets sort of hard to find what you're looking for in all those open windows. It can also slow things down a bit.

This is where Firefox's tab feature comes in handy. To see how it works, try it out yourself right here and now. Open your Firefox browser by clicking the launcher on the top GNOME Panel (or going to **Applications ▸ Internet ▸ Firefox Web Browser**); then Google the word *nyckelharpa* using Firefox's handy search box, which is next to the word *Go* at the top-right corner of the browser window (see Figure 4-7). By default, Firefox will perform searches for keywords entered in the search box using Google. You can, if you like, select other search engines by clicking the G icon in the search box and then making your selection. Amazon.com, eBay, and Yahoo! are available, to name a few, and you can even add others. For now, however, let's stick to Google for our present search, by typing **nyckelharpa** in that search box. Once you've finished typing, press the ENTER key, after which a page of Google results should appear in the main pain of the Firefox window.

NOTE *While tabbed browsing is no longer as unique as it once was (Safari has the feature built in, though you have to enable it yourself, and Internet Explorer now has the same functionality available as a downloadable add-on), it is implemented and enabled by default in Firefox.*

Figure 4-7: Performing a Google search from the Firefox search box

The top result should be the American Nyckelharpa Association, and you are now going to open that page in a new tab, rather than in the same or a new window. To do that, right-click the link, and in the popup menu that appears, select **Open Link in New Tab**. You can, if you prefer, make things a tad easier and dispense with the popup menu selection step by simply clicking the link with both mouse buttons simultaneously or by holding down the CTRL key as you click the link. Either way, the new page will appear in a new tab, while your original page of search results remains, ready and waiting in the other tab (see Figure 4-8). I am pretty confident in saying that, once you get used to this feature, you will wonder how you ever got along without it.

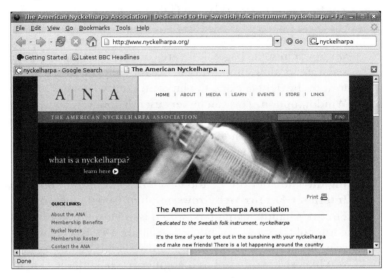

Figure 4-8: A link opened in a new tab in Firefox

Other Firefox Features: Popup Manager

Firefox has a number of other useful features. One is its Popup Manager, which suppresses those annoying popup windows that often appear when you access a new web page. You can enable or disable this feature from the Preferences window (**Edit ▶ Preferences**) by clicking the **Web Features** icon in the left pane of that window and then checking or unchecking the box next to the words *Block Popup Windows*. You can also permit certain sites to provide popup windows (some popups are not only useful, but necessary for the correct functioning of a site) by clicking the **Allowed Sites** button next to that Block Popup Windows entry and inputting the URL for the site in question.

Project 4: Installing Firefox Extensions

One of the coolest things about Firefox is that it allows you to further expand its functionality by adding various extensions. These extensions include all sort of things; many are quite functional, while others are just plain fun and goofy. They range from blog-writing tools to image viewers. For this project, however, we will be installing a cool weather station of sorts, called Forecastfox, that allows you to view not only the current weather conditions in your area (or any other area of your choosing), but also a two-day local forecast, Doppler radar maps, and more—all from AccuWeather.com. All of this is available at the click of a button from the Status or Menu bars, or the Bookmarks or Navigation toolbars—your choice (Figure 4-9).

Figure 4-9: The Forecastfox extension installed in Firefox

4-1: Downloading and Installing the Forecastfox Extension

To get started with the process of installing any Firefox extension, you have to first, quite logically, find and download one. To do this, go to the Firefox **Tools** menu, and select **Extensions**. The Extensions window will then appear (Figure 4-10), showing you the extensions you already have installed, which at this point should be only one. To add more, click the **Get More Extensions** link at the bottom-right corner of the window, which will bring your browser to the Firefox Add-ons site.

Figure 4-10: Seeing what extensions you have and getting more in Firefox

At this point, you would normally browse for things that seem of interest to you, check to make sure they don't have any special requirements (such as Microsoft Windows—a few do), and then download and install the extension that has struck your fancy. In this case, we already know what we are going to install, so I'll just tell you where to find it.

To find the Forecastfox extension, first try having a look at the Top Downloads section of the page, as it is often there. Otherwise do a search for it in the search box on the Extensions page. You might also just type the URL where it is currently residing: https://addons.mozilla.org/firefox/398. Once you've found it, click the **Install Now** link for that item, and then wait. Sometimes the download will take a bit of time, sometimes less. Either way, just be patient, and don't keep clicking the link. The extension will be in the process of downloading even if seems as if nothing is happening, and when it is done, a window will appear telling you so (Figure 4-11).

Figure 4-11: Firefox seeks your permission
before installing an extension

Once the window appears, all you have to do is click the **Install Now** button. The Extensions window (previously seen in Figure 4-10) will then pop to the front of the currently open Firefox window and indicate the progress of the download. When the download is done, the new extension will be added to the list of extensions with a message telling you that Forecastfox will actually be installed once you restart Firefox. The implicit command thus being: restart Firefox.

4-2: Setting Up the Forecastfox Extension

When Firefox first starts up after you've installed the Forecastfox extension, you will see the Forecastfox Options window (Figure 4-12). In that window, type your zip or postal code (or that of any other area for which you want weather information) in the text box next to the word *Code*. If you're not sure what the zip or postal code for your desired locale is, click the **Find Code** button to select that location by name.

Figure 4-12: The Forecastfox Options window

In the Forecastfox Options window, you can also choose whether you want the temperatures shown in Fahrenheit or Celsius and where you want the information to appear in your browser window. The Status bar at the bottom of the browser window seems to be the least intrusive location, so that is what I've chosen. Of course, you are free to place it where you like. When you're done, click the **Apply** button and then the **OK** button, and you'll be on your way to intense meteorological entertainment.

Email with Evolution

Evolution is the default email program in Ubuntu, and it could probably best be described as a better-groomed, spunkier clone of Microsoft Outlook (see Figure 4-13). It allows you to send and receive mail, make appointments, and keep a list of tasks. It can also filter junk mail, which is a necessity these days, and even synchronize with your PalmPilot, if you still have one of those. Also, if such things are important to you, it is a much more handsome program to look at than Outlook.

Figure 4-13: Ubuntu's default email client—Evolution

To use Evolution, just click the email launcher on the top panel or go to the **Applications** menu and select **Internet ▶ Evolution Mail**. When you first run Evolution, you will be greeted by a setup wizard, so have the account details you received from your Internet service provider handy. These should consist of your POP host address for receiving mail, your SMTP host address for sending mail, and your mail password, which is very often different from your Internet logon password. Your mail password is not actually entered during the various wizard steps, so check the **Remember this password** checkbox when filling in the POP details. When you first connect to your mail server, you will be prompted for your mail password, so you can type it at that time, and you won't have to deal with it again.

An Email Alternative: Thunderbird

Evolution is, without a doubt, the most popular email software in the Linux world, but despite its obvious attractions and popularity, I have to say that I don't much like it, though I can't quite put a finger on the reason why. I just prefer the more straightforward Thunderbird for my email chores. In contrast to the multifunctional Evolution, Thunderbird (Figure 4-14) is a more mail-oriented program that is very straightforward to use, yet includes most of the most important email functions you've come to expect, such as junk mail filters. In fact, it is remarkably similar to Outlook Express in terms of appearance and handling. It also lacks the quirkiness that always seems to squirrel its way into Evolution in some form or another. The fact that Thunderbird is also available in both Mac and Windows versions means that you may already be familiar with it, or prepared to deal with it if you find it in use on another system you happen to be using.

Figure 4-14: The Thunderbird email client

Thunderbird does not come bundled with Ubuntu, so if you would like to try it out, you will have to download it and install it yourself. Now that you have set up your machine to connect to the Internet, however, you can easily do this after going over the contents of Chapter 5 (okay, so I'm jumping the gun a bit again). Just do a Synaptic search for *thunderbird*, and then mark **mozilla-thunderbird** for installation. Once it is installed, you can then run it from the **Applications** menu by selecting **Internet ▸ Thunderbird Mail Client**.

As I mentioned, both Evolution and Thunderbird are equally capable and possess essentially the same features in terms of mail handling. The difference is primarily a look-and-feel matter. Why not try both Evolution and Thunderbird and see which you like better?

By the way, if you find that you prefer Thunderbird to Evolution, you can add a panel launcher for it so as to make things easier on yourself when you want to run the program. Just go to **Applications ▸ Internet ▸ Thunderbird**

Mail Client, right-click that entry, and then in the popup menu that appears, select **Add this launcher to the panel**. You can then remove the Evolution launcher, if you are so inclined.

Other Internet Applications

What I've covered thus far in terms of Internet applications is just the tip of the iceberg (might as well use that worn-out phrase before there aren't any icebergs left, right?). Ubuntu also comes with a couple of other Internet applications that you might want to consider. These include the Instant Messenger client called Gaim (**Applications ▸ Internet ▸ Gaim Internet Messenger**), which allows you to do use any one of your MSN/Windows Instant Messenger, Yahoo! Messenger, AOL Instant Messenger (AIM), ICQ, Gadu-Gadu, Napster, GroupWise, IRC, or Jabber accounts . . . or all of them simultaneously. If you want to give Internet telephony a try, Ekiga Softphone (**Applications ▸ Internet ▸ Ekiga Softphone**) also comes bundled with your distribution, so you need not despair.

There are still more Internet applications that you might want to consider downloading and installing after you've completed the next chapter. These include the two applications I've already mentioned in this chapter, WiFi Radar and Thunderbird, but there are a host of others. If this all sounds pretty enticing to you, get those fingers of yours flipping and move on to the next chapter—the mother lode awaits!

5

ROUNDING OUT THE BIRD

Downloading, Installing, and Updating Programs the Easy Way

One of the handiest things about Ubuntu is that it is equipped with a very simple-to-use application installation mechanism. The engine, using the term loosely, behind this is a mechanism called Advanced Package Tool (APT), which allows you to easily download, install, update, and remove software packaged in DEB archives, or *packages*.

APT is a rather foolproof way of installing programs; nothing will go missing, since it automatically downloads and installs any files that the main application you are installing requires to run. Tracking down such files, called *dependencies*, proves to be a significant headache for most Linux users. The painful quest of finding and then installing this file or that, as well as any dependencies that those files themselves might have, has led to the missing dependency problem being referred to as *dependency hell*. APT makes that pretty much a thing of the past.

The one thing about APT that some people, especially beginners, might consider a problem is that it is a command-driven application. This means that you control it via commands in a command Terminal. Fortunately, Ubuntu has two different graphical front ends for APT that allow you to bypass the command line and make everything about as easy as you could hope it would be.

Project 5A: Installing Applications via Synaptic

As I mentioned, Ubuntu comes with two graphical front ends for APT: the simpler, though arguably more attractive, GNOME App Install; and the main application handling workhorse, Synaptic. Because Synaptic is the more full-featured of the two applications, and because GNOME App Install also utilizes it for its settings chores, we'll start things off with Synaptic.

To get a look at Synaptic, go to the **System** menu, and select **Administration ▶ Synaptic Package Manager**. Because APT installs things in your system in areas that are write protected (more on that topic in Chapter 6), you will be prompted for your password in a separate window before Synaptic actually appears. The password is just your usual user password (users of other Linux distros take note), so that should be easy enough to remember. Type your password when prompted to do so, and click **Continue**. Synaptic, shown in Figure 5-1, will soon appear.

Figure 5-1: Synaptic Package Manager

Although the Synaptic interface may seem rather simple at first glance, it is a very powerful program. It not only allows you to search for, download, and install applications, but it also allows you to find and install the less glamorous, but equally important, libraries and support files that you might need for use with other applications that come bundled with Ubuntu (such as MP3 support), or those you install by other means. You can also use Synaptic to find other things such as fonts, foreign language localization files, and less common utilities, and to update the software you have installed on your system when such updates are available.

Of course, if you don't know what you're looking for, you can browse through the packages available via Synaptic by clicking the **Sections** button at the bottom-left corner of the window, selecting a category of interest in the pane above that, and then clicking the name of a specific package in the top-right pane, after which a description of that package will appear in the pane below.

5A-1: Adding APT Repositories via Synaptic

It is important to know that the packages that APT (and thus both Synaptic and GNOME App Install) searches for, downloads, and installs are located in a set of specific online *repositories*. These repositories are basically online servers in which a great number of applications, support files, and more are stored for use with your particular system. All of the files that originally come bundled with your system, including the system (kernel) itself, and updates, when available, are stored there.

Only the main application and update repositories are activated by default in Ubuntu, but the real gold mine of applications is located in what are called the *universe* and *multiverse repositories*. These repositories contain software that is prepared and maintained by the Ubuntu community, but not officially supported by Ubuntu. In order to really make your Synaptic experience (and your GNOME App Install experience, for that matter) worthwhile, and to follow along with future projects in this book, you will, therefore, need to activate the universe and multiverse repositories.

To do this, go to the Synaptic **Settings** menu, and select **Repositories**. When the Software Preferences window appears, you will see all of the repositories that are currently activated (Figure 5-2). To activate the universe and multiverse repositories, scroll down the list of repositories in the main pane (under the word *Channels*), and then check the boxes for all of the entries followed by *(Binary)*.

After you've done that, click the **Add** button, and once the Add Channel window appears, check the boxes next to *Community maintained (Universe)* and *Non-free (Multiverse)*. After that, click the **Add** button to save your changes and close the window.

Once back at the Software Preferences window, click **Close**. A new window will then appear telling you that you will have to click the Reload button in order for your changes to take effect. Click the **Close** button in that window, and then click the **Reload** button in the main Synaptic window as you were just instructed to do.

Synaptic will then begin downloading package lists from each of the repositories you just added to its package database. A window like that in Figure 5-3 will show the progress of the download and will disappear when the process is complete. There will then be a brief period during which all of the panes in the main Synaptic window will be gray, but don't worry; this is only temporary.

Figure 5-2: Synaptic's repository list

NOTE   *Because the contents of the various repositories change quite often, it is advisable to reload the repository lists by clicking the Reload button every time you take Synaptic out for a spin.*

Figure 5-3: Download progress indicator in Synaptic

Adding New Repositories to Synaptic

You don't need to do it right now, and you may, in fact, never have to at all, but it is worth knowing that you can add new repositories to Synaptic. In fact, you will learn how to add one later in Chapter 9, but just for future reference, I will lay out the process here. It is basically the same as that for adding the universe and multiverse repositories, albeit it with a little twist.

To add a repository, just follow these steps:

1.   Go to the Synaptic **Settings** menu, and select **Repositories**.
2.   In the Software Preferences window that then appears, click the **Add** button.
3.   In the Add Channel window that then appears, click the **Custom** button.

4. Yet another window will then appear. In the text box in that window, enter the APT line for the repository you want to add. For example, take a look at the following APT line for Wine, which you'll learn about in Chapter 9 (you can add the line at that time, if you're interested).

```
deb http://wine.budgetdedicated.com/apt dapper main
```

5. Once you're done, click the **Add Channel** button in that window. The window will disappear, and the new repository will appear checked in the Software Preferences list.

The new repository, just like the universe and multiverse repositories, can be deactivated by simply unchecking the box below its entry in the Software Preferences window.

5A-2: Installing Monkey Bubble

Let's start using Synaptic by installing a game called Monkey Bubble just to see how things work. What you will be doing is basically the standard method you would use to search for and install any package via Synaptic, so it is a process well worth remembering. Here are the steps:

1. In the main Synaptic window, click the **Search** button.
2. A Find window will appear. Be sure to select **Description and Name** in the Look In menu (to provide a more forgiving search), type monkey in the Search box, and then click the **Search** button.
3. After a short period of time, a list of results will appear in the upper-right pane. Look for **monkey-bubble**, and click it once to select it. A description of that file will then appear in the bottom-right pane.
4. Right-click that same entry, and select **Mark for Installation** in the popup menu that appears.
5. A window like the one in Figure 5-4 will open, telling you what is going to be installed. The libraries you will find there are the dependencies required for Monkey Bubble to run. Click **Mark** in that window.

Figure 5-4: Synaptic lets you know what additional packages will be installed

6. You are now ready to roll, so just click the **Apply** button in the main Synaptic window, after which yet another window (Summary) will appear, telling you what is going to be installed, what is going to be changed, and what is going to be left alone.

7. Click **Apply** in that Summary window, after which Synaptic will begin the installation process, showing you its progress in a separate window (very much like the progress window you saw in Figure 5-3, in fact).

8. When the installation is complete, a new window like that in Figure 5-5 will appear to let you know. Click **Close** in that final window, and then wait until Synaptic snaps out of its temporary state of grayness, which signals the complete end of the installation process.

Figure 5-5: Synaptic lets you know when it's done doing its thing.

You can now run Monkey Bubble (Figure 5-6) by going to the **Applications** menu and selecting **Games ▶ Monkey Bubble**.

Figure 5-6: Monkey Bubble

Installing the Flash Player Plugin for Firefox

To get a little more practice, let's use Synaptic to install the Flash Player plugin for Firefox. Given the fact that more and more web pages out there contain significant amounts of Flash content, this installation will make your web surfing endeavors much . . . well, let's just say less annoying, since you won't have to repeatedly stare at messages such as "Additional plugins are required to display all the media on this page" or "Click here to download plugin" (an especially annoying message, since the click-to-install approach doesn't seem to work—not yet anyway).

To do the deed, click the **Search** button in the main Synaptic window, type `flash` in the small Find window that then appears, and then click **Search** in that window. In the list of results that then appears, scroll down until you find **libflash-mozplugin**, and click it once to select it. Once you've done that, right-click that same entry, and select **Mark for Installation** in the popup menu that appears. Click **Mark** in the window that appears, click the **Apply** button in the main Synaptic window, and then click **Apply** again in the Summary window that appears.

When the installation is done, you can check things out to make sure that Flash is at work by opening Firefox (and, yes, you must restart it if it was open while you were installing the Flash plugin) and going to www.adobe.com/products/flash/about. If you don't see any of the annoying you-need-this-click-here-to-install-that messages that I mentioned earlier, you can sit back and smile. Success has once again come your way. Hoola.

Removing Applications via Synaptic

To remove applications installed from a DEB package via Synaptic, GNOME App Install, or any other means, search for the application you wish to remove either by clicking the **Search** button and typing the name of the application you wish to remove, or by clicking the **Status** button in the bottom-left corner of the Synaptic window, clicking **Installed** in the pane above that, and then scrolling through the list of installed packages that then appears in the top-right pane. Once you find the application in that list, right-click on its name, and select **Mark for Complete Removal** to remove the application and any setting or configuration files for that application. When the window that tells you what is going to be axed appears, check through it carefully so as to make sure you aren't inadvertently uninstalling something you would mourn the loss of—like your whole desktop environment, for instance. Assuming everything looks okay, click the **Apply** button, after which the process will be the same as that for installing applications.

Upgrading Applications via Synaptic

As I mentioned, you can also use Synaptic to upgrade applications installed in your system. To do this, click the **Status** button in the bottom-right corner of the Synaptic window. In the pane above that button, then click the entry **Installed (Upgradeable)**, after which a list of the installed applications with available upgrades will appear in the upper-right pane. Right-click on any application listed there that you would like to upgrade, and select **Mark for Upgrade** in the popup menu that then appears. Repeat the right-click procedure for any other application you want to upgrade, then click the **Apply** button. The procedure from then on out will be the same as that for installing packages.

Project 5B: Installing Applications via GNOME App Install

While Synaptic is great for just about everything, when it comes to browsing to see what cool or handy applications are available for you, Ubuntu's other APT front end, GNOME App Install, is probably a more satisfying way of going about things, due to its graphical nature.

To get a feel for that application, make sure Synaptic is closed (you can't run Syanptic and GNOME App Install at the same time), and then open GNOME App Install by going to the **Applications** menu and selecting **Add/ Remove**. The Add/Remove Applications window, shown in Figure 5-7, will then appear.

Figure 5-7: GNOME App Install

As you can see, items in GNOME App Install are categorized pretty much in the same manner as in the Ubuntu Applications menu itself. If you click any of the category icons in the left pane of the window, you will see a list of all the items available for that category in the top-right pane—installed items are checked, while those that are not installed are unchecked. Not surprisingly, you will find that the checked items within each category mirror those in the relevant submenu of the Applications menu.

5B-1: Selecting Applications for Installation

GNOME App Install, like Synaptic, can install multiple applications simultaneously, so to give it a whirl, we'll try installing a couple of applications that might be of interest to you. Before getting down to selecting the applications, however, be sure to check the two boxes located between the top- and bottom-right panels: the one next to the words *Show unsupported applications* and the one next to the words *Show proprietary applications.* Doing this will enable you to view everything that is available to you in the repositories you activated via Synaptic in Project 5A on page 66.

Now that all that there is to be seen can indeed be seen, let's start out by selecting the very cool and decidedly useful address book application called Rubrica (shown in Figure 5-8). To select Rubrica, just click the **Office** category in the left pane of the Add/Remove Applications window, scroll down the list of available applications in the top-right pane, and check the box next to the words *Rubrica Addressbook.*

Figure 5-8: Rubrica—a very cool address book

Let's also select a handy audio application called SoundConverter that converts audio files from one format to another—MP3 to Ogg Vorbis, for example (you'll learn more about SoundConverter in Chapter 16). To select it for installation, click the **Sound & Video** category in the left pane of the window, scroll down in the top-right pane, and check the box next to the word *SoundConverter.*

NOTE   *Be careful not to uncheck the boxes next to any of the already checked applications listed in GNOME App Install. Doing so will result in their being removed once you go on to Project 5B-2 on page 74.*

5B-2: Downloading and Installing Selected Applications

Once you've made your selections, click the **OK** button at the bottom of the Add/Remove Applications window. A new window, like that in Figure 5-9, will appear showing what you are about to install. Click **Apply** in that window, after which you will be prompted for your password, just as you were for Synaptic (and for the same reasons), so type your user password, and click **Continue**. GNOME App Install (APT, actually) will then begin the download and installation process, showing its progress via the same progress windows you saw when installing applications with Synaptic.

Figure 5-9: GNOME App Install tells you what it is about to install.

When it's done, GNOME App Install will close itself down, and you'll be ready to run your new applications. You can run the applications by going to the **Applications** menu and then looking in the submenu that matches the category in which each application was located within GNOME App Install. That would be **Office** for Rubrica, and **Sound & Video** for SoundConverter, which you'll learn more about in Chapter 16.

As you can see, installing applications via GNOME App Install is quite simple, and if you paid heed to my warning, you also know how easy it is to uninstall applications. Just check, and click Apply to install; uncheck, and click Apply to remove. Can't get much easier than that, you have to admit.

Performing System Upgrades via the System Update Panel Applet

At the beginning of this chapter I mentioned that there were two graphical front ends for APT, but I must now admit that I understated things a bit—there are actually three, though that third front end is strictly used for updating your system. Before updating individual packages via Synaptic, therefore, it is probably a good idea to save yourself some time by first checking for available updates via the System Update panel applet.

To perform the update, make sure that Synaptic and GNOME App Install are both closed (you just can't run two APT front ends at the same time, as I told you), click the **System Update** panel applet, type your password when prompted for it, and press the **Continue** button. A Software Updates window (Figure 5-10) will then appear.

Figure 5-10: Upgrading packages en masse via the System Update panel applet

In that window, a list of all of the available updates will appear. You can scroll through that list and uncheck the box for any application you don't want to upgrade, but if you don't really know what you're doing, you had better just leave it as is. Either way, once you're ready, click the **Install Updates** button, after which the updates will be downloaded and installed, with the same windows you saw in Synaptic and GNOME App Install showing you the progress of the process. Once the installation is complete, you will be notified in a separate window. Click **Close** in that window, and then do the same in the Software Updates window. Depending on what you installed, another small window may appear telling you that you will have to restart your system in order for changes to take effect. If so, it is best to be obedient and reboot.

6

A TIDY NEST

File and Disk Handling in Ubuntu

No matter which operating system you are using, you have to deal with files. Some people are very organized, placing every file in a logically named folder as soon as that file is saved for the very first time. Then there are people like me, who save everything to the desktop until it is so full of junk that they can no longer make out the wallpaper, and only at that point do they start organizing in earnest (if placing all of those files in a single folder called March17Cleanup can be called organizing). Ah.

Of course, files not only get stored on your hard disk, but they are also copied to and from CDs, DVDs, external hard disks, flash drives, and other storage media and devices. They are also often saved in archives, which are then compressed to reduce their spatial footprint, making them easier to send via email or to fit onto spatially challenged removable storage media.

With that intro, you may have already guessed that in this chapter I will be dealing with file handling in Ubuntu, particularly in relation to the Nautilus File Manager, which is at the heart of GNOME's file-handling capabilities.

Nautilus: Your File Manager

As I mentioned, the program that creates the file viewing and organizing interface in your system is called Nautilus, and it comes as part of the GNOME desktop environment. You may not have thought of an operating system's file manager as a program before, but in fact, that is what it is. (The Windows file manager is called Windows Explorer.) To have a look at Nautilus, just go to the **Places** menu, and select **Home Folder**.

When Nautilus opens up to your home folder, you should find nothing the first time out other than a folder titled Desktop (shown in Figure 6-1), which, if double-clicked, will show everything you have stored there (a lot in my case; most likely nothing in yours). There is also another folder, called Examples, which is the same as the one that appears on the Desktop when running Ubuntu off the live CD. It contains sample files that give you an idea of what Ubuntu has in store for you, along with that Nelson Mandela video I mentioned in Chapter 3.

You can create additional folders and, of course, files to your heart's content, so this rather spartan state of affairs is sure to change once you get down to really using your system. In fact, you will be creating a number of folders in Chapter 7, which will make everything look a bit more lived in.

Figure 6-1: The contents of your home folder as viewed in a Nautilus window

The Side Pane

Nautilus has a lot of interesting features that deserve mention, and the most obvious of these is the side pane, which appears at the left side of the window. The side pane allows you to view a variety of information via selectable views. You can make your choices by clicking the drop-down menu at the top of the side pane (Figure 6-2).

Figure 6-2: Selecting views
for the Nautilus side pane

The default view in Ubuntu is Places, which is a sort of quick navigation tool. In Places you will find icons representing various data-storage locations available to your system, such as your home folder, desktop, full filesystem, any network shares you are connected to (more on that in a moment), and any removal storage media or devices you have in or connected to your system. Double-clicking any of these icons will show the contents of that location in the right panel of the Nautilus window.

There are, of course, other views, such as Tree, which provides you with an expandable hierarchal view of your filesystem, and History, which shows you where in your filesystem you have been most recently, much in the way the history function works in a web browser. There are still other views for you to choose from, a couple of which you will work with in Chapter 7.

Now You See It; Now You Don't

The side pane is a rather handy feature, but there may well be times when you would prefer to have more space to view the contents of your window and thus want to get rid of the pane temporarily. You can do this quite easily by going to the **View** menu of a Nautilus window and then deselecting **Side Pane**. The check mark next to that entry will then disappear, as will the side pane. To get it back, just return to the **View** menu, and select **Side Pane** again. The check mark will then reappear, as will the side pane itself.

There is another way to hide the side pane that many people seem to stumble upon accidentally, usually resulting in a bit of unnecessary panic. If you look at the gray border at the right side of the side pane, you will notice that there is a small ribbed section in the center (see Figure 6-3). Clicking that ribbed section acts as a toggle to hide or show the side pane. The panic most users suffer is a result of the fact that when the side pane is hidden in this way, the Side Pane entry in the View menu is still checked, indicating the side pane is still in view, though your eyes tell you differently.

So there it is—the side pane's little secret. No, it's not a particularly interesting secret, but one that should not only provide you with an added layer of convenience, but also some peace of mind.

Figure 6-3: Showing and hiding the Nautilus side pane

File Handling in Nautilus

Since Nautilus is primarily a file manager, it only makes sense to get down to the business of using it at that level. Of course, most folks who use computers today are already familiar with the basics of drag-and-drop and a few other means of creating folders and copying, cutting, and moving files. But for those who are unfamiliar with one way or another of performing these essential procedures, I thought it best to spell it all out. If you find this all a bit redundant, please bear with me for the good of the masses.

Creating, Naming, and Renaming Folders

Creating a folder is a simple enough task, and there are two ways of going about it. The easiest (in my opinion) is to right-click in any empty space within a Nautilus window, and select **Create Folder** in the popup menu that appears. If you prefer using menus to right-clicking empty space, you can instead start things rolling by going to the Nautilus **File** menu, and selecting **Create Folder**.

Regardless of where you made your Create Folder selection, a new folder with the name *untitled folder* will appear in the Nautilus window. The name box of the folder will be highlighted and surrounded with a black box, which means that you can immediately give that folder a name by simply typing one—nothing to click or do other than that. Press ENTER or click any open space in the Nautilus window to complete the job.

If you later decide that the name you gave your folder needs some tweaking or even a complete revision, you can rename it by right-clicking it and selecting **Rename** in the popup menu. Alternatively, you can click the folder once to highlight it, and then select **Edit ▶ Rename**. After that, you can type the new name for the folder and then press ENTER or click any open space in the Nautilus window to seal the deal.

Moving Files and Folders

Perhaps the easiest of all file manipulations you can perform in Nautilus is moving a file by means of drag-and-drop. I am pretty sure that anybody who has wielded a mouse is familiar with that particular move. There is another way of moving files and folders, however: cut and paste.

The easiest way of doing this is to right-click the file (or folder) you want to move, and then select **Cut** from the popup menu (**Edit ▶ Cut** will also do the trick). At this point, it will seem as if nothing has happened, as the file will still be there, so don't worry. After that, right-click any open space in the folder to which you wish to move the file, and then select **Paste** in the popup menu. The file will then disappear from its original location and appear in its new one.

Can you use key combinations to do this, you ask? Sure. Simply follow the directions I just gave, but use CTRL-X to cut and CTRL-V to paste.

Copying Files and Folders

Based on the instructions I just gave, you can pretty well imagine the methods for copying files and folders, as they are essentially a variation on the same theme. Just right-click the file you want to copy, select **Copy** from the popup menu, right-click any open space within the target location, and then select **Paste**. Keystroke-wise, that would be CTRL-C to copy and, as before, CTRL-V to paste.

It is also possible to copy folders and files via the wonders of drag-and-drop, though this involves more hands than required for a simple drag-and-drop move; fortunately, the two you have will do nicely. Just press and hold the CTRL key while you drag the file or folder you want to copy to the target location. Be sure to release the mouse button and then the CTRL key (releasing in the opposite order will not work), and you will find a copy of the file in its new location.

Navigating in Nautilus

Navigating through your various folders and subfolders in Nautilus is quite straightforward. In fact, all is conceptually pretty much the same as what you are accustomed to in Windows and Mac OS. You can simply move into and out of folders through a combination of double-clicking folders and clicking the Back, Forward, and Up buttons.

Tabbed Browsing in Nautilus

In addition to the hierarchal view option provided in the side pane, there is another handy feature that can make your navigation chores even easier: Nautilus's tabbed browsing feature. These tabs (they look like buttons, actually) appear in the navigation bar for each folder you opened on the way to the one you are currently viewing.

Say, for example, that you have a folder called gooseberries inside a folder called Dalarna inside a folder called SwedeStuff inside a folder called NordicStuff, which itself is in your home folder. As you click your way to that gooseberries folder, starting with a double-click on the NordicStuff folder, Nautilus will display a tab for that folder . . . and any folder opened before it. Take a look at Figure 6-4 to see what I mean.

Figure 6-4: Tabbed navigation in Nautilus

As you can see, there is a tab button for each of the folders within the path from your home folder (mine, in this case) to your target: gooseberries. So what, right? Well, say you want to go back to the NordicStuff folder to open a file in which there's some text that you want to copy and then paste into a doc within the gooseberries folder. Sounds like a minor pain, right?

Well, rather than goof around with the Back button, you can instead simply click the NordicStuff tab button, and the contents of that folder will be there before you. Need to go back to gooseberries? Just click the gooseberries tab button. Back to SwedeStuff, you say? Just click the SwedeStuff tab button. All quite *fantastisk*!

Spelling It Out—Typing File Paths in Nautilus

If you prefer typing to clicking, you will be happy to know that you can navigate to a folder by typing its path. Just go to the **Go** menu, and select **Location**, or keyboard shortcut lovers can just press CTRL-L. A search box will then appear in the location bar (Figure 6-5), in which you can type the path to your target folder, and then press ENTER. In the case of my berried example, that path would be: /home/rg/NordicStuff/SwedeStuff/Dalarna/gooseberries.

Figure 6-5: Typing the path to your target folder

Bookmarks Within Nautilus

With all this clicking away to deeply buried subfolders, it is worth mentioning another very handy feature of Nautilus: bookmarks. Yes, Nautilus lets you bookmark folders to which you have navigated. While you are no doubt familiar with creating bookmarks for web pages that you frequent, you may be wondering why on earth you would want to create bookmarks within your filesystem.

Well, imagine that you have a folder that you need to use often, but it is even more buried away than my gooseberries folder in the previous section. Getting there would take an excessive number of mouse clicks, and all that clicking is bound to eventually give you a bad case of carpal tunnel syndrome. While that is great for your HMO, it is most decidedly not good for you. Instead of maiming yourself, you could click your way to that folder once, and then, in the **Bookmarks** menu of the Nautilus window, select **Add Bookmark**. After that, whenever you want to get back to that buried folder, you can just click the **Bookmarks** menu, and the folder will be right there waiting for you in the drop-down list.

Another handy thing about Nautilus bookmarks is that they also appear in Save As dialog boxes, such as when you save an OpenOffice.org document or download a file via Firefox. In any Save As dialog box, just click the **Save in folder** button, and you will find your bookmarks.

Using Nautilus as a Network Browser

Another handy Nautilus feature is its ability to function as a network browser. You can, for example, see what networks and shares are available to you on your home or office network by going to the **Places** menu in the GNOME Panel and selecting **Network Servers**. You can do the same from within a Nautilus window by going to its **Go** menu and selecting **Network**. Icons for any networks or computers on that network would then appear in the Nautilus window, as you can see in the case of my own home setup in Figure 6-6. From that window, you can then double-click your way to a share that you have permission to access, such as the Shared Documents folder of a Windows machine or the public folders of a Mac.

Figure 6-6: Network browsing in Nautilus

By the way, in case you are wondering what a share is, I'll clear that up for you. Basically, a *network share* is a location on a computer, such as a folder, where other users on a network can access and save files. The Shared Documents folder on a Windows system is a good example. Other users on a network can copy files from and (usually) write files to the Shared Documents folder, whereas they cannot access any other part of the filesystem on that host machine.

If the share you are trying to open requires a username and password, you will be asked for those in a new window (Figure 6-7). Note that in this case, the username and password you need to enter are those for the machine to which you are trying to connect—not the ones you're using in Ubuntu (unless the usernames and/or passwords happen to be the same, of course). You can then copy files to and from that share as if it were a folder on your own hard disk.

Figure 6-7: Entering network usernames and passwords for the machine to which you're trying to connect

In some cases, especially when trying to access shares on a Mac running OS X, the double-click method will not work. You will not be able to access any share on a particular machine, even though an icon for that machine appears in the Nautilus window. In such cases, double-click the icon for the machine you are tying to access, and then once open (to an empty window), go to the **Go** menu, and select **Location**. A text box will appear in the location bar (just like in Figure 6-5) with the location of the machine you are trying to access already listed.

To that location, add a forward slash (/) followed by the username used on the target machine. For example, if the target machine is called cowboycats, and the username is mewtoyou, the location would be smb://cowboycats/mewtoyou. You can also narrow things down to a particular folder on the machine, as long as you know the path to that folder, by adding to the path you've already typed, smb://cowboycats/mewtoyou/Documents, for example.

NOTE   *In case you are wondering, the* smb *at the head of that path means* Samba, *which is software used by Unix-based systems (such as Linux and Mac OS X) in order to interact with Windows networks.*

Once you've made your way to the folder you wish to browse on the networked machine you've connected to, it might be a good idea to use the bookmark function in Nautilus to bookmark that open share window. You can then easily access that share in the future by choosing the share's name in the Nautilus Bookmarks menu. Pretty cool, if I do say so myself.

Using Nautilus as an FTP Client

Nautilus not only allows you to browse and mount shares on local networks, but it can also act as an FTP client, say for instance when you want to change the files for your website on a remote server. To do this, go to the Connect to Server window (**File ▶ Connect to Server**), and then select **FTP (with login)** for Service Type. Then type the information provided by your website host, and click the **Connect** button. An FTP Network Share icon will then appear on the desktop and in the side pane. Double-click that icon, type your password (for that account—not the one for your Ubuntu system, unless it happens to be the same) when prompted to do so, and then you will be able to view and add to the files you have there.

File and Folder Permissions Within Nautilus

As you make your way in the world of Ubuntu, you will find that occasionally you'll come across files or folders emblazoned with emblems such as those shown in Figure 6-8. These emblems signify that the file or folder in question is in some way locked, either in terms of your being able to read it, being able to alter it, or both. These readability and alterability states of being are referred to as *permissions*.

can't read   can't write   can't read or write

Figure 6-8: Restricted permissions emblems in Nautilus

Now you may be (legitimately) wondering what the point of this permissions business is, so in order to help you understand, I will give you some examples of how it can be useful. Let's say that you have some files that you don't want your spouse or kids to see—some bad poetry or a Christmas shopping list, for example. By denying read permission to those files, or to a folder containing those files, no one would be able to sneak a peek unless they were savvy at changing permissions and had the permissions necessary to change permissions for those files or folders.

As another example, imagine you have a file that you have worked many hours on and have finally completed. To alleviate fears that you might accidentally trash it in some way, you could deny write permissions. By doing this, you wouldn't be able to do anything to that file without changing its permissions. In fact, if you tried to move that file to the Trash, or even to the desktop or another folder, you would be greeted with a no-can-do message, such as the one shown in Figure 6-9.

Figure 6-9: Nautilus tells you when permissions
restrict your freedom of movement.

Changing File and Folder Permissions in Nautilus

To change file or folder permissions in Nautilus, just right-click the file
or folder in question, and then select **Properties** from the popup menu.
Once the Properties window opens, click the **Permissions** tab, and you will
see who the owner of the file or folder is and what you are allowed or not
allowed to do with it (see Figure 6-10).

Figure 6-10: Changing permissions in a Nautilus
Properties window

You might find this permissions business a bit confusing, but it is really
quite simple to understand. As you can see in Figure 6-8, permissions can be
granted or denied to the *owner* of the file or folder (you), to a specified *group*,
or to *others* (everybody else). These permissions are:

Read   Permission to view the contents of a file or folder

Write   Permission to alter the contents of a file or folder

Execute   Permission to run a program or script

In general, you needn't worry all that much about setting permissions
for your own files, as you are really the only one who has access to your user
account. One of the main exceptions to this is when you transfer files from

CD to your hard disk. In this case, the files will be write protected, meaning that you cannot alter the files until you change the permissions for them. You can change the permissions of such files in order to allow yourself to alter them by clicking the checkbox in the Owner row next to the word *Write*. Once you are done, click the **Close** button, and you'll be on your way.

Keeping Your Home Folder Private

Another exception to my you-don't-need-to-worry-about-permissions claim, and a potentially important one at that, is the state of permissions for your home folder, particularly when other people have user accounts on your machine. In Ubuntu, when someone logs in to their own account on your computer, they can click their way to your user folder and view its contents.

To remedy this situation—and thus protect the sanctity of your home folder, the privacy of its contents, and the peace of mind of its owner (you)— you can change the permissions of your home folder. Here's what you need to do:

1. Open up a Nautilus window, and then double-click **File System** in the side pane. The contents of your entire hard disk will then appear in the right pane of the Nautilus window.

2. Look for and then double-click the folder named home. When the contents of the home folder you just clicked appear in the right pane, there should only be one folder there—your own home folder, which will have the same name as your own username. Mine, for example, is named rg.

NOTE *The folder named home is not your home folder, but rather the folder that contains the home folders for each of the user accounts on your machine.*

3. Right-click your home folder, and then select **Properties** in the popup menu.

4. In the *username* Properties window (mine says *rg Properties*), click the **Permissions** tab.

5. In the Permissions tab, uncheck all of the boxes except the three next to the word *Owner*. When you're done, your window should look like mine in Figure 6-11. If so, click **Close**.

Reading Data CDs and DVDs

Dealing with data CDs and DVDs in Ubuntu is quite simple, as everything is automatic. To read a CD or DVD with data on it, rather than music or video, place the disk in your drive, and a CD or DVD icon (they look the same) will automatically appear on the desktop. A Nautilus window displaying the disk's contents will also appear, after which you can copy files from the CD or DVD to your hard disk using standard drag-and-drop procedures.

When you want to remove the CD or DVD, just close its Nautilus window, right-click the desktop icon for that disk, and in the popup menu, select **Eject**. The disk will then be ejected automatically.

Figure 6-11: Changing the permissions of a home folder for privacy

Burning Data CDs and DVDs

Burning data CDs and DVDs in GNOME is extremely easy. All you have to do is place a blank CD-R (CD-Recordable) or DVD (DVD-RW, DVD-R, and DVD-RW are all supported by Ubuntu) in your drive, making sure to select a media format supported by your drive, and a window will appear asking you what you want to do with the disk. Click the **Burn Data CD** button, or in the case of a blank DVD, the **Make DVD** button. Nautilus's CD/DVD Creator window will then appear, which as you no doubt notice looks pretty similar to other Nautilus windows, save for the brown band below the location bar and the Write to Disc button (Figure 6-12).

Figure 6-12: A Nautilus CD/DVD Creator window with files ready to be burned to disk

Once the CD/DVD Creator window is open, copying the files you want to burn to disk is pretty much a simple drag-and-drop maneuver. Just open a new Nautilus window, and drag the files you want to burn to disk from that window over to the CD/DVD Creator window. If you prefer to do things in a decidedly Windows-esque fashion, you can select the files you want to transfer to disk by clicking each file once, holding down the CTRL key while doing so, for multiple selections. If you want to select multiple consecutive files, you can click the first file in the group, press and hold SHIFT, and then click the last file in the group, automatically selecting all the files in between. Once you've made your selections, release the CTRL or SHIFT key, right-click any of the highlighted files, and select **Copy** in the popup menu. After that, go back to the CD/DVD Creator window, right-click any open space, and then select **Paste** in the popup menu.

It is probably worth mentioning that the files you copy to the CD/DVD Creator window are not actually copied. Instead, what you see in the Creator window are essentially aliases pointing to the original files in their original locations. Thus, if you move one of the files from its original location before burning the contents of the CD/DVD Creator window to disk, the file will automatically vanish from the window, and it will not be burned to disk when you finally get around to that step. This is not problematic, but it is something worth being aware of.

Once you have copied all of the files you want to burn to disk, click the **Write to Disc** button, after which a window (shown in Figure 6-13) will appear, telling you, among other things, how many megabytes of files you have selected to write to disk. In this window, you can give your disk a title and adjust the speed at which your disk will be burned (slower speed = fewer chances for errors), though you can just as well accept the defaults.

Figure 6-13: Setting options before burning a CD or DVD

Once you are ready to burn the disk, just click the **Write** button, and the CD/DVD Creator will do its work. In some cases a warning window will appear telling you that some of your files may not be suitably named for Windows compatibility. Just click **OK** if you come face to face with such a window, unless you do intend to transfer the files to a Windows system, in which case, you had better go back and rename the files according to Windows naming conventions before you get down to the actual burning. In particular, avoid special characters and diacritics (such as umlauts and accents), and do not use the following characters, which are reserved for Windows system functions: / : ? * " < > |.

Once the burning gets under way, its progress will be shown in a new window, and then when the job is done, you will be asked what you would like to do next. Assuming you are done with your disk burning for the day, click **Eject**, and then click **Close**.

In case you are wondering, the disks you burn in Linux *will* be readable in other operating systems.

Dealing with CD-RW Disks

CD-RW disks are pretty much like CD-R disks except that they can be erased and then written to again. They are also quite a bit more expensive than CD-R disks and, generally, cannot handle faster burning speeds.

Using CD-RW disks is much like working with CD-R disks. If the disk is blank, there is no difference in the process at all, which makes things quite simple. And, if the CD-RW disk already has data on it that you wish to replace with something else, the process is only slightly different.

One of these differences is that Nautilus will treat your CD-RW disk as a regular data disk rather than a blank one. This means that when you pop your disk into the drive, a regular Nautilus window will automatically open, rather than a CD/DVD Creator window.

To write to the disk, you will need to manually switch from the Nautilus window to a CD Creator window, which is easily done by selecting **CD/DVD Creator** in the **Go** menu of the Nautilus window opened for that disk. Once you've done this, the window will become a CD/DVD Creator window. Now drag the files you want to burn to CD to that window, and, once you are ready to burn, click the **Write to Disc** button.

As is the case with regular CD-R disks or DVDs, a Write to Disc window will appear. When you click the **Write** button in that window with a used CD-RW disk in the drive, however, a slight difference occurs. At this point, a new window like that in Figure 6-14 will appear telling you that the disk seems to have files already written on it. Click the **Erase Disc** button in that window, and the CD/DVD Creator will erase the files already on the CD-RW and replace them with the new ones that you dragged to the CD/DVD Creator window. Not bad at all, eh?

Figure 6-14: Erasing a CD-RW disk with Nautilus

Burning ISO Images to Disk

When you download Fedora Core or other Linux distributions from the Internet, you usually download them in the form of one or more disk images, which are commonly referred to as ISOs because such files end in the .iso extension. An *ISO* is an image of a CD's file contents, which means that it is the CD minus the media itself. To put it another way, if CDs had souls, the ISO would be the soul of a CD; take away the CD's metal and plastic, and the remaining data would be an ISO.

As it is impossible to download a physical CD over the Internet, the bodiless ISOs are the next best thing. For example, to get a working copy of Ubuntu from the Web, you need to download an ISO, which you then burn onto a blank CD in order to give the images their bodies back, so to speak. In the process you create the working installation disk that you need to install Ubuntu.

Fortunately, burning an ISO to disk is a pretty simple chore. Just open a Nautilus window, and locate the icon for the ISO file you want to burn to disk. Right-click the ISO file, and in the popup menu that appears, select **Write to Disc**. Once you do this, the Write to Disc window will appear; just click the **Write** button, and you'll be on your way.

Duplicating Data CDs

Duplicating CDs and DVDs is also easily accomplished in Ubuntu. Just right-click the desktop icon for the disk you want to copy, and then select **Copy Disc** in the popup menu. The Write to Disc window will then appear. Click the **Write** button in that window, and the Nautilus CD/DVD Creator will begin copying the contents of the disk as a disk image to your hard disk. This may take a bit of time, so don't worry. When it is done, you will be prompted to insert a blank disk into your drive. Once you've done that, the Creator will begin copying the disk image to the blank disk.

If you want to know how to duplicate audio CDs, hang on until you get to Chapter 15.

Burning Multisession CDs

If you are coming from the Windows environment, you are no doubt familiar with multisession CDs. These are CDs on which data is added one session at a time. For example, you burn a few files to disk today, add a few more to the disk tomorrow and a few more files the day after that. Each time you burn additional files to the same disk, you are adding a session, which explains the name *multisession*. If that explanation seems a bit obtuse, you can basically think of them working like floppy disks (albeit with considerably more storage capacity). While Nautilus can read and display the contents of such multi-session disks, it cannot (yet) write multisession disks. To do that, you will need a different disk-burning application. I recommend GnomeBaker.

You can download and install GnomeBaker via Synaptic (search for *gnomebaker*). Once installed, you can run it from the **Applications** menu by selecting **Sound & Video ▸ GnomeBaker**.

To burn the first session to CD, insert a blank CD-R disk (just close or cancel any Nautilus windows that pop up in response), and then drag the files that you want to burn during the session to the bottom pane of the GnomeBaker window, under the Data Disk tab (Figure 6-15). You can drag files from the file browser in the top two panes of the GnomeBaker window, from a Nautilus window, or from the desktop.

Figure 6-15: Using GnomeBaker to create multisession disks

When you have all the files in place that you want to burn, click the **Create Data Disk** button at the bottom-right corner of the screen. A new window, Create Data CD, will appear. In that window, click the drop-down menu button next to the word *Mode*, and select **tao** instead of default. Once you've done that, click **Start**, and the burning process will begin. GnomeBaker will eject the disk when the burn is complete.

Burning Subsequent Sessions

To add a new session to a multisession disk, make sure that the bottom pane of the GnomeBaker window is empty (click the **Clear** button if it isn't), and then insert the multisession disk into your drive. After your drive has finished its spinning and you have pushed the Navigator window for that disk out of the way, click the **Import** button above the bottom pane of the GnomeBaker window. A small window will appear asking you to select the drive where the multisession disk is located. You most likely only have one drive, so the correct device should already be displayed. If so, click **OK**.

The files burned in previous sessions will now appear in the bottom pane, and they are identified by a CD icon to the left of the filename. To add additional files to burn to the disk (thus creating a new session), just follow the procedures you used for burning the initial session.

USB Storage Devices

No chapter dealing with file handling and storage would be complete without touching upon the topic of USB storage devices, so that is exactly where I will now turn. Unless you have been under a digital rock for the past few years, you are no doubt well familiar with USB devices. Your printer is very likely a USB device, as is your scanner. And although your digital camera is not a USB device in the traditional sense, chances are that every time you connect it to your computer in order to transfer photos, you are doing so via a USB connector.

Among the most popular USB devices out there are those for file storage. These include external hard disks, flash memory card readers, and the tiny, finger-sized devices known as *flash drives* (Figure 6-16). Flash drives are especially popular today, and deservedly so: they are quite inexpensive; extremely handy when you need to transfer fairly large, but not gigantic, amounts of data from computer to computer (from work to home, for example); and pretty safe in terms of cross-platform (including Linux) compatibility.

Figure 6-16: USB storage devices

Putting USB Storage Devices to Work

Let's start with some good news here by pointing out that working with USB storage devices is really easy. Just plug the device into one of the USB ports on your computer. The LED on the device will do a bit of blinking as the system reads what's on it, and after that, a disk icon for that device will appear on your desktop. A few moments later, a Nautilus window will open, revealing the contents of the device. You can then copy files to and from the device using the drag-and-drop or copy-and-paste procedures I mentioned earlier in this chapter.

Once you are done and wish to remove the device, right-click its desktop icon, and select **Unmount Volume** in the popup menu. A progress bar will appear in a small window as the system writes the new data to the drive. When the process is complete, the contents of the Nautilus window should revert to a view of your home folder, and the desktop icon will be gone. You can then safely remove the device from the USB port.

Project 6: Creating and Extracting Compressed Files

Since I have been talking about file storage, it seems only fitting to wrap things up in this chapter by teaching you how to create and extract compressed files. In the Windows world, these are generally referred to as Zip files, while in the Linux world, *tarball* is the operative name. The Linux name, in case you're wondering, comes from the application that is used to create the archive for such files, Tar.

Anyway, to get some of the hands-on stuff down, we'll be creating a Windows/Linux/Mac–friendly Zip file, and then extracting it. We can get down to business by opening a Nautilus window and creating a couple of dummy files to work with. You can do this by going to the Nautilus **File** menu and selecting **Create Document ▸ Empty File**. A new file will appear in the Nautilus window, with its name highlighted. You can now just type a name for the file, such as the one I'm using: *dogwood.* Now repeat the process to create a second file. I'll be calling that one *violet.* Use something equally evocative for yours.

Now that we have two files to work with, let's start creating the compressed archive by following these steps:

1. Select the two files either by clicking your mouse to the side of the files, and then dragging the cursor (with the mouse button still pressed) over both files until they are highlighted, or by holding down the CTRL key and clicking on each file individually.

2. Once both files are highlighted, right-click either one, and select **Create Archive** from the popup menu.

3. In the Create Archive window that then appears, type **blossoms** in the Archive text box, and then select **.zip** from the drop-down menu button to the right of that. Once everything looks like what I've set up in Figure 6-17, click the **Create** button, after which a compressed archive of your two files (blossoms.zip) will appear in your home folder.

Figure 6-17: Creating a compressed archive

Now that you know how to put things together, let's get back to work and learn the equally simple task of ripping it all apart—well, okay, *extracting* it.

1. Drag the original dogwood and violet files to the Trash to get them out of the way.
2. Double-click the **blossoms.zip** file you've just created. A window showing the contents of the file will then appear (Figure 6-18).

Figure 6-18: Extracting a compressed archive

3. In that window, click the **Extract** button, after which another window, Extract, will appear. Click the **Extract** button in that window, and within a second (two at the most), you will find two new copies of dogwood and violet in your home folder.

Now you've created and extracted a compressed archive, which is in this case a Zip file. You can also create a compressed tarball in the future by following the same procedure (hopefully with real rather than dummy files), but when it's time to select an archive type, select **.tar.gz** instead of .zip. Other than that single step, it is the same creation and extraction process.

7

DRESSING UP THE BIRD

Customizing the Look and Feel of Your System

 Before entering the world of Linux, I had used just about every desktop operating system around. Despite the differences among them all, however, one thing that I eventually suffered from in each case was a kind of visual boredom. I suppose you might call it GUI fatigue.

It wasn't that I was tired of using a graphical interface; it was just that I couldn't help but get sick of looking at the same old icons, window borders, and color schemes. Of course, there were some changes that could be made, but it just wasn't possible to get around the basic look and feel without add-ons that demanded a price in terms of performance.

One of the features of Linux that pleased me to no end, and continues to do so, is that users can drastically change the look of things. I don't mean just the icons and backgrounds, but everything, including the actual window borders and controls. Add to that the variety of graphical desktop environments and window managers available for Linux, and you have a totally customizable system. Is it any wonder that there are so many more Linux desktop screenshots out there on the Web than for any other system? If you don't believe me, just have a look at a site dedicated to Linux screenshots, www.lynucs.org, and click the **Screenshots** link.

You may not be as fickle as I am in terms of the look and feel of your system, but you can learn to use and enjoy all the graphical customization power that Linux offers you as you work through this chapter.

Project 7A: Creating a New User Account

If you are reluctant to alter the look of your present setup, you can create a new user account and experiment with making the changes in this chapter when logged in to the new account. If you opt to go this route, your regular home environment will remain untouched because look-and-feel customizations that are performed in one user account do not affect other user accounts. When you are all done with the project, you can then simply delete the new user account. Either way, it's up to you.

To set up a new user account, follow these steps:

1. Go to the **System** menu, and select **Administration ▸ Users and Groups**.

2. When prompted for your password, type it, and then click **Continue**. The Users and Groups window will open.

3. In the Users and Groups window, click the **Add User** button, which will bring up a User Account Editor window.

4. Type a new username: **graphika**. In the Real Name field, you can type whatever you like; I used *Graphics Lover* in the example. Then move on down to the Password section of the window, skipping over Contact Information, and type an easy-to-remember user password in the two password boxes; in this case, the one you're using for your present account will do just fine. Once you've done all this, your window should look more or less like that in Figure 7-1.

5. If everything looks fine and dandy, click **OK** to close the window and get back to the Users and Groups window, which will now list your new user account right below your current one (see Figure 7-2).

Before using the graphika account, you need to give yourself user privileges to install software while logged in with it. Normally, this privilege is disabled by default on new user accounts, as you probably don't want your kids, workmates, or anyone else with their own user account on your computer installing all sorts of weird stuff and screwing up your system settings.

Figure 7-1: Creating a new user account

Figure 7-2: The new user account displayed in the Users and
Groups window

To change the privileges for the graphika account, click the **graphika**
entry within the User list to highlight it. Once you've done that, click the
Properties button. A new window, Settings for User graphika, will then
appear. In that window, click the **User privileges** tab, and then check the
box next to the words *Executing system administration tasks* (as shown in
Figure 7-3). Once you're done, click **OK**, and then exit the Users and
Groups window by clicking **OK** again.

Figure 7-3: Changing user account privileges

Logging In to Your New Account

To use this new account, go to the **System** menu and select **Log Out** (or just click the **Logout** button at the far-right corner of the top panel). When the logout window appears, click **Log Out**. After a few seconds, you will be back at the login screen. Type your new username in that window, and then press ENTER. After that type the new password for the account, and press ENTER again. You will soon be at the desktop for your new user account.

Switching Users

It's worth knowing that there is another way to switch users other than simply logging out of one account and into another. This alternative approach is logically referred to as *switching users.* Switching users differs from the logout/login approach, in that you remain logged in to your original account while you log in to your other account (or while someone else with an account on your computer logs in to theirs). Going this route keeps all of the windows or applications you have open. These windows will not appear in the account you are switching to, but they will be there, conveniently waiting for you, when you switch back to the account from whence you came.

This is a good way to proceed if you plan to be switching back and forth between your two accounts. It is also a good approach when, say, your child needs to log in to his or her account for a moment to do a quick email check, burn a CD to play on the way to the beach, or print a file for school. When your child is done, you can quickly get back to what you were doing before without having to reopen files, web pages, or whatever else you happened to be dealing with at the time of the switch.

You can switch users in much the same way you would using the logout/login approach. After clicking the **Quit** button in the top panel, you can click **Switch User** instead of Log Out. You are then delivered to the login screen where you type the username and user password for the other account (each step followed by a press of the ENTER key), just as you would normally log in.

To get back to your original user account after going the switch-user route, just click the **Quit** button at the right corner of the top panel, click **Switch User** (if you plan to return shortly to the new account) or **Log Out** (if you don't plan to return soon), and then once back at the login screen, type your original username, press ENTER, type your password, and press ENTER again. In the small window that then appears, click the **Return to previous login** button.

Another window will appear, in which you must type the user password of the account you are returning to. Type your password, click **Unlock**, and you will be back at your original desktop, with everything as it was when you last saw it, open windows and all. Pretty cool.

Logging In to Another Account in a Separate Window

If switching back and forth between accounts seems like too much of a hassle to you, there is yet another, almost surreal, alternative—logging in to another account in a separate window while still in your regular user account.

This being-two-places-at-the-same-time approach requires a little bit of work up front, but it provides a lot of convenience in the long run, not only when going through Project 7B on page 102, but also whenever one of those "Hey 'rents, can I check my email for a second?" moments arises. To set things up so that you can do this, you need to install, set up, and use an application called Xnest. Here are the steps:

1. Run Synaptic, do a search for *xnest,* and install it.

2. Once Xnest is installed, close Synaptic, go to the **Applications** menu, and select **Accessories ▸ Alacarte Menu Editor**.

3. When the Alacarte Menu Editor window appears, click **System Tools** in the left pane, and then check the box next to *New Login in Nested Window* in the right pane. Click **Close** to finish.

After performing these steps, you can log in to your new account by going to the **Applications** menu and selecting **System Tools ▸ New Login in Nested Window**. An Xnest window will appear, and after a few seconds, the Ubuntu login screen will appear within that window. In that screen, type your new username (*graphika,* or whatever name you chose) and password as you would during any other login. Your new desktop will soon appear in the Xnest window (Figure 7-4).

When you are done with your Xnest session, click the **logout** button at the far right of the top panel, and then click **Logout** in the set of choices that appears. The Xnest window will automatically close after you have been logged out of that session.

Figure 7-4: Using Xnest to log in to another account while still in your own

Project 7B: Customizing Your Desktop Environment

Whichever user account you've decided to play with, you are now ready for
action. We are going to start off easy by just creating folders, but by the time
we get to the end of the process, you will have created a much wilder, and,
depending on how you look at things, gaudier desktop environment than
you've ever seen before. All of this is in good fun, of course, and when you
are done, you should be able to completely and confidently customize things
the way you want on your own. So let's go.

7B-1: Creating Folders

To get started, open your home folder. Unless you've been working on your
own without me, there should be nothing there at this point except for the
Examples folder, which I mentioned in Chapter 3, and a folder called Desktop,
which basically contains any files, folders, and shortcuts to programs that you
have put on your desktop. If you are anything like me, you will want to put an
end to this rather empty state of affairs by creating some folders in which you
can organize your files in the future.

   The first folder you will create will be for your documents, which you'll
call Documentia, though you can, of course, change the name later if you
like. You can create a folder quite easily, much like you do in Windows, either
by clicking the Nautilus **File** menu and then selecting **Create Folder** or by
right-clicking in an empty space within the window and then selecting
Create Folder from the popup menu. An untitled folder will appear.

Having a folder called untitled is, of course, a tad goofy, so you will want to change that. The text in the box below the folder will already be highlighted, so just type `Documentia`, and press ENTER. Once you have done that, the folder will show its new name.

Now you can repeat the process and create four more folders: Photos (for your photos, of course), Downloads (where you can dump any used files you will download along the way in this book), PDFs (for PDF files), and Music (for music files you will later learn to rip from music CDs with the program Sound Juicer). Once you have done all this, your home folder window should look like that in Figure 7-5.

Figure 7-5: Adding folders to your home folder

7B-2: Adding Emblems to Folders

You must admit, things do indeed look a bit better than before, but this is just the beginning. To graphically remind yourself what each folder is for, you can add little folder-top icons called *emblems*. These can be added to any folder or file. For now, let's add one to the **Documentia** folder by right-clicking it and then, in the popup menu, selecting **Properties**. When the Properties window appears, click the **Emblems** tab and then scroll down until you see the emblem called Documents (Figure 7-6). Click the checkbox next to **Documents**, and then click the **Close** button. The emblem should now appear on your folder.

Now, for additional practice, try adding the **Sound** emblem to your Music folder. Just use the same steps as before, and substitute the appropriate items and entries.

Figure 7-6: Choosing emblems for your folders

7B-3: Setting Window Backgrounds (and Emblems Again)

Once you've added those two emblems, your folders should look a bit spunkier. Nevertheless, the background of the Nautilus window is still white. You need not stand for that if you don't want to; you can change it as well. To do so, just go to the menu bar of your home window, click the **Edit** menu, and select **Backgrounds and Emblems**. The Backgrounds and Emblems window will then appear (see Figure 7-7).

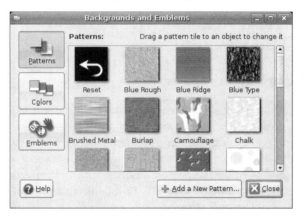

Figure 7-7: Choosing a background for your Nautilus window

From this window, you can drag any pattern into your home window, or into any other Nautilus window for that matter, and the pattern will then become the background for all your Nautilus windows. So, for experience's sake, scroll down to find the pattern swatch called **Manila Paper**, and then drag it to the white space in the main pane of your home window. Once you've done that, the previously white window area will look like the wallpaper in a lawyer's office. Very nice, if you like that sort of thing. You can change it to a different background in the same way, of course, or you can go back to the default white by dragging the **Reset** swatch into the window.

NOTE *If you prefer to use an image of your own for the Nautilus window background, you can also do so quite easily. Just locate the image in a new Nautilus window, click it with both the left and right mouse buttons (or just the middle mouse button, if you have a three-button mouse), and then drag the image to any open space within the target window. When you release the buttons, select **Set as Background** in the popup menu that then appears.*

In addition to the buttons for pattern and color swatches, there is a third button in the Backgrounds and Emblems window called Emblems. Clicking the Emblems button reveals all of the emblems you saw in Project 7B-2 on page 103, thus providing you with another way to add emblems to your folders. This method is far handier when adding emblems to several folders or files in the same go.

To see how this works, click the **Emblems** button. Then drag the **Camera** emblem onto your Photos folder, **Package** onto your Downloads folder, and **Special**, for lack of a better choice, onto your PDFs folder. The selected emblems will then immediately appear on those folders.

7B-4: Dolling Up the Side Pane (and Emblems Yet Again)

Now let's change the look of the Nautilus side pane. Keeping the Backgrounds and Emblems window open (if you already closed it, open it again), click the **Places** menu button in the Nautilus side pane, and select **Information**.

You can add a different background pattern to the side pane now as well, but for practice let's add a color instead. To do this, click the **Colors** button in the Backgrounds and Emblems window. The window will now be filled with swatches of color. Drag the **Grapefruit** swatch to your side pane, and it will turn from gray to, of all things, grapefruit (albeit a very dark and unusually colored grapefruit). You can also create a two-color gradation effect by adding yet another color. Drag the **Mango** swatch to the bottom of the side pane (but still within the pane), and you should have a grapefruit-to-mango, top-to-bottom gradation within the pane. Of course, if you are not pleased with this tropical color set, you can get back to your original default gray panel by dragging the **Reset** swatch onto the area. When you're done, you can close the Backgrounds and Emblems window.

The side pane of your Nautilus window provides yet a third way to work with emblems. But before I let you in on this third, and last, way, you will need to add two more folders to your home folder. Create one folder and name it Finances, which you can use to store files dealing with your relative worth in the modern scheme of things, and then create another and call it MyFaves, where you can place . . . well, your favorite files.

After you've created the new folders, go to the side pane, click the **Information** drop-down menu, and select **Emblems**. A list of emblems will appear within the side pane. Select the **Money** emblem, and drag it onto your Finances folder. Next, select the **Favorite** emblem, and drag it onto your

MyFaves folder. Your window should now look like that in Figure 7-8. Once you are done, go back to the drop-down menu and select **Information** to get everything back to relative normalcy again.

Figure 7-8: Selecting emblems from the Nautilus side pane

Even if it's not your cup of tea, you have to admit that your Nautilus window is definitely more colorful now. You can, of course, change it to look however you want it to, but I'll ask you to hold off on that a little while longer, because you are going to be doing a some more playing around with it shortly.

7B-5: Changing the Desktop Background

Now that your home folder window is all gussied up (or gaudied up, depending on your aesthetic sense of things), you may feel that your desktop looks rather drab in comparison.

Changing the desktop background (often called *wallpaper*) is easily achieved by right-clicking any open space on the desktop and selecting **Change Desktop Background** in the popup menu. This will bring up the Desktop Background Preferences window (see Figure 7-9).

Installing Additional Wallpapers

As you can see, the default wallpaper in Ubuntu is called Ubuntu Lagoon, but other than that there really isn't much for you to choose from. To remedy the situation, you need to provide some images of your own. These could be photos from a digital camera, works of art you created on your computer, or just about anything you want to put there. In this case, however, you are going to venture out onto the Web to get and then install some wallpaper. A number of sites provide free desktop wallpaper, such as those for automobile manufacturers, singers, television shows, and so on.

Figure 7-9: Changing your desktop background

Two sites specifically geared toward Linux users are www.kde-look.org and http://art.gnome.org, but for this chapter, I will be downloading some wallpaper from the Slovak LinuxOS.sk site. If you want to follow along using the same Tux-chases-the-Windows-varmints wallpaper that I use, go directly to the wallpaper image by pointing your web browser to www.linuxos.sk/downloads/wallpapers/4.jpg. When the picture appears in the browser window, right-click it, and then select **Save Image As**. In the Save Image window, give it a unique name (*4.jpg* doesn't tell you much, after all) or use the one I gave it, *windowsroundup.jpg*, and click **Save**. If you prefer, you can download any wallpaper you like from wherever you like, as long as it is in a supported format, such as BMP, PNG, or JPEG. It's all up to you.

Once you've downloaded your wallpaper, place it in your Downloads folder. After that, you can install it by going to the Desktop Background Preferences window and clicking the **Add Wallpaper** button. In the Add Wallpaper window that then appears, navigate to your new wallpaper, click it once to highlight it, and then click **Open**. The wallpaper will then appear highlighted in the Desktop Background Preferences window and will soon thereafter appear on the desktop itself (Figure 7-10). Once it does, click **Finish** to complete the process.

Hiding the Bottom Panel

By the way, you may have noticed that you can barely see the panel at the bottom of the screen in Figure 7-10. This is because the panel obscured the bottom of the new wallpaper, which irritated me. I went to the Panel Properties window by right-clicking some empty space in the bottom panel and selecting **Properties** in the popup menu. In the Panel Properties window, I clicked the checkbox next to the word **Autohide** and then clicked **Close**. The autohide function works just like it does in Windows or Mac OS X—the panel stays out of view until you move your mouse into the general vicinity of where it should be. You can make the same change if you like, but that is an aesthetic matter that I will leave up to you. Ah, the sweet taste of artistic freedom.

Figure 7-10: The newly wallpapered desktop

7B-6: Downloading and Installing the Art Manager (GNOME Art)

Searching the Internet for wallpaper to install can in itself be a rather fun adventure, but sometimes it can also feel like quite a chore. Fortunately for you, me, and all involved in such things, there is an even easier way: the Art Manager. The Art Manager, also known as GNOME Art, is a handy application that searches the art.gnome.org site, and downloads a list, with thumbnails, of all the wallpapers that are available there. It can also do this for the various window border, controls, and icon theme sets that you can use in the following parts of this project. Using the thumbnailed lists, you can easily download and install whatever you want—all without ever placing a cursor in your web browser. Needless to say, the Art Manager is decidedly cool!

Unfortunately, the Art Manager is not installed by default; however, after having gone through Chapter 5, you know how easy it is to download and install applications like the Art Manager. All you have to do is run Synaptic, do a search for *gnome-art*, and then install it.

You can then run Art Manager by selecting **System ▸ Preferences ▸ Art Manager**. The GNOME Art window will then appear with absolutely nothing in it. To put it to use, and relieve that emptiness, go to the **Art** menu, and select **Backgrounds ▸ GNOME**. (You can select **All** instead of GNOME if you like, but it will take longer to download the list of available wallpapers.)

Once your selection is made, the Art Manager will begin downloading a list of all that is available for you at the art.gnome.org site. When it's done, you will see a list of thumbnails for you to choose from (Figure 7-11).

Figure 7-11: Installing desktop wallpapers using the Art Manager

You can now install a wallpaper by scrolling down until you find one that suits your fancy, clicking it once to highlight it, and then clicking the **Install** button. Art Manager will then download it, install it, and then automatically open the Desktop and Background Preferences window so that you can immediately apply it to your desktop if you like. As I said before, it's a very handy tool to have, especially since you'll be using it more soon within this project.

7B-7: Changing Window Borders, Controls, and Icon Sets

Now we get to my favorite part of this journey through the world of digital cosmetic surgery—changing the way window borders and controls look in GNOME. Let's set about doing just that.

The procedure is really quite easy. Go to the **System** menu, and select **Preferences ▸ Theme**. The Theme Preferences window will open and show you a list of the themes that are installed on your system (see Figure 7-12). The default theme in Ubuntu is called Human, but, as you can see, there are many others as well.

To get the hang of things, have a look at each of the themes listed by clicking them one by one. The changes will take effect immediately. Just clicking on a theme will change your window borders, controls, and even, if you take a peek in your home folder, the icons. This is especially noticeable when you click Crux or Grand Canyon.

Each theme consists of a window border, a set of controls, and a collection of icons. This being the case, it is possible to mix and match these elements on your own. For example, let's say that you like the look and color of the bubbly controls in Grand Canyon, but you prefer the window borders in Mist and the icons in Ocean Dream. Well, you needn't despair, because you can create a custom theme consisting of these three different elements.

Figure 7-12: Selecting a theme in GNOME

To create your own mix-and-match theme, just click the **Theme Details** button in the Theme Preferences window. A new window will open, and you will find three tabs: Controls, Window Border, and Icons. From within each of these tabs you can select the components you prefer. First click the **Controls** tab, and select **Grand Canyon**. Then click the **Window Border** tab, and select **Mist**. Finally, click the **Icons** tab, and select **Sandy**, which is the icon set for the Ocean Dream theme.

Now keep the Theme Details window open, but open your home folder and take a look at what you've done. Hmm . . . not bad. But, perhaps you don't really like the look of those Mist window borders all that much. To find something that suits you better, click the **Window Border** tab again, and scroll down until you see something you do like (Crux seems to do the trick for me), and click that. Better? Now that you are satisfied, you can click the **Close** button.

You will now be back at the Theme Preferences window, where you will notice that at the top of the list, there is a new theme entry called Custom Theme. If you want to save this new combination for later use, click the **Save Theme** button. Doing so will open a dialog box in which you can name your theme and write a brief comment about it. So, name your theme, write a comment if you like, and then click **Save**. Your new theme will now appear in alphabetical order within the theme list under the name you chose.

Once that's all done, your home folder window should look like that in Figure 7-13 (and take a look at your panel and Applications menu while you're at it). Ah, trés cool!

Figure 7-13: Changing the look of the home folder window

7B-8: Installing Additional Window Borders, Controls, and Icons

If you are excited about this customization thing but you're not satisfied with the theme choices included with the system, you can download and install still other window borders, controls, and icons. To show you how to do this, I will walk you through creating a faux Mac theme, which will look fairly similar to the standard Aqua theme of Mac OS X, as you can see in Figure 7-14.

Figure 7-14: An Aqua-fied Ubuntu desktop

Getting and Installing the Files You'll Need

To get the files you'll need to do this, take the Art Manager for another ride. Once it is up and running, go to the **Art** menu, and select **Backgrounds ▸ Other**. Once the list of available wallpapers appears in the Art Manager window, scroll down until you find one called **Real shoot**, install it, and then apply it in the Desktop Background Preferences window, which will automatically open.

Now to get an appropriate window border for your new theme, go back to the **Art** menu, but this time select **Desktop Themes ▸ Window Border**. Look for one called **Hacked**, and install it. When the Theme Preferences window automatically appears, click the **Theme Details** button, and click the **Window Borders** tab. In the list that appears in that tab, click **Hacked**. Close the Theme Details and Desktop Background Preferences windows to complete the task.

Next get a set of matching application control widgets by going back to the Art Manager **Art** menu and selecting **Desktop Themes ▸ Application**. When the list is downloaded, look for a file called **Yattacier 3**, and install it. In the Desktop Background Preferences window that then appears, click **Theme Details** as you did before—but this time around click the **Control** tab, and select **Yattacier3** in the list within that tab.

To round things up, let's add some new icons to the mix by going back to the Art Manager, heading to the **Art** menu, and selecting **Desktop Themes ▸ Icon**. Once the list is downloaded, look for and install **Snow-Apple**. After that it's basically a repeat of the previous step, but this time around, click the **Icons** tab in the Theme Details window, and then select **Snow Apple**.

Finishing Touches

Well, things are certainly sort of Mac-ish now, but there is even more we can do to emphasize the effect. First, open a Nautilus window, click the **Computer** button, and then drag the **Filesystem** icon to your desktop. This will create an alias of your hard disk there. Next, go to the bottom panel, and remove everything except Trash. After that, open the Preferences window for your bottom panel by right-clicking the area to the far right of Trash and selecting **Properties** in the popup menu. In the **General** tab of that window, uncheck **Expand**, and then increase the size of the panel to around 54 pixels. When you're done, click **Close**, and then start adding launchers for the applications you use most.

Finally, go to the top menu, and remove the three icons next to the System menu. After that, add a Window Selector applet, so that you have some way to navigate through your open windows. You might also want to change the background in your home folder, since the warm tones presently there no longer match your new cooler configuration.

The transformation is now complete, and if you followed along correctly, your desktop should look something like mine back in Figure 7-14. You can stick with your new OS X–ish theme, or switch to something else. For consistency's sake, I will switch back to *Human* now. By the way, if you do decide to keep the faux-Aqua theme, remember to click the **Save Theme** button in the Theme Preferences window and give the theme a name.

As you are already aware, unlike Windows, Mac OS X, or other Linux distributions, Ubuntu has a completely empty desktop upon installation. A lot of people advocate this approach because it discourages the permanent use of the desktop as a location to store files and program launchers. After all, as the argument goes, you don't place your trash can or file cabinet on the desktop in your office, do you?

All such logic aside, there are still many people who prefer to have their trash can, hard disk, and home folder on their desktops, thank you very much. If you are one of them, as I am, here's what you need to do:

1. Press ALT-F2 to bring up the Run Application window. This keyboard shortcut is the equivalent of clicking the Run Application panel applet that you placed on the panel in your original user account.

2. Run the GNOME Configuration Editor by typing `gconf-editor` in that window and then pressing ENTER.

3. When the Configuration Editor window appears, click the small arrow next to apps, scroll down to nautilus, and click the small arrow next to that.

4. Click **desktop** in that expanded nautilus section, after which the options for that item will appear in the right pane of the window (Figure 7-15).

Figure 7-15: The Configuration Editor

5. Check the boxes next to the items you would like to appear on the desktop. You have four unchecked choices to choose from: computer_icon_visible (like My Computer in Windows), documents_icon_visible

(to create a link to your Documents folder, if you have one), home_icon_visible (for quick access to your home folder), and trash_icon_visible (for you-know-what).

6. When you're done, close the Configuration Editor.

NOTE   *Changes made in the way I just described will affect all user accounts. If you choose, for example, to show the trash can on the desktop for one user account, it will appear there for all others.*

Project 7D: Changing Your Login Screen

You may have noticed while working with the Art Manager that there is a menu selection (**Art ▸ Other Themes**) for something called Login Manager. The Login Manager is your login screen, also known as a *greeter*—the screen where you type your username and user password when you first log in to your system. The Login Manager is another thing that you can customize, but be forewarned that any changes you make will be system-wide, not just for you; whatever Login Manager theme you install and choose will be the Login Manager theme that everyone else with user accounts will see when they use the machine. Of course, if you are the only one using your machine, this point is moot.

7D-1: Downloading a Login Manager Theme

In order to try customizing the Login Manager, run the Art Manger, and select **Art ▸ Other Themes ▸ Login Manager**. Once you've done this, browse through the various themes in the list, and choose one or two that you want; I give you free rein on this one, but I'll be choosing the theme called SVG Sakura, in case you want to follow along exactly.

Unlike your other experiences with the Art Manager up to now, Login Manager themes can only be downloaded, and you have to do the installation yourself. That being the case, once you've made your selection, click the **Download Only** button. Once the download is complete, you will find the file in archive form, with a tar.gz ending, in your home folder, or any other folder you decided to save it to. You do not need to extract, or *untar*, the archived file.

7D-2: Installing Your New Login Manager Theme

Once you've downloaded a theme or two of your liking, you need to open the Login Screen Setup window. To do this, go to the **System** menu, and select **Administration ▸ Login Window**. A dialog box asking for your password will then open. Type the password for the account you are currently using, and click **OK**. The Login Window Preferences window will soon appear (see Figure 7-16), showing a thumbnailed list of the greeters available.

You can add the greeters you just downloaded to this list by dragging the files directly to the list. A small window will then appear, asking if you're sure that you want to install the file you've just dragged to the list, and since you do want to install the file, click **Install**.

Figure 7-16: Customizing the Login Manager

To select the greeter you wish to use, just click the round button next to its name in the list in the Login Window Preferences window, and then click the **Close** button. Of course, to see your greeter in action, you will have to log out first so you can log back in, but you needn't restart or shut down the machine. You can then see your new greeter when the login screen appears (Figure 7-17), though yours may well be different.

Figure 7-17: The new login screen

Project 7E: Changing Your Splash Screen

Well, now you've changed just about all there is to change system-wise, but there is actually one more item that you can tinker with—your splash screen. In case you're not familiar with the term *splash screen*, it's the screen that appears when GNOME is starting up right after you log in but before you get to your desktop. The default screen, shown in Figure 7-18, is pleasant enough, but you can choose something a bit wilder or at least more colorful if you are so inclined.

Figure 7-18: The default Ubuntu splash screen

7E-1: Installing New Splash Screens

Ubuntu does not come with any alternative splash screens for you to play with, so in order to make changes, you first need to download and install some splash screens with which to work. This can be done quite easily by opening Art Manager (**System ▸ Preferences ▸ Art Manager**) and following these steps:

1. Go to the **Art** menu, and select **Other Themes ▸ Splash Screen**. Art Manager will then download the available splash screens.

2. Once the download is complete, scroll through the offerings, and select one that suits your fancy by clicking it once.

3. After your selection has been made, click the **Install** button, after which Art Manager will download and install the file. When it's done, the GNOME Splash Screen Preferences window will appear, showing the newly installed screen.

4. Go back to the Art Manager, and repeat steps 2 and 3 to add a few more screen choices to your repertoire.

5. Once you have installed three or four splash screens, close Art Manager.

Enabling Automatic Login

While the Login Window Preferences window is open, it is as good a time as any to mention an option that may well be of interest to you. If you find it a bit of a drag to type your username and password every time you start up your machine, you'll be happy to know that you can bypass the whole login process. If you share your machine with other users, of course, this isn't something you'd want to do because anybody with access to your machine would thus have access to your user account. I also wouldn't recommend doing so on a laptop, since they are more easily lost or stolen, thus leaving your data at risk to absolute strangers.

To enable automatic login, click the **Security** tab in the Login Window Preferences window, and then click the checkbox at the top of the page, next to the words *Enable Automatic Login.* After that, click the arrow at the right side of the drop-down menu, next to the word *User,* and select your username from the list. Once you're done, click the **Close** button. The next time you start up your machine, you will bypass the login screen and be delivered directly to the desktop.

7E-2: Selecting and Activating Splash Screens

When you have multiple splash screens installed on your system, you can select and then activate them via the GNOME Splash Screen Preferences window (Figure 7-19), which should already be open. When it isn't, you can bring it up by going to the **System** menu and selecting **Preferences ▸ Splash Screen**.

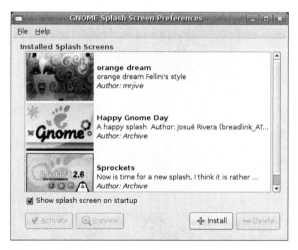

Figure 7-19: Choosing a new login screen

To select and then activate a splash screen, make your selection by clicking on the splash screen of your choice once, and then click the **Activate** button. You will then see your splash screen in action when you next log in to your system.

Choosing a Screensaver

Screensavers used to be a must-have (and must-use) item for computer users who wanted to prevent damage (burn-in) to their monitors. Video display technology, however, has now advanced to the point where screen-savers are no longer completely necessary. Nevertheless, screensavers are cool to look at, and one very nice thing about Ubuntu is that it comes with an unusually extensive collection of screensaver modules—nearly 200 of them! There are so many that you are sure to find at least a few you like. The screensaver settings are preconfigured to switch between modules randomly, changing the current module every few minutes. You can change these settings by going to your **System** menu and selecting **Preferences ▸ Screensaver**.

The Screensaver Preferences window, shown in Figure 7-20, allows you to do a variety of things, such as set the length of time between module changes and the length of idle time before the screensaver starts up. You can also opt to use only one screensaver module or no screensaver at all. In random mode, you can also omit the modules that you don't like by unchecking the boxes next to the undesired modules' names. This can be quite useful, especially if certain screensavers seem to tax the graphic capabilities of your machine.

Figure 7-20: Setting screensaver preferences

Project 7F: Wrapping Things Up—Installing and Applying Firefox Themes

It's time to bring this rather lengthy exercise in customization to a close. Now that you know how to do most of the things you might want to do in this area, you can return to your own user account and use what you've learned to make changes that suit your own tastes and desires.

If you've really gotten hooked on this customization thing, you'll be happy to know that there are always more things you can bend to your will. In addition to being able to customize your system sounds, the splash screen that appears after you log in, and the system fonts that are displayed in your menus and folders, you can also play around with the many applications that allow customizations through the use of skins designed specifically for those apps.

Perhaps the most notable of these customizable applications is Firefox, which you first met in Chapter 4. Firefox allows you to change the look of its buttons, application controls, and even background colors through the use of *themes*, some examples of which you can see in Figure 7-21. You will be glad to learn that downloading and installing these themes is a fairly straightforward process, so to finally wrap things up, I will end this chapter by providing you with the steps you need to follow:

1. In Firefox, go to the **Tools** menu, and select **Themes**. The Firefox Themes window will then appear.

2. In the bottom-right corner of that window, click the **Get More Themes** link.

3. A new Firefox window listing available themes will then appear. Click any of the links to see a preview of that theme, or browse the available themes categorically by clicking the category links at the left side of the page.

4. When you find a theme you like, click the **Install Now** link on the page for that theme.

Figure 7-21: Firefox themes

5. A confirmation window will then appear, asking if you're sure that you want to install the theme in question. Click **OK**.

6. Once the theme is downloaded and installed, it will appear in the list of available themes in the left pane of the Themes window (Figure 7-22). Select the theme you want to use by clicking it once, and then click the **Use Theme** button.

7. Restart Firefox to see your new theme in action.

Figure 7-22: Selecting Firefox themes

8

SIMPLE KITTEN WAYS

Getting to Know the Linux Terminal and Command Line

Many people shy away from Linux because they envision it as a system for compu-geeks, an environment in which you do everything the hard way—by command line. In this era of graphical interfaces, the idea of typing commands to get things done seems a dreadful throwback to the days of DOS, and that puts many people off—especially those who remember what it was like in the "old days."

This reaction is fair enough, but it is not really an accurate reflection of the reality of the Linux world. After all, most Linux users today utilize some sort of graphical interface. They can, and often do, achieve all that they hope to achieve through drop-down menus and mouse clicks alone. Many are able to survive quite happily without ever once opening their Terminal. The same could be true of you.

Be that as it may, there is still much to be said for the power and convenience of the command line. The fact that the command line can now be utilized within a graphical environment also makes it much less forbidding. The Terminal is just a tiny text-based island in a sea of graphical bodies (see Figure 8-1). Using the command line can be as pain-free as anything else you do on your system, and it can actually provide you with a little fun if you are willing to give it a try.

Figure 8-1: Putting the Terminal in perspective

Unfortunately, many guides to using the command line are written by hard-core command-line junkies, whose enthusiasm for what they see as a really good thing inadvertently makes what they write seem even more off-putting to the recent Linux immigrant or wannabe.

For your sake, I will try to curb my own enthusiasm so as not to scare you right back to Chapter 5 and the more comfortable world of Synaptic. I will also try to help you keep things in perspective by teaching you, whenever possible, to use the command line as a complement to the various graphical tools that you have at your disposal, rather than presenting it as the sole way of going about things. Of course, I am not going to cover every possible angle in this regard—just enough to give you some exposure and experience and, hopefully, make you feel at least a little more at ease with the command line. Who knows; could you actually come to think of using the command line as . . . fun? Well, I won't get too carried away.

Meet the Terminal

The Linux Command Terminal application in your Ubuntu system can be run by going to the **Applications** menu and selecting **Accessories ▸ Terminal**. When the Terminal opens, it will, in all its simplicity, look much like Figure 8-2.

Figure 8-2: The Terminal application

As you can see, all it says is `rg@RG-Vaio-on-Ubuntu:~$`. In this case, the `rg` is my username, `RG-Vaio-on-Ubuntu` is the name I gave my computer during installation, and the tilde (`~`) signifies that I am in my home folder. If it were to say `~/Music`, for example, it would mean that I am currently in the Music folder within my home folder. Of course, all this will be different in your case, as your username and computer name will be different. If your username is *frog* and your computer's name is *wetrock*, for example, the command line will say `frog@wetrock:~$`. If all this is sounding rather obtuse to you, just think of it this way: *username@computer_name*`:~$` in the Terminal is the equivalent of your home folder in Nautilus.

Typing in the Terminal is straightforward enough; you just type as you usually do. You can also delete and insert letters or phrases by using the DELETE and BACKSPACE keys and the cursor keys. For practice, try the following:

1. Type `I like strawberries so very much`.
2. Change `strawberries` to `cherries` (because cherries are, in fact, so much better). Just use your left cursor key to move the cursor in front of the first *s* in `strawberries`.
3. Tap your DELETE key as many times as necessary to erase the word `strawberries` (uh, that would be 12 times, methinks).
4. Just type `cherries`, and then use your right cursor key to move the cursor back to the end of this meaningful sentence.

Now that you've completed this fascinating bit of typing practice, press the ENTER key. As you will almost immediately see, the Terminal's response to your efforts thus far is merely a dismissive `bash: I: command not found`. Although you've typed a string of text that has meaning to you, it means absolutely nothing to your system. In fact, the system was so shortsighted that it could see nothing other than the first word you typed in the Terminal (I); and because I is not a valid command, the system had no idea what do to with it.

Shells

You may be wondering what this bash business is all about and why it is talking to you. Well, Bash (Bourne Again Shell) is one of the many shells that are used in Linux systems, and it's the one that happens to come with your Ubuntu distro (and most others, for that matter). A *shell* is a program that interprets the commands you type into the Terminal and delivers them, so to speak, to your system so that it can act upon them. I like to think of it as a command-handling subsystem, for which the Terminal acts as a graphical front end. Some scripting languages, as you will find out in Project 8C on page 142, also have their own shells; but other than those few exceptions, you generally need not be unduly concerned with shells other than to know what they are and what people are talking about when referring to them.

Some Goofy, Yet Useful, Fun with the Command Terminal

A rather cool thing about typing in the command Terminal is that it has what you might call short-term memory. Try it out by typing the word **cherry** and then pressing ENTER. Ignoring the command-not-found message, go on and type **vanilla**, and press ENTER. Now type **icecream**, and press ENTER. So far, so dumb, right? Well, not really. Let's type everything we've typed thus far again, but this time let's do it with only one key.

Huh?

Yes, just press the up cursor key once, and what do you see? That's right—the last command you typed appears, which in this case would be icecream. Press the up cursor key again, and the command that you typed before that will appear—vanilla. One more time? Yes, cherry. And one more time for the grand finale . . . I like cherries so very much.

Considering what we have thus far, this may all seem a bit silly, but imagine that you're not typing goofy little words and instead have to deal with considerably longer strings, such as a simple copy command (which you'll learn about later in this chapter) like

```
cp Photos/mypics/stpierre/coastal/onthebeach1_27.jpg /home/frog/
photos_for_mom/stpierre
```

By typing that string, you are copying an image called onthebeach1_27.jpg from the coastal folder to another folder called stpierre. If you wanted to copy another photo in the coastal folder, onthebeach1_16.jpg, for instance, you could simply press the up arrow key once, use the left cursor key and DELETE key to move over to and delete the 27, replace it with **16**, and then use the right arrow key to get back to the end of the command. All in all, it would be much simpler and much faster. It would also help you avoid mistakes in typing. Not so dumb anymore, eh?

Nontoxic Commands

As you now know, all of this typing is easy enough, but in order to actually do something useful with your Terminal, you need to type commands—and there are more of them than you could ever hope or need to know. To get you started, we will begin with some commands that are easy to understand, nontoxic, and completely kitten-friendly.

$ whoami

There is no command as easy, safe, or even as seemingly useless, as whoami. Rather than help those with multiple-personality disorders discover who they are at any given moment, the whoami command simply tells you which user is currently logged in. Try it out by typing **whoami** after the $ and then pressing the ENTER key. Remember that commands are case sensitive, so type accordingly.

The Terminal will now tell you the username of the person currently logged in. If you are logged in as frog, you should get frog as the answer to your command.

$ finger

If you enjoyed discovering who you are with the whoami command, then you might enjoy finding out even more about yourself using the finger command. The finger command can be used in a number of ways, but a very simple one is finding out about a particular user. Try this out on yourself by typing **finger** and then your username. In my case, that would be **finger rg**. Once you've typed the command, press ENTER and see what you get. You can see my results in Figure 8-3.

```
rg@RG-Vaio-on-Ubuntu: ~
File  Edit  View  Terminal  Tabs  Help
rg@RG-Vaio-on-Ubuntu:~$ finger rg
Login: rg                          Name: Rickford Grant
Directory: /home/rg                Shell: /bin/bash
On since Wed May 17 12:12 (EDT) on :0 (messages off)
On since Wed May 17 13:24 (EDT) on pts/0 from :0.0
    2 hours 53 minutes idle
On since Wed May 17 16:21 (EDT) on pts/1 from :0.0
    1 second idle
No mail.
No Plan.
rg@RG-Vaio-on-Ubuntu:~$ finger rg
```

Figure 8-3: Output from the finger command

As you can see, my login name is rg, my real name is Rickford Grant, my home directory is /home/rg, I am using the bash shell for typing my commands, I have been logged on since Wed May 17 at 12:12 EDT, my computer was idle for 2 hours 53 minutes (I went out to buy a toaster oven, in case you were wondering), and I have no mail or plan. It doesn't tell you my social security number or my mother's maiden name, but it is pretty cool, don't you think?

I mentioned that the results said I had no plan, and you may well be wondering what that is all about, so I'll fill you in. A .plan file is a small file kept in your home folder that other users see when they use the `finger` command on you. Traditionally, a .plan file contained information about where you were going to be or what you were working on. These days, however, most people use them to leave odd little messages, quotations, or whatever, much as they do in email signatures. Take a look at Figure 8-4 to see what happens after I add a .plan file to my home folder.

```
                    rg@RG-Vaio-on-Ubuntu: ~
File  Edit  View  Terminal  Tabs  Help
rg@RG-Vaio-on-Ubuntu:~$ finger rg
Login: rg                          Name: Rickford Grant
Directory: /home/rg                Shell: /bin/bash
On since Wed May 17 12:12 (EDT) on :0 (messages off)
On since Wed May 17 13:24 (EDT) on pts/0 from :0.0
   44 seconds idle
On since Wed May 17 16:21 (EDT) on pts/1 from :0.0
   2 minutes 8 seconds idle
On since Wed May 17 16:42 (EDT) on pts/2 from :0.0
No mail.
Plan:
"I was the victim of a series of accidents... as are
we all"
rg@RG-Vaio-on-Ubuntu:~$ █
```

Figure 8-4: Output from the finger *command with a plan*

You can now see my plan, which is a quotation from Kurt Vonnegut's *The Sirens of Titan* (or Al Stewart's song by the same name, for that matter), though you can put anything you want in your own. You will get the chance to create your own plan file in Project 8A on page 136, so if this all seems fun to you, just hang in there.

Before moving on, I should mention that you can also use the `finger` command to do a little domestic espionage of sorts. Let's say your child, Chris, has a user account on your machine. Chris, who wants your permission to go to the movies, claims to have been hard at work on the computer all day writing up a report for school. Having your doubts, you could type `finger chris` to see what the facts actually are. It may be a bit underhanded and rotten, but it works. It also works both ways, so others can check up on you as well. You can give it a try right now by seeing when the last time you logged in to your graphika account was. Just type **finger graphika**, and then press ENTER.

You can even use the `finger` command to find out facts about people on other systems, providing their network's finger service is active and you know their email address. Typing something like `finger` *username@hostname*.com would do the trick. Kind of cool, but also kind of spooky, I suppose.

$ pwd

If you know who you are but aren't exactly sure where you are, pwd (print working directory) should come in handy. The pwd command tells you exactly where the Terminal is in your directory tree.

Let's say, for example, that my Terminal is in my personal home directory (which is actually called rg) in the system's home directory (which is actually called home, and which is where all the user account directories are located) when I use the pwd command; I would, after pressing the ENTER key, get /home/rg printed to my Terminal. You should get similar results if you try it out.

NOTE   *The word* print, *in this case, has nothing to do with your printer; it merely means that the response will be printed to, or displayed in, the Terminal.*

$ df

Another safe and easy, but much more useful, command is df (disk filesystem). The df command tells you how much disk space you have used, as well as how much space you still have available, on each of the partitions on your various mounted disks. Try it out by typing **df** and then pressing ENTER. Your output should look something like that shown in Figure 8-5 (depending, of course, on the size of your mounted disks and how they are set up).

```
rg@RG-Vaio-on-Ubuntu: ~

File  Edit  View  Terminal  Tabs  Help

rg@RG-Vaio-on-Ubuntu:~$ df
Filesystem           1K-blocks     Used Available Use% Mounted on
/dev/hda1             37721596  2007748  33797700   6% /
varrun                 127864       84    127780   1% /var/run
varlock                127864        4    127860   1% /var/lock
udev                   127864      152    127712   1% /dev
devshm                 127864        0    127864   0% /dev/shm
lrm                    127864    18956    108908  15% /lib/modules/2.6.15-2
2-386/volatile
/dev/sda2             1907988    86468   1821520   5% /media/ipod
/dev/sdb1              246004   162656     83348  67% /media/TOSHIBA
rg@RG-Vaio-on-Ubuntu:~$ █
```

Figure 8-5: Output from the df command

As you will notice, the sizes are given in kilobytes (KB) rather than the gigabytes (GB) and megabytes (MB) you are probably more used to, but there is a way around this. Many commands accept a *flag*, or *option*, to further fine-tune how the command performs. These flags are written directly after the main command and are preceded by a space and a hyphen.

In this case, you can try using the -h (human readable) flag to have your figures come out in the way you are most familiar with. Try this out by typing **df -h** on the command line and pressing ENTER. The output should now appear in a more familiar format (see Figure 8-6).

Figure 8-6: Output from the df command with the -h flag

$ ls

Another harmless but handy command is ls (list directory contents). The ls command shows you what is in your current directory. This is the non-graphical equivalent of double-clicking a folder in Nautilus to see what is inside. Try it out by typing **ls** and then pressing the ENTER key.

If you've been following *my* commands so far, your results should list all of the folders in your home directory. You can also use the -R flag to show not only the list of files in the folder, but also what is within the subfolders. Of course, you should have no subfolders in any of the folders you created in Chapter 6, so you can hold off experimenting with this for a while. Instead, try typing **ls -a** to see your invisible, or *hidden*, files.

$ sudo

When you ran Synaptic back in Chapter 5, you were first asked to input your password before you could run the program. The reason for this, as I mentioned then, is that Synaptic installs the files it downloads in various folders throughout your system, almost all of which are write protected. By supplying your password, you are telling your system that you, as holder of the password, have the right to allow Synaptic to do that.

The command version of that same password-giving process is the sudo command. To perform an operation in a folder that is write protected, you would first type sudo and then the command you want to perform. For example, if you wanted to copy an icon image, let's call it myicon.png, to the globally located and write-protected pixmaps folder (/usr/share/pixmaps), you would type sudo cp myicon.png /usr/share/pixmaps.

After typing a command preceded by the sudo command and pressing ENTER, you will be prompted for your password. Once you type your password and press ENTER again, the command will be executed. I should mention that once you input your password, it will stay in memory for about 15 minutes. This means that you will not be prompted for your password when using the sudo command again within that time frame.

$ locate

In contrast to the seemingly lightweight commands you have learned so far, the locate command is really quite useful. In fact, you might well find it a much easier, faster, and more effective method of finding files than the graphical search tool in the Places menu. Using the command is quite easy: you simply type the command followed by a space and the name of the file you are searching for.

Before you can use this command, though, you will need to create a database of filenames for locate to use. This is quite easily done by using the sudo command, which you just learned about, and then typing **updatedb** (Whoa, Nellie! Yet another command!), followed by a tap on the ENTER key (that would be sudo updatedb). After you type your password when asked to do so, it will seem that nothing is happening for a while, but don't worry. As long as the cursor in your Terminal is blinking, progress is being made, and when your user prompt returns, you will have successfully created the database file. After that, you can go on and use the locate command.

To take this new command out for a test drive, let's look for the openofficeorg-20-writer.png file that we worked with in Chapter 3. Just type the following, and press ENTER:

```
locate openofficeorg-20-writer.png
```

Your results should look like those in Figure 8-7.

Figure 8-7: The results of a locate search

$ calendar

I'll let you experiment with this one on your own. Just type **calendar**, and press ENTER to see the somewhat interesting results.

$ exit

The exit command is a simple one that allows you to exit the Terminal. Just type **exit**, and press ENTER. The Terminal window will close.

Commands with Some Teeth

The simple commands you have tried so far are all of the safe-and-sane, fire marshal–approved variety; they merely print information to your Terminal. Now you are going to try to get some real tangible results from the commands you use. These commands are also essentially safe and sane if you follow my instructions.

$ mkdir

You have already learned how to create folders by means of menus and your mouse, but you can also do this using the command line. The command is mkdir (make directory), and it is easy as pie to use (though I've never been quite sure how pie is easy).

To see how this command works, and to work with the commands that follow, use the mkdir command now to create a folder called command_exp (for command experiments). All you have to do is type **mkdir command_exp** in a new Terminal window, and press ENTER. The new folder should appear in your home folder, so go ahead and check to see if it is there by clicking the home icon on your desktop.

Okay, good, *bra, bueno*! Now let's create another new folder within that new folder—a *subfolder*, if you will. We'll call this one sub. So, just type **mkdir command_exp/sub**, and press ENTER. You can now go take a peek and see if the subfolder appears within the command_exp folder, if you like.

$ mv

The next command is the mv (move) command, but before we experiment with it, we need to create a dummy file—we need something to move, after all. We can do this by using another command—touch. To make the file, and let's call it expfile.txt, go to the Terminal, type **touch expfile.txt**, and press ENTER. The new file will now appear in your home folder.

To move the file that you've just created, you will use the mv command, of course. Just type **mv expfile.txt command_exp/sub** (this tells the system which file to move and where to move it to), and press ENTER. The file will now be in your sub folder.

$ cd

Until now, you have been using the command line from your home folder. With the cd command, you can change your Terminal's location to another folder. This is a very handy command that you will be using quite a lot when doing the other projects in this book. To take it out for a spin, let's get inside the command_exp folder by typing **cd command_exp** and pressing ENTER. If you've done this correctly, the prompt in your Terminal should now read *username@computer_name:~/command_exp$*. If so, you can pat yourself on the back.

While you are there, you might as well try out the ls command with the -R (recursive) flag to see how that works. Just type **ls -R**, and press ENTER. Your Terminal should now show that you have a subfolder there called sub and a file inside that subfolder called expfile.txt.

That is all you really want to do in there for now, so to get back to your home directory, just type **cd**, and press ENTER, which will take you back home, so to speak.

For future reference, it is worth noting a couple of other cd command shortcuts. If you are within a subfolder of a subfolder and want to move back a step, so to speak (from /home/rg/peas/pudding to /home/rg/peas, for example), you can do so by typing **cd ..** (with a space between cd and ..) and pressing ENTER. You can also type **cd -** (with a space between cd and -) in order to get back to a directory where you were previously (from /home/rg to /home/rg/peas/pudding, for example).

$ cp

Being fickle, as humans are by nature, you might decide that you not only want your expfile.txt file in the sub folder, but that you also want a copy in your home directory, where it was in the first place. To copy expfile.txt, you can use the cp (copy) command.

To do this, the command needs to know where the file you want to copy is, what it is called, and where you want to copy it, which in this case is to your home folder. Normally you would type `cp command_exp/sub/expfile` `.txt /home/`*`username`* to do this, but if you recall my mention of it near the beginning of this chapter, you can abbreviate the `/home/`*`username`* portion of the command string to `~/`, which means the same thing, and is an important tip to remember, as the tilde is frequently used in online instructions. As reducing wear and tear on the fingers is always a desirable goal, type the following command, and then press ENTER:

```
cp command_exp/sub/expfile.txt ~/
```

Be sure to put a space between the file you are copying and its destination (in this case, between the `expfile.txt` and `~/`).

Once you've done this, you should have two copies of expfile.txt, one in your home folder and one in your sub folder. Go have a look to see the fruit of your endeavors.

$ rm

When you were a kid, you may well have experienced the joy of building a castle out of LEGO bricks and then the even greater joy of tearing the whole thing down (preferably by hurling D cell batteries at it). We will now embark on a similar move. The first tool in this nostalgic endeavor is the rm (remove) command, with which we can trash files.

The rm command, albeit very useful and easy to use, should be used with caution. Once you remove a file with this command, there is no going back—the file will not be placed in the Trash; it is gone for good.

To play it safe, let's try out the rm command by getting rid of that new copy of expfile.txt that we just created in the home folder. The basic rm command structure consists of the command itself, rm, followed by the name of the file that you wish to remove. In this case, you want to remove the file called expfile.txt located in your home folder. Assuming your Terminal shows you to be home, remove the file by typing `rm expfile.txt` followed by a tap on the ol' ENTER key. The file will then be gone, and gone for good.

Now, double your pleasure by getting rid of the version of expfile.txt that is located in the subfolder sub. In this case, you need to specify where the file is because it isn't in the folder that the Terminal is in. Just type `rm command_exp/sub/expfile.txt`, and then press ENTER. Oooh, very cool. Brings ya back, doesn't it?

$ rmdir

You will now continue the fun with the `rmdir` (remove directory) command, which is a bigger and more powerful version of the `rm` command.

The `rmdir` command, like the `rm` command, should be used with caution. There are no do-overs with `rmdir`. Once you remove a directory or folder with this command, it is gone for good.

To try this command, you can get rid of that sub folder you created. Type `rmdir command_exp/sub`, and press ENTER. The sub folder should now be gone. Finally, to round out the fun, use the `rmdir` command once more to get rid of the command_exp folder that we created earlier. You've probably got it down by now, but just in case you haven't, type `rmdir command_exp`, and then press ENTER.

$ chmod

In Chapter 6, you learned how to change file permissions via the Nautilus interface. This is without a doubt the easiest way to go about such things, but when you have a folder full of files, perhaps copied to your hard disk from CD, that are write protected, it can be quite tiring to change the permissions of such files one by one. In this case, the command-line approach proves to be much easier to deal with.

The command for changing file permissions is `chmod` (change mode). To use it, just type the command followed by the permissions you want to extend to a file, and then the location of the file itself. For example, let's say that you copied a JPEG file, mybirthday.jpg, from a CD to the personal subfolder within the Photos folder on your hard disk, and the file is write protected. To change the file so that you have write permissions (meaning that you can alter the file), you would type the following and then press ENTER:

```
chmod 744 ~/photos/personal/mybirthday.jpg
```

To change the permissions of all the files and subfolders (and all the files within those subfolders) in one fell swoop, you can add the -R (recursive) flag to the `chmod` command. The command would thus be as follows:

```
chmod -R 744 ~/photos/personal
```

The number *744*, by the way, extends read, write, and execute (run) permissions to you, the owner, but gives read-only rights to everyone else—a pretty safe choice when in doubt. If you want to figure out permission numbers for yourself, it is pretty easy. You are basically dealing with three number positions, each of which has eight numerical possibilities (0–7). The left slot represents permissions for the owner; the center slot represents permissions for the group; and the third slot represents permissions for others.

The meanings of the numbers themselves are as follows:

7   Read, write, and execute permissions

6   Read and write permissions

5   Read and execute permissions

4   Read-only permissions

3   Write and execute permissions

2   Write-only permissions

1   Execute-only permissions

0   No permissions

Figure 8-8 points out the meaning of each of these numbers and what each number slot represents. In fact, if you don't mind a bit of simple addition, things are even easier to understand. To start out with, remember that 1 = execute, 2 = write, and 4 = read. Add any of those numbers together, and you get the other permissions combos. For example, 1 (execute) + 4 (read) = 5 (read and execute). As you can see, permissions aren't all that complicated.

Figure 8-8: The meaning of permissions numbers

Now if you're more of a letters than numbers sort of person, you'll be happy to know that there is another way to change permissions that is probably even easier. In this approach, you only have to deal with two groups of letters and the symbols + and −.

The first group consists of the following:

u   User (owner of the file)

g   Group (specified group of users)

o   Others (anyone who is not the user or a member of the group)

a   All (all of the above)

The second group consists of:

r Read

w Write

x Execute

You might already be able to figure out how this is all going to work, but I'll spell it out just in case your intuition is worn out for the day. Let's say you want to change the permissions of a file (butterhaters.txt, for example) so that all users on your machine can read and write to it. After opening a Terminal window, you can make the change by typing `chmod a+rw butterhaters.txt` and pressing ENTER.

Oops! Just remembered that you don't want anyone changing the content of the file, eh? Well, to take back the write permissions for that file, you just need to type `chmod a-w butterhaters.txt` and then press ENTER. As you can see, the + gives permissions, while the - taketh away.

Much simpler, you've got to admit.

A Couple of Other Biters You'll Be Using Soon

This is as good a place as any to introduce two more commands that you will be called upon to use in this chapter and elsewhere in the book: `ln` and `tar`. You needn't practice with these yet, as you will be using them very soon, but you might as well know what they are all about.

$ *ln*

The `ln` (link) command is used to create a link file that launches or activates another file located in a separate folder. This is very useful when trying to activate a file that is buried deep in the subfolder of a subfolder of a subfolder somewhere on your hard disk. The command is very often used with the `-s` (symbolic) flag, which provides essentially the same thing as the shortcut you've come to know in Windows, or the alias on the Mac.

The easiest way to use the `ln` command is to first use the `cd` command to change the Terminal's location to the folder where you want to place the link. Then you can type the `ln` command on the command line, followed by the path of the file you wish to link to. For example, let's say that you want to put a link in your home folder for an OpenOffice.org Writer file of your autobiography called myLife.sxw. The file is pretty well buried in a nest of subfolders deep within your home folder: /home/*username*/Documentia/personal/self/autobiography/myLife.sxw. To create the link, you would open a new Terminal window, type the following command string, and then press ENTER:

```
ln -s Documentia/personal/self/autobiography/myLife.sxw
```

Once you are finished, the link will appear in your home folder as an icon matching the original file in appearance, albeit sporting an arrow to signify that it is a link.

$ tar

In Chapter 6 you learned to create and extract archives, or tarballs, but did you know that you can also create and extract tarballs using the command line? The tar command is your key to doing this.

To create an archive, you would simply type tar -cvf, followed by the name the final tarball will be, and then the name of the folder or file you are trying to archive. For example, let's say that you want to create an archive of your photos folder, and you want to call it pics4pals. In this case, you would type the following command, and then press ENTER:

```
tar -cvf pics4pals.tar photos
```

As you no doubt noticed, there are some flags after the tar command in that string. The *c* tells the tar program to *create* a new archive. The *v* tells the program to be *verbose*, or, in other words, to tell you what it is doing in the Terminal as it is doing it. Finally, the *f* tells the program that what follows is the *file information*.

If, after creating the archive, you suddenly remember that there is one more file you want to add to the mix, you can use the -r flag to append the archive. For example, to add a file called cranky.png to the archive, you would type the following and then press ENTER:

```
tar -rvf pics4pals.tar cranky.png
```

Of course, chances are that you will be doing more tarball extracting than creating, so you no doubt want to know how to do that. Fortunately, the process is pretty similar to what you use when creating the tarball. The main difference is in the first flag. Rather than using the tar command with the -c flag, you would instead use it with the -x flag, which tells the tar program to *extract* the specified archive. So if you want to extract a tarball called spicyfood.tar, type the following command, and press ENTER:

```
tar -xvf spicyfood.tar
```

What you have been doing thus far is creating and extracting archives, which are basically just collections of files. They are not, however, compressed. In fact, most tarballs you find will be compressed, and you can tell by the ending *tar.gz*. That *gz* means that the archive was compressed using the gzip program. Extracting a compressed tarball is just as easy as extracting a straight tar archive; all you have to do is add the -z flag, which tells your system to use the gzip program to decompress the archive. For example, if you want to extract a compressed tarball called goosedown.tar.gz, type the following command, and press ENTER:

```
tar -xzvf goosedown.tar.gz
```

Well, now that you know how to decompress and extract a gzipped tarball, you probably want to know how to create one. This is, again, little different than creating the tar archive itself; you would just add the -z tag to tell the program to use gzip to compress the folder. For example, to create a compressed version of your Documentia folder, which we'll call tightdocs.tar.gz, for example, you would type the following, and press ENTER:

```
tar -czvf tightdocs.tar.gz Documentia
```

It's worth mentioning at this point that you may also come across some files compressed with the bzip program. Such files are recognizable by some variation on the .bz file extension. Dealing with these files should pose no problem, as the commands are almost identical to those for gzip. Just substitute -j for -z in the command string.

Compressing and Extracting Compressed Single Files

If you want to compress or decompress a single file, there is no real need to use the tar program at all, since its purpose is to create archives consisting of several files. You can instead use the gzip and gunzip commands directly. For example, to compress a file called matilda.png, you would type gzip matilda.png, and press ENTER. The matilda.png file would then become matilda.jpg.gz. To decompress the file, you would type gunzip matilda.jpg.gz, and press ENTER, after which the matilda.jpg file would be back to normal.

So can you compress an archive you've already created with the tar command? Sure. For example to compress the spicyfood.tar archive we mentioned before, you would type gzip spicyfood.tar, and voilà—you've got yourself a compressed spicyfood.tar.gz archive. Pretty cool, don't you think?

Project 8A: Creating a Plan

Well, now that you have a bit of command experience, it's time to get some practice and put all those commands to good use. In this project we start off easy by creating a .plan file, like I mentioned in the section "$ finger" on page 125. The actual .plan file is a hidden file (as you can see by the period before its name), which contains the plan or message that you add to that file. That message will appear in the output of someone's Terminal when they use the finger command to find out more about you. You may not need such a .plan file, but it is an easy enough way to get started working a bit more with commands and the Terminal itself, so let's give it a try.

To start out, we are going to open the Terminal-based Pico editor to create the .plan file. To do this, open a Terminal window, type **pico .plan** (being sure to put a space between pico and .plan), and press ENTER. Your Terminal should now look a bit different, as you can see in Figure 8-9.

Figure 8-9: The Pico editor

You will now be looking at your new, and totally empty, .plan file within the Pico editor. All you have to do now is type your plan or message. Once you've done that, press CTRL-X to exit the Pico editor, and it will ask you if you want to save your work. You do, so type Y, after which you will be presented with a set of save options. You have already named the file .plan, as you can see near the bottom of the screen, so all you have to do is press ENTER. You will be back at your now-familiar user prompt in the Terminal window.

To wrap things up, you want to change the permission of the new .plan file by typing **chmod 644 .plan** in the Terminal window and then pressing ENTER. The .plan file should now be in your home folder and visible by all, so go on and test your work by typing **finger *username*** and pressing ENTER. The message you entered in your .plan file should now appear in the results in place of the no Plan you found there earlier. If you want to change the contents of your .plan file later on, just follow the same steps, and change the text when the .plan appears in the Pico editor.

NOTE   *The name of the .plan file is preceded by a period, which means that it is a hidden file. Thus, if you take a look in your home folder, you will not be able to see the file unless you have checked the box next to the words* Show hidden and backup files *in the Nautilus Preferences window.*

Project 8B: More Command Practice with pyWings

Now let's get some more experience behind the Terminal by installing a simple, and admittedly kind of silly, oracle program called pyWings (see Figure 8-10). pyWings will give you cryptic guidance in response to whatever questions you may ask it.

Figure 8-10: Seeking wisdom from pyWings

To use pyWings, you type whatever your confusion is in the input box, click one of the concern icons on the left (self, another, world), one of the realm icons on the right (love, work, truth), and hit the big button that looks like half an eye. The oracle will then tell you what it has to say. As an example, I asked the oracle why I haven't become rich yet, and I picked *self* as my concern and *truth* as the realm. Figure 8-11 shows the wisdom that was bestowed upon me.

Figure 8-11: PyWings bestows its wisdom

As you can see, the oracle told me, "Release is not necessarily freedom," which I will interpret as one of those "dreams come true, not free" sort of pieces of advice.

Great.

pyWings was written in a programming language called Python, which actually creates scripts rather than true conventional programs. You will learn a little more about this distinction in Chapter 9, but one of the differences I can mention right off the bat is that you don't actually have to install pyWings; you are simply going to put it on your hard drive in your home folder and run it from there, more or less as is.

8B-1: Getting pyWings

You are just about ready to begin "installing" pyWings, but before you do, you've got to get it from the project's home page at http://pywings .sourceforge.net/download.html. Just scroll down the page to the section below the words *Unix/Linux/X11*, and click the **HTTP** link, which will get you the file pywings-1.0.1.tar.gz (*.tar.gz* tells you that this is a *tarball*—the Linux world's answer to Zip files). Be sure to place the file in your home folder so that you can follow along easily.

8B-2: Creating a LocalApps Folder for pyWings

As I mentioned before, you will be installing the pyWings program locally in your home folder. Installing a program *locally* means that you are installing the program and all its support and data files in your home folder. This makes things a bit easier, but it also means that the program will not be available to other users. It also means that, if you're not careful, you might inadvertently delete it.

To make things a bit easier and safer for you, you are going to create a folder in your home folder in which to place pyWings and all other applications that you install locally on your machine in the future. You will, logically enough, call the folder LocalApps.

Let's make the folder by command, in order to get some more practice. Go to the Terminal, make sure you are in your home folder, type the following command, and then press ENTER:

```
mkdir LocalApps
```

8B-3: Extracting the pyWings Tarball

Now it is time to extract the tarball. You can do this by the double-click method you learned in Chapter 6, but since we're working with the command line, let's use that instead.

To start out, we're going to place the tarball in the same folder into which we extract its files. Usually this isn't necessary because the contents of most tarballs are already packaged in a folder of their own. By double-clicking the tarball to open it up in File Roller, you can see whether things are packed in a folder or simply as a group of files. In the case of pyWings, it is the latter, so follow these steps:

1. Create a pywings folder by typing `mkdir pywings` and pressing ENTER.
2. Move the pyWings tarball into that folder by typing `mv pywings*.gz pywings` and pressing ENTER.

You can see that in this step we used an asterisk (*) to save some wear and tear on our fingers. The asterisk is a wildcard character that in this case told your system to move any file beginning in *pywings* and ending in *.gz*. Fortunately we had only one item matching those criteria.

3. Move over to the new pywings folder by typing **cd pywings** and pressing ENTER.

4. Now we get down to the process of extracting the tarball itself using the tar command. To do this, type **tar -xzvf pywings*.gz**, and press ENTER.

    Again, notice that we used the asterisk to save ourselves some keystrokes, though we could just as well have typed **-1.0.1.tar** in its stead.

5. Finally, type **cd**, and press ENTER to bring the Terminal back to your home folder.

8B-4: Moving the pyWings Folder to Your LocalApps Folder

The extraction process is now complete. Before going on to running pyWings, however, let's move it to the new LocalApps folder you created in Project 8B-2 on page 139. To do this, type the following command, and then press ENTER:

```
mv pywings LocalApps
```

8B-5: Running pyWings

Now that you have pyWings in place and ready for action, let's start up the great oracle right now so that you can get a better perspective on how to deal with the aspects of life that trouble you.

In the Terminal, make sure you are in your home directory, type **LocalApps/pywings/pywings.py**, and press ENTER.

If all went according to plan, pyWings should be up and running and will soon be making you a wiser person.

8B-6: Creating a Launchable Link for pyWings

The method of running pyWings that you've just used works well enough, but it is a pain in the posterior to open your Terminal and type that somewhat lengthy string every time you want to find out what fate has in store for you. Let's find a way to make things easier in the future.

To run an application from the Terminal, you generally type the name of that application or, to put it more precisely, the name of that program's executable file; the application's name thus acts as a sort of command. In order for your system to recognize that command, however, the command (the executable file, or a link to it) must be in a location where the system can find it. Whenever you run a command of any sort, your system checks a series of locations (most of which are *bin folders*, where executable files are located) to find that command.

You can easily find out where these locations are by typing **echo $PATH** in a new Terminal window and then pressing ENTER. As you will see, on your Ubuntu system, these locations are:

- /usr/local/bin
- /usr/local/sbin
- /sbin
- /usr/sbin

- /bin
- /usr/bin
- /usr/bin/X11
- /usr/games

If the command you typed is in one of those locations, the program, or script, will run. As you no doubt know, however, pyWings is not in any of those locations. It is in /home/*username*/LocalApps/pyWings and is thus, in a sense, out of your system's sight.

To remedy this situation, you could add the path of your pyWings script to the list of paths that the system checks for run commands, so as to make the system aware of your new application's existence. However, let's try another method that I think is easier. What you will do is create a link to pyWings, a sort of launchable alias, in one of the locations your system does check for commands.

To create this link, you will be using three commands: cd (to change directories), sudo (to give yourself write access to the destination folder), and ln -s (to create the link).

1. In the Terminal, type **cd /usr/games**, and press ENTER. This puts you in one of the folders your system searches when you enter commands.

2. Type **sudo ln -s /home/*username*/LocalApps/pyWings/pywings.py pywings**, and press ENTER. (Note that there is a space between the words pywings.py and pywings at the end of that command string.)

   The pywings at the end of that command string is the name that you are giving the link; the name of the link thus becomes the command you will use to run the application. If you type nothing, the link will be called pywings.py, which would mean three more keystrokes for you every time you wanted to start the program.

3. Type your password when prompted to do so, and then press ENTER.

4. Type **cd**, and press ENTER to return the Terminal to your home folder.

8B-7: Running pyWings Again

Now that you have created the link, you should be able to run the pyWings program much more easily. To try it out, quit pyWings (if it is still running), type **pywings** in the Terminal window, and press ENTER. Your personal pyWings oracle should appear again.

You've managed to cut down on the number of keystrokes required to run pyWings from the Terminal. However, if you are really into this pyWings thing and want to use it often, it will probably be handiest to add a launcher to your panel, a drawer, or the Applications menu.

To add a pyWings panel launcher, for example, right-click any open space in the panel, and select **Add to Panel**. When the Add to Panel window appears, click the **Custom Application Launcher** button. In the Create Launcher window that appears, type `pyWings` in the Name section, anything you want in the Comment section (`Your Obtuse Guru`, for example), and, assuming you created a launchable link in Project 8B-6 on page 140, type `pywings` in the Comment section. For an icon, click the **No Icon** button, and then look around until you find an icon that suits your fancy. I like gnome-eog.png myself. Once you've made your selection, click **OK** in the Browse Icons window, and then click **OK** in the Create Launcher window.

8B-8: Adding Emblems to Your LocalApps Folder

Now that pyWings is successfully installed and working, it is probably a good idea to add an emblem to your new LocalApps folder so that you don't inadvertently dump it in the Trash someday. You have already learned how to do this in Chapter 7, so I won't give you the step-by-step instructions.

Project 8C: Command Practice Review with Briscola

If you would like to reinforce the skills you've put to use in the previous project, why not go a bit Continental, and try out Briscola—a simple, yet very traditional, Italian card game (see Figure 8-12). Unlike pyWings, which is a Python script, Briscola is a script of a different flavor, written in a scripting language called Tcl, which uses something called Tk to create its graphical interface.

Figure 8-12: Briscola

8C-1: Getting Briscola

You are just about ready to begin "installing" Briscola, but before you do, you must get it. You can get Briscola by going to the project's home page at www.rigacci.org/comp/software and downloading in the traditional manner, but since we're working with commands, let's instead get Briscola by using a new command: wget.

To do this, just open a Terminal window, type the following command string, and then press ENTER:

```
wget http://www.rigacci.org/comp/software/briscola/briscola-4.1.tar.gz
```

In your Terminal window you will see wget in action as it connects to the site where Briscola is stored and then downloads the file. When it's done, you will find the Briscola tarball in your home folder.

8C-2: Extracting the Briscola Tarball and Renaming the Briscola Folder

Extracting the Briscola tarball is essentially the same process as that for pyWings; however, Briscola is already packaged within its own folder, so you won't have to create a special folder for it.

Although I am sure you now know the drill, I'll tell you again. Just open a Terminal window, type the following command, and press ENTER:

```
tar -xzvf briscola*.gz
```

A new folder, Briscola-4.1, will now appear in your home folder with all of the Briscola files in it. To make things easier to deal with in the future, let's shorten the name of the folder to simply *briscola*. We already know how to do this via the right-click method, but this time around let's to do it via the command line. To do this, you use, perhaps surprisingly, the mv command followed by the name of the file whose name you are going to change, followed by the new name of the file.

Give it a go by typing the following command and pressing ENTER:

```
mv briscola-4.1 briscola
```

8C-3: Preparing the Briscola Script

Most applications that come in tarball form include a README file, which includes information on what you need to do in order to install and use the application. If you double-click the **README** file in the briscola folder in Nautilus, you will see that the "HOW TO START" section tells you to adjust the first line of the briscola.tk script to point it to your Tk shell, and to adjust the second line of the script to point to the directory where the various Briscola files are located.

To perform the adjustments as instructed in the README file, just follow these steps:

1. Find the Tk shell, called Wish, by typing `locate wish` in the Terminal window and pressing ENTER, and then note the location given on a piece of paper. It should be /usr/bin/wish.
2. Direct the Terminal to the briscola folder by typing `cd briscola` and pressing ENTER.
3. Use the Pico editor, which we used in Project 8A on page 136, to edit the briscola.tk file by typing `pico briscola.tk` and pressing ENTER. The briscola.tk file will appear in the Pico editor in your Terminal window.
4. Change the very first line of the briscola.tk file from #!/usr/local/bin/wish to `#!/usr/bin/wish`.
5. In the second line, change /usr/local/games/briscola to `/usr/share/games/ briscola`, which is where you will place Briscola in just a bit.
6. Press CTRL-X on your keyboard.
7. Type `Y`, and press ENTER to save your changes.
8. Type `cd`, and press ENTER to return the Terminal to your home folder.

8C-4: Moving the Briscola Folder to a Global Location

We could move the briscola folder to the LocalApps folder and play it from there, as we did with pyWings, but this time around, let's do things a bit differently by moving the whole thing to global territory. This not only keeps it safe from our obsessive housekeeping tendencies, but also allows all users on the same computer to play the game. We will need to use the sudo command to do this so that we can have write access in those protected folders.

To do this, just type the following command in the Terminal window, and press ENTER:

```
sudo mv briscola /usr/share/games
```

When you are prompted for your password, type it, and press ENTER.

8C-5: Creating a Launchable Link for Briscola

Even though we've moved Briscola to a global location, we still can't run it with a simple one-word command because the briscola.tk file itself is not in the system's command search path. Just as we did for pyWings, we will now create a launchable link for Briscola to solve that problem. Here are the steps:

1. In the Terminal, type `cd /usr/games`, and press ENTER.
2. Now create the link by typing `sudo ln -s /usr/share/games/briscola/ briscola.tk briscola`, and press ENTER.
3. Type `cd`, and press ENTER to return the Terminal to your home folder.

You can now easily run Briscola by typing `briscola` in the Terminal and pressing ENTER.

Can I Do the Same Thing with pyWings?

Sure. If you want to move pyWings to a global location, just follow the same procedure for moving the pywings folder and creating the link as you did for Briscola, making the necessary substitutions, of course. You will have to remove the previously created pyWings link, though, by typing the following command and pressing ENTER:

```
sudo rm /usr/games/pywings
```

After that, move the pywings folder to global territory by typing **sudo mv ~/LocalApps/pywings /usr/share/games/pywings**, and pressing ENTER. When prompted for your password, type it, and press ENTER. You can then create the launchable link by typing **cd /usr/games**, pressing ENTER, typing **sudo ln -s /usr/share/games/pywings/pywings.py pywings**, and pressing ENTER once more.

Playing Briscola

As I already mentioned, Briscola is easy—about as easy a card game as there is. It is a trick-taking game, which means that you put out a card, then your opponent puts out a card, and the one who puts out the higher point-value card wins the hand, or *trick*. Points are awarded on the basis of the cards involved in that trick. The winner of the trick then goes on to *lead* the next trick, meaning that the winner puts out his or her card first the next time around. When all the cards are played, the points for each player are then tallied, and the player with the higher points wins. All much simpler to do than it is to describe.

The Cards and Their Rankings

Like many other Italian and Spanish games, Briscola is played with a 40-card deck, consisting of the following cards: K, Q, J, 7, 6, 5, 4, 3, 2, and the Ace. Traditionally, it is played with either French-suited cards (hearts, diamonds, clubs, and spades) or Italian-suited cards (swords, coins, batons, and chalices), usually dependent upon the region in which it is played. In the software version you have just installed, you will be playing with French-suited cards in the regional pattern of Tuscany.

Unlike most card games you are probably familiar with, the ranking and point values of the cards in Briscola is somewhat different, as you can see in the following chart.

Ranking of Cards	Point Value
Ace	11
3	10
King	4
Queen	3
Jack	2
7, 6, 5, 4, 2	0

While this ranking arrangement might seem odd, it is actually fairly common in card games from the southern and Catholic regions of Central Europe. With that bit of information in mind, it should all be pretty easy enough to fathom, taking a religious view, that God (Ace) and the Holy Trinity (3) rank higher than the quasi-mortal royals (K, Q, J) and their decidedly mortal subjects (7, 6, 5, 4, 2). The rankings are thus quite sensible, albeit slightly ironic, given that some religions frown upon playing cards, calling them "the devil's tool."

Game Play in Briscola

Once Briscola starts up, it will deal three cards to each player. It will then take the seventh card and place it face up under the downward-facing pile of undealt cards, known as the *stock* or *talon*. That seventh card is called the *Briscola* (from which the game gets its name), and it determines the *trump suit* for that particular game. This means that any card of the same suit as the Briscola will beat any card of any other suit, even one of a higher ranking. Of course, when you play a trump card against another trump card, the normal rankings of the cards come back into play.

It is important to note at this point that unlike many other trick-taking games, you are neither required to follow the suit of the card led in a trick in Briscola, nor are you required to beat it if you can. This means that if your opponent plays a club card, you can play a card of any suit you like, even if you have a card that can beat it, all depending on your own strategy for ultimately winning the game.

Before getting started, it is a good idea to first go to the **Options** menu and select **Show Score**. This will allow you to know how you're doing as you play. Once you've done that, you are ready for action, and as your computer opponent is always kind enough as to allow you to lead, you can begin by clicking the card you want to put into play. Your compu-opponent will then play its card.

Once you've assessed the situation, click on one of the blank spaces in your hand, and the points for that trick will be displayed in the box labeled *You* (if you won the trick) or the box labeled *Me* (if the computer won the trick). Of course, if the trick only involved the 7, 6, 5, 4, or 2 cards, no points will appear, as those cards have no point value.

Want to Know More?

If you would like a more detailed set of rules for playing Briscola (and just about any other card game in the world), check out www.pagat.com.

Customizing the Terminal

As you now well know, the Terminal is a very simple application in terms of looks. It doesn't have to be, however, because you can spice things up a bit if you're so inclined. Not only can you change the background and text colors in the Terminal, but you can even display one of your favorite photos as a background (as shown in Figure 8-13) or make the background transparent . . . well, kind of transparent anyway.

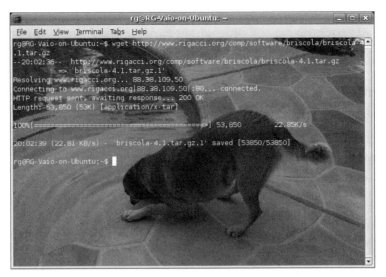

Figure 8-13: A Terminal window with customized background and font colors

To change the Terminal background, go to the Terminal **Edit** menu, and select **Current Profile**. When the Editing Profile window appears, click the **Effects** tab, select **Background image**, and then click the **Browse** button to navigate your way to the image you want to use (Figure 8-14). Depending on the image you use for your background, you may find it rather difficult to see the text once your image appears in the Terminal. If so, try moving the slider under the words *Shade transparent or image background* in the Editing Profile window. If that still doesn't do the trick, click the **Colors** tab, deselect **Use colors from system theme**, and then try some of the preset Foreground and Background combinations from the menu button next to the words *Built-in schemes* (I used White on Black in Figure 8-13).

Figure 8-14: Customizing the Terminal window

If you just want to make the background transparent, select **Transparent background**, and drag the slider near the bottom of the Editing Profile window to the far left. You can also use the slider to adjust the shading of your background image if you choose to go that route.

NOTE *The transparency effect used in the Terminal is a pseudo-transparency, as it is really just a mirroring of the desktop image. You will thus find, if you have any icons on your desktop, that when you pass the transparent terminal across such icon-laden areas, those icons will not appear in the seemingly transparent Terminal window—all you will see is the desktop wallpaper or background color.*

Depending on the colors present in your background image or in your desktop wallpaper (if you've gone the transparent route), you may also want to change the font color for your Terminal to make things easier to see. To do this, click the **Colors** tab, deselect **Use colors from system theme**, and then make the appropriate font color selection.

Tabbed Shell Sessions in the Terminal

To wrap things up in this chapter, I thought I might mention one particularly convenient feature of the GNOME Terminal: tabs. Just as you can view multiple web pages in one Firefox web browser window through the use of tabs, tabs in the Terminal application allow you to have more than one shell session running at the same time without having more Terminal windows open (see Figure 8-15). This reduces the amount of desktop clutter and generally makes things easier to deal with. You can open a new tab within the Terminal by going to the Terminal **File** menu and selecting **Open Tab ▸ Default**.

Figure 8-15: Running multiple shell sessions in tabs within the GNOME Terminal

9

DINING ON TARBALLS, BINARIES, JAVA, AND EVEN RPMs

More Ways to Install Programs

In the past few chapters, you learned how to install applications via Synaptic and run script-type applications from the command line, which gives you quite a variety of applications to choose from. It is now time, however, to expand your application-gathering repertoire even further.

In this chapter you will learn how you can add applications to your system in four other ways: compiling applications from source, converting Red Hat Package Manager (RPM) packages for use in your Debian-based system environment, running binary tarballs and Java-based applications, and—say it ain't so—even running some Windows applications. When you are done, you will have more options at your disposal than you'll know what to do with . . . and that's not a bad position to be in.

Compiling Programs from Source

For the beginner, just the mention of compiling a program from source seems off-putting enough. The words *compile* and *source* seem to instill a sense of foreboding in the heart of the new user. That certainly was the case for me, anyway.

However, this method of installing programs is a lot easier than it sounds. In fact, now that you have some experience using the Terminal and command line, it is just plain easy—a sort of one, two, three, and you're done process.

Of course, you can live long and prosper without ever bothering to compile anything on your system. You can move along quite happily with your system as is, or you can just install programs by means of the very convenient Synaptic application, which you learned about in Chapter 5.

So why would you want to bother compiling programs from source? Well, although there are a lot of DEB packages that Synaptic can ease into your system, not every bit of software in Linuxdom is available in that file format. Or perhaps you want the newest version of the software you have your eyes on, but the version available via Synaptic is a slightly older version. Of course, there is that good old human nature factor at play as well—there may well come a time when curiosity gets the better of you, and you will want to move just one step beyond the way you've grown accustomed to doing things. After working through this short project, you will be able to do just that, and I am sure you will find that your initial worries will have been for naught.

What Is Source?

In order to understand what *source* is, you should understand a bit about how a program actually gets from its primitive state on the programmer's computer to an up-and-running application on your machine. First the programmer writes a program in a programming language. You have probably heard of programming languages such as BASIC or C, and there are many others. What the programmer actually writes with such a language is a set of instructions called the *source code*, or *source.* Your computer, however, cannot actually understand any of that source on its own. It is as if the computer speaks ancient Greek, and the source code is all written in French. The computer therefore needs some sort of interpreter to help it out.

The various languages that programmers use are called *high-level languages*—they are relatively easy for programmers to read. The computer, on the other hand, only understands *low-level languages*, which are quite difficult for most mere mortal programmers to deal with. To convert the high-level language instructions to a low-level language, the computer needs some other program to translate.

This can be done while a program is running, in which case the translator program is called an *interpreter.* Applications that run using an interpreter are usually *scripts.* The pyWings and Briscola applications in Chapter 8 are examples of such script applications.

The problem with such scripts is that they can be slower than most of the applications you're familiar with because the computer must run an interpreter, interpret the source code, and run the actual application all at the same time. This is like having a French book translated into Greek by a live interpreter—very slow indeed.

As an alternative, most programs use a compiler instead of an interpreter. A *compiler* translates the high-level source code into low-level *machine code*, or *object code*, that the computer can understand before the application is actually run. Once this translation is done, the computer never has to bother with the high-level instructions again; it can merely read the translated version each and every time it runs the program. This is like having a translated version of a foreign book that you can read any time you want to. Because computers can run compiled programs without simultaneously using an interpreter, compiled programs run faster than scripts. Most applications for all operating systems are, therefore, compiled.

Tarballs: The Containers of Source

Almost all source packages come in the form of tarballs (tarballs, DEBs, and even the RPMs, such as those used in Red Hat–based systems, are all referred to as *packages,* which is why the icon for such files looks like a little parcel-post box). As you learned in Chapters 6 and 8, tarballs consist of a group of files that have been archived into a single file, which is most often compressed to save disk space, much like Zip files on Windows systems or SIT (StuffIt) files on Macs. In Linux, the most common method of creating such archives is through the *tar program,* from which the tarball gets its name, while the compression of that archive is usually accomplished by means of the gzip program. Compressed tar files, or *tarballs,* can thus be recognized by their file endings, which are *.tar.gz,* or when compressed with the bzip program, *tar.bz2.*

As you learned in Chapter 8, the files archived in tarballs can be extracted by using the command line, but to keep things easy in this chapter, you can just use the simple double-click method that you used in Chapter 6, if you prefer.

The Basics

As I mentioned before, the process of compiling an application from source and then installing it is actually simple. Basically, after untarring the source tarball, you would use the following commands to accomplish the task:

./configure   To configure a *makefile,* which provides instructions for the make command

make   To translate the source code into object code that the computer can understand

sudo make install   To give yourself write privileges in protected folders and then install the application

make clean   To clean up the leftovers once the process is complete (to clean up the mess)

I know that sounds like a lot of commands, but as I always say, it is easier to actually do than it looks like on the page, so fear not.

Installing the Tools You Need

Because Ubuntu is designed with the average computer user in mind, it does not come with the various applications and libraries you need to compile applications from source. Fortunately, however, just about everything you need to get the job done is available via Synaptic. To get ready for the work at hand in this chapter (and many other jobs you are likely to do on your own in the future) perform searches for and install the following packages:

- build-essential
- checkinstall
- libgtk1.2-dev

I should mention that although there are only three packages you need to mark for installation, Synaptic will download and install quite a few more necessary packages in addition to these—a total of 29 packages, to be exact. Nothing to worry about though, just a heads-up so that you don't go into a mid-1960s freakout.

Project 9A: Compiling and Installing Xmahjongg

To get some hands-on experience with compiling a program from source, you will be working with a game called Xmahjongg, which you can see in Figure 9-1. If you've tried out the version of Mahjongg that comes with your Ubuntu distribution, you will notice that this one is much easier on your eyes and is a bit more colorful (check out the project site at www.lcdf.org/xmahjongg to catch a glimpse of it in its full four-color glory).

Figure 9-1: The Xmahjongg game

Xmahjongg, the version of Mahjongg that we'll be working with, is available via Synaptic, so it is not absolutely necessary to install it in this manner, but Xmahjongg provides a perfect opportunity to learn how to compile a program from source. The amount of source code isn't all that great, so it won't take too much time to do, and it requires no tinkering.

In case you are not already familiar with this genre of Mahjongg game, the idea is simple enough. Each tile has an image and there are four of each tile in the pile. You must match pairs of like tiles that are open on at least one side. When you click the two matching open tiles, they will disappear. The object of the game is, thus, to remove all the tiles from the board. A very simple solitaire game.

9A-1: Downloading and Extracting the Xmahjongg Files

To get started, you will first have to download the Xmahjongg source code. You can get this from the Xmahjongg project page at www.lcdf.org/xmahjongg. Download the tarball xmahjongg-3.7.tar.gz or a newer version if there is one. Do not download any of the other file types available on that page.

If you prefer, you can instead download the Xmahjongg tarball by using the wget command that you learned in Chapter 8. Just open a Terminal window, type the following command, and then press ENTER.

```
wget http://www.lcdf.org/xmahjongg/xmahjongg-3.7.tar.gz
```

Once you have the file on your hard disk, untar the xmahjongg-3.7.tar.gz file either via the command line, as you learned to do in Chapter 8, or via the simple double-click method. To make it easier for you to follow along with the directions I'll be giving you, be sure to place the untarred Xmahjongg folder in your home folder. Then you will be ready to roll.

Normally at this point, you would look through the folder to find some instructions for dealing with the package, just as you did in Chapter 8 for Briscola. In most source code packages, this information is included in an INSTALL file like that in the xmahjongg-3.7 folder (Figure 9-2). To read the INSTALL file, just double-click it, and it will open in Gedit.

In this case, you can simply close the INSTALL file, as it prescribes the same steps as I've listed below. However, in the future, when you install other programs from source, you will need to follow the instructions in the INSTALL files that come with the source files for those programs. With most INSTALL files, the instructions will match those that follow, though I would suggest using the alternative method I'll be presenting as a substitute for the make install step.

Of course, it may well occur that you take a look at the contents of the INSTALL file and start wondering what alien tongue it is written in. In such cases when you have no idea what the INSTALL file is going on about, which sometimes happens, just look for a configure file in the package folder. If you find one, then just try doing things the way you will learn in this project.

Figure 9-2: Identifying a package's INSTALL file

9A-2: Running configure and make for Xmahjongg

Now that you have downloaded and untarred the Xmahjongg tarball, installation is pretty standard, though we will be finishing up in a slightly different way. Here's what you need to do:

1. Open a Terminal window, and then move into the new folder by typing **cd xmahjongg*** and pressing ENTER.

    The next step is sort of a setup phase that runs the configure script in the xmahjongg-3.7 folder. The configure script checks what files, compilers, and other things it needs, and then it searches your computer to see if those things are there, and if so, where. Based on this information, it writes a file called a makefile, which is a set of instructions that will tell the make command in the subsequent step how to set things up specifically for your system configuration.

2. Configure the program by typing **./configure** and pressing ENTER.

    While you are running configure, you will see lots of odd and mysterious things flowing through your Terminal window; this is essentially a running account of what is going on, each step of the way. Depending on the program you are dealing with, this could take a bit of time—a few seconds or a few minutes. Either way, you needn't worry. As long as the mysterious text keeps flowing and you don't get an error message at the very end of the whole process, all will be well.

When configure has done its thing, you will see your prompt again, and you can go on to the next step, which is the translation, or *compilation*, step. The make command reads the makefile, created by configure, to see how things need to be set up on your machine. Then it proceeds to call on the compiler to translate the high-level source code into low-level, machine-readable files that can be installed in the subsequent step.

3. To perform this translation, type **make**, and press ENTER.

Again, you will be treated to more mysterious text flowing through the window and a short wait, usually a tad longer than for the configure process. Once make has done its job and you see your prompt again, you are ready to install the program.

Up to this point, you have not changed your system in any way. All the changes thus far have taken place in the xmahjongg-3.7 folder only. Your system is still as pure as the day you started. Of course, all that is going to end right now when you perform the final installation step.

9A-3: Installing Xmahjongg

Normally at this point of the process, you would type sudo make install and press ENTER, after which the files that were compiled in the make step would be installed in various locations throughout your system. You would then follow this up with the make clean command to tidy things up in the Xmahjongg folder by getting rid of any unnecessary files.

This traditional approach works fine enough, but things can get a bit messy if you find yourself wanting to upgrade or remove the application later on, as you have to keep track of where everything is and remove each item piece by piece using a series of sudo rm commands. Sometimes an application package will provide a make uninstall routine, but such routines don't always work perfectly, aren't available for every package, and require you to keep the project folder on your hard disk in order for you to perform the procedure.

If you are a traditionalist, you can go ahead and install Xmahjongg in this traditional manner. In the same Terminal window that you performed the ./configure and make steps, just type **sudo make install**, and then press ENTER. You will be prompted for your password, so type it, and then press ENTER again. Xmahjongg will then be installed and ready for use.

The Alternative Installation Method

The traditional installation step is fine enough, but because of the limitations I mentioned in terms of removing the application, I recommend finishing things off in a slightly different way. What you are going to do, assuming you are willing to go this route, is to skip the make install step and instead convert the compiled, but uninstalled, application into a DEB package, and then install that. By doing this, you can remove the package quite easily using Synaptic whenever the desire strikes. Having a DEB package for your application, you don't need to keep the project folder, and you can save on hard disk clutter.

To create and install the DEB package, here's what you need to do:

1. Assuming you are using the still-open Terminal window in which you entered the make command, type **sudo checkinstall**, and then press ENTER.

2. A message will soon appear in the Terminal telling you that the ./doc-pak directory does not exist, and asking you if the program should create it. You want it to, so type **Y**, and press ENTER.

3. The checkinstall program will then begin performing a mock install, after which it will create the DEB package. Before completing the process it will ask you for a description of the package. Type something like **An easy-to-see Mahjongg game**, press ENTER, and then press ENTER again.

4. You will then be presented with a screen, such as that in Figure 9-3, giving you the chance to change the package information. You don't need to change anything, so just press ENTER.

Figure 9-3: Accepting checkinstall's default package information

5. The checkinstall program will then finish up the packaging of the DEB package, install it, and then let you know when it is done.

And that is that. The Xmahjongg game is now installed on your system, and you will find an Xmahjongg DEB package within the Xmahjongg folder. You should move that DEB package to a safe place, such as a Tarballs or Software folder (or whatever else you choose to call it) so that you can use it again should you someday need to reinstall your system. Once you've moved the DEB package, dump the Xmahjongg folder, assuming it is in your home folder, by typing **cd ; sudo rm -r xmahjongg*** and pressing ENTER.

NOTE   *The semicolon, surrounded by spaces on either side, is used to separate commands written on a single line. In following the directions just given, you are really performing two operations in a single line:* cd *and* sudo rm –r xmahjongg*.

9A-4: Running Xmahjongg

As a general rule, programs compiled from source do not automatically install a launcher in your Applications menu; you must instead run them by command. Although you can run a program for the first time by typing a command in the Run Application panel applet, it is better to run the program for the first time by typing the command in your Terminal window. If anything has gone amiss during installation, the Terminal will tell you what the problem is, whereas the Run Program method would just leave you wondering what's going on.

To run Xmahjongg, just type **xmahjongg** in a Terminal window, and then press ENTER. If everything goes as it should, you can create a program launcher for Xmahjongg in your Applications menu, on the GNOME Panel, or in a panel drawer.

Project 9B: Converting an RPM for Use in a Debian-Based System: Skype

As you already know, Ubuntu is a Debian-based system, which means that most applications available for it, such as those you install via Synaptic, come in DEB packages. Other systems, such as Mandriva and Fedora Core, however, are RPM based, which is the program packaging system developed by Red Hat. It is possible, in many cases, to use RPMs in Debian-based systems by converting the RPMs to DEB packages. In this project, we are going to be doing just that in order to install the very handy Internet telephony application Skype.

Skype, shown in Figure 9-4, is Voice-over-IP (VoIP) software that allows you to speak to other Skype users over the Internet with the clarity of a regular telephone line, and it doesn't cost anything—even if you call users overseas. There are also for-fee services, such as Skype Out, which allows you to call regular mobile and land line telephone numbers from your computer at a fraction of what it would normally cost you to do so from a regular telephone.

While it is true that Ubuntu comes bundled with a VoIP package of its own, called Ekiga Softphone, it is not compatible with the much-better-known and more widespread Skype. Since it is very likely that the majority of people you know who are using a VoIP software package are using Skype, it only makes sense to go the Skype route so that you can easily communicate with them. It's nice software anyway.

Figure 9-4: Internet telephony made
easy with Skype

9B-1: Installing Alien

Before downloading, converting, and installing the Skype RPM, you have
to first install Alien, which is the application that allows you to perform the
conversion. Fortunately, Alien is available via Synaptic, so all you have to
do is perform a search for *alien*, and then follow the standard installation
procedures, making sure that you have met all the necessary dependencies
for the application you are going to install. If you don't know beforehand
what those dependencies are, you will find out when you try to install the
file; a list of unmet dependencies will then appear.

9B-2: Getting the Skype RPM

Once Alien is installed, you need to download the Skype RPM. You can get this
from www.skype.com/download/skype/linux. On that page, click **RPM for
Mandriva 10.1 and newer**. There are other versions on the page that might
work, but there are more problems involved in dealing with them.

Once the download is complete, make sure to place the RPM in your
home folder.

9B-3: Converting the Skype RPM

Now that the Skype RPM is in your home folder, you can convert it to an
Ubuntu-friendly DEB package using Alien by typing the following command,
and pressing ENTER:

```
sudo alien -d skype*.rpm
```

After typing your password when prompted to do so, nothing much will seem to happen. Once Alien is done doing its thing, however, you will get the message skype_1.2.0.21-2_i386.deb generated (or something like that) in the Terminal window. If you look in your home folder you will then find the newly generated DEB package along with the original RPM.

9B-4: Installing Dependencies

Before going on to install the Skype DEB package, you need to install a library upon which it depends: libqt3-mt. Fortunately, you can get this easily enough via Synaptic by doing a Synaptic search for *libqt3-mt* and then installing the file.

9B-5: Installing the Newly Generated Skype DEB Package

You can now install the newly generated Skype DEB package by using the dpkg (Debian package) command with the -i (install) flag, and then pressing ENTER. The command should be:

```
sudo dpkg -i skype*.deb
```

If I haven't won you over to the world of commands (not that I'm trying to), and you still prefer going about things graphically whenever possible, you will be happy to know that you can install a DEB package by simply double-clicking the file in question. Doing so will bring up the Gdebi Package Installer window (Figure 9-5).

Figure 9-5: Installing individual DEB packages graphically

In that window, click the **Install Package** button, and a new window will appear telling you that you need to grant administrative rights in order to install the package. Click the **Grant** button, and you will be prompted for your password before installation of the package will begin. When the process is done, you will be notified in the installation progress window. Just click **Close** in that window, and the process is done. You can then close the Package Installer window as well.

9B-6: Running Skype

Once all the pieces have been installed, you can run Skype by going to the **Applications** menu and selecting **Internet ▸ Skype**. After setting up a Skype user account, I would advise restarting your computer. Skype seems to work better in terms of sound quality after that initial restart. Also remember, while on the topic of sound quality, that it is best to use Skype with a headset. Trying to talk with a stick microphone could cause feedback or echoes because the microphone will pick up sounds from the speakers and transmit them.

Project 9C: Running Other Precompiled Binaries

Applications that are compiled and can be run as-is by your operating system are called *binaries*. When you compiled Xmahjongg from source code, you were in essence creating a binary for the application that you later installed. DEB packages and RPMs are essentially precompiled binaries with a built-in installation mechanism.

There are, however, quite a few other programs that come in binary form but are not DEB packages or RPMs. Instead, they come as tarballs, and, once extracted, can be run either locally from within your home folder or, with a just a bit more work on your part, globally.

Such binary packages come in two flavors, so to speak: dynamic and static. *Dynamic binaries* are dependent on other libraries and bits of software installed on your system. If you don't have the dependencies installed, you can't run the application, or at least not with all of its functions. *Static binaries*, on the other hand, don't depend on anything else in your system, as they come with everything they need to run. Of course, such convenience comes at a price, because the size of a static binary package is usually considerably greater than that for a dynamic binary package. That means longer download times and more used disk space for you.

G-Sudoku

In this project you will be working with a dynamic binary package called G-Sudoku (Figure 9-6), which is a sudoku game generator and solver. It depends on GTK, a widget library used by many applications in the creation of their user interface. Since GTK is present in just about every Linux distribution out there, G-Sudoku should run right out of the box, as they say.

Figure 9-6: G-Sudoku

9C-1: Getting the G-Sudoku Tarball

To start out, you will first need to download the G-Sudoku tarball, which you can easily do by going to www.yzonesoft.com/gsudoku/gsudoku.html and clicking the **Downloads** link. On the Downloads page, go down to the Linux section, and download the file listed there (*tar.gz.file* is all it says). If you prefer to go the wget route that you learned about in Chapter 8, you can instead open a Terminal window, type the following command string, and then press ENTER to download the tarball.

```
wget http://www.yzonesoft.com/gsudoku/files/gsudoku_02_linux.tar.gz
```

Either way you go, once the G-Sudoku tarball is on your hard disk, extract it via the command line or the double-click method, and then make sure to place the application folder in your home folder.

9C-2: Running G-Sudoku

You can run G-Sudoku in one of two ways. You can either double-click the G-Sudoku binary file itself to launch it (the icon looks like a lavender diamond), or you can open a Terminal window, type the following command, and press ENTER:

```
cd gsudoku* ; ./gsudoku
```

G-Sudoku is an open source application, but it wasn't always. In the past, you had to pay for G-Sudoku, which might explain why when you start it up there is a small, though not unattractive splash screen (splash window, actually) that appears, announcing that the application is sponsored by Raja Tea. Strangely, that splash screen actually causes a few problems, because if you close it too soon, you can inadvertently close the whole program.

To avoid this problem in the future, go to the **Settings** menu, and select **Settings**. When the Settings Dialog window appears, click **Preference** in the left pane, and then deselect **Show splash screen at start up**. There is no OK button in the window, so just close it to save the changes.

When you are ready to play, just click the **New** button in the main window, and G-Sudoku will generate a new game for you to play.

9C-3: Moving G-Sudoku to a Global Location

If you would like to move G-Sudoku to a global location so that everyone who has a user account on your machine can play it (or so that you don't toss it out by accident), you can do so in the same manner you did with Briscola in Chapter 8.

First, shorten the name of the G-Sudoku folder from *gsudoku_02_linux* to *gsudoku*. After that, just type the following command, and press ENTER:

```
sudo mv gsudoku  /usr/share/games
```

Because you used the sudo command, you will be prompted for your password, so type it, press ENTER, and the job will be done.

9C-4: Creating a Launchable Link for G-Sudoku

With G-Sudoku in its new global location, running it is a bit more tiring on the fingertips, as you must now type /usr/share/games/gsudoku/gsudoku in order to run it. Well, to make things much easier, we can create a link in one of the directories within the system's command search path. This is the same thing we did for Briscola in Chapter 8.

To create the link for G-Sudoku, here's what you need to do:

1. In the Terminal, type **cd /usr/games**, and press ENTER.
2. Create the link by typing **sudo ln -s /usr/share/games/gsudoku/gsudoku**, and press ENTER.
3. Type **cd**, and press ENTER to return the Terminal to your home folder.

You can now run G-Sudoku by typing gsudoku in the Terminal or Run Application panel applet and pressing ENTER.

Project 9D: Running Java Apps: Risk

In Chapter 8 you learned to run a couple of applications based on scripts, such as the Python-based pyWings and the Tcl/Tk–based Briscola, but it just wouldn't be right to finish up our discussion of applications without mentioning what might be well considered the granddaddy of all scripting languages—Java. In this project, you will learn how to install the Java Runtime Environment and how to install and run the Java-based version of the classic board game, Risk.

9D-1: Installing the Java Runtime Environment

In order to run Java-based applications, or scripts, you need to first install the Java Runtime Environment. This is easily done via Synaptic by doing a search for *j2re*. When the search is complete, mark the file **j2re1.4** for installation, and if you want to also install the browser plugin at the same time, mark **j2re1.4-mozilla-plugin**, as well. After that, go through the usual steps for installing a package via Synaptic. During the installation process, a small window will appear (Figure 9-7), spelling out the license terms for the package. Check the box next to the words *Do you agree with the above license terms* (don't be bothered by the fact that the terms are actually listed *below*), and then click the **Forward** button to get back to the installation.

Figure 9-7: Agreeing to the Java Runtime Environment licensing terms

9D-2: Getting the Risk File

Risk, as well as many other Java-based applications, is available from www.sourceforge.net, but to make things easier, just point your browser directly to the Risk project home page at http://jrisk.sourceforge.net (and don't forget the *j* at the beginning of that URL). On the main page, click the **Download** link. Then, on the Downloads page, click the **Risk jar and source** link. You will then be taken to a page of download locations, so click the one closest to you, and wait for your download to begin.

Risk comes as a Zip archive, so once the download is complete, you will have to unzip the file using one of the methods you've learned thus far. Once you're finished, you will have a new Risk folder within your home folder. If you take a look in that folder, you will notice the file Risk.jar. This is the game that you will be running via the command line. In the future, should you choose to download other Java-based applications, the file with the .jar extension will be the one you will be trying to run.

9D-3: Running Risk

Now that you've installed the Java Runtime Environment and downloaded and extracted the Risk Zip file, you are ready to run Risk without any further work. To get going, open a new Terminal window, and do the following:

1. Move into the Risk folder by typing **cd Risk** and pressing ENTER.
2. Type **java -jar Risk.jar** (be sure to place a space between java and -jar), and press ENTER. Risk (shown in Figure 9-8) will soon appear, after which you can start playing.

Figure 9-8: Risk

In case you're wondering, here's what you did in that last line: The first part of the command string, java, calls the Java Runtime Environment into action; the -jar flag after that tells Java that you are going to be running a JAR file; and the last part is the actual file you are going to run, Risk.jar. In the future, if you choose to run other Java-based applications, just follow the same pattern: java -jar *application_name*.jar.

Running Windows Applications with Wine

Now that you've learned just about every way there is to add applications to your system, I might as well throw in one more—running Windows applications. Despite the fact that there is a Linux equivalent to most of the Windows programs that people use or need, there may be one or two programs that you will come to miss. For me it has long been the freeware version of the Austrian card game Schnapsen. Fortunately, it is possible to run some Windows applications from within Linux with the help of a program called Wine.

The folks at Wine seem keen on pointing out that Wine is not a Windows emulator, preferring to call it a *Windows compatibility layer*. In fact, even the name itself drives home the point, as Wine is a recursive acronym for *Wine Is Not an Emulator*. Whatever way you choose to look at it, its function is to allow you to run Windows apps without having Windows installed on your machine.

It is only fair to point out that Wine continues to be a work in progress. It works fairly well with some programs and not at all with others. Things have improved, however, and Wine now seems to work better with more applications. Until the latest release, for example, I had been unable to get my beloved Schnapsen game to run. Now it does, and pretty well at that (Figure 9-9).

Figure 9-9: A Windows application (Schnapsen) running under Linux

If you are curious as to which apps are known to run under Wine, and to what degree of success, check out the Wine home page at www.winehq.org, and click the **AppDB** link. And if you are curious about Schnapsen and aren't afraid of wading through a bit of German, get the program at www.members.a1.net/zillinger. You can also learn the rules of Schnapsen (and any other card game in the world) at www.pagat.com.

Installing Wine

It is possible to install Wine via Synaptic from the repositories you have already activated thus far. Unfortunately, the version available there (as of this writing, anyway) has some quirks that make it an undesirable choice. Instead, it is better to add WineHQ's repository to your Synaptic repository list, just as in the example given in Chapter 5, before downloading and installing Wine. Just remember that the APT line you want to add to the repository list is:

```
deb http://wine.budgetdedicated.com/apt dapper main
```

After you have added the repository and reloaded the package lists, perform a search for *wine*, and then mark and install it.

Setting Up Wine

Once Wine is installed, you will need to allow it to create a fake Windows C: drive within your home folder. One way to do this is by running the Wine configuration manager, Winecfg, even though you don't really need to do any configuring at this point in the game.

The first time around, it is probably best to run Winecfg via the command Terminal so that you can see evidence in the Terminal ouput that Wine is indeed creating your fake C: drive. Just type **winecfg**, and press ENTER. Wine will then create the fake C: drive, after which Winecfg (Figure 9-10) will appear. As I said, you don't need to configure anything at this point, so you can have a look at Winecfg and then close it. In the future, you might want to check out the online documentation at www.winehq.org.

Figure 9-10: The Wine configuration manager—Winecfg

Installing a Windows Application in Wine

To get a feel for how you can go about installing a Windows application to use under Wine, I will point you to one that will definitely work—a pretty cool tabbed text editor called NoteTab Light (Figure 9-11).

Figure 9-11: NoteTab Light

To get NoteTab Light, go to www.notetab.com, and click the **EXE Package** button in the NoteTab Light 4.95 section. Firefox will then launch a window asking you what you want to do with the file. Accept the default, *Open with Wine*, by clicking **OK**. A few moments after that, the same setup wizard that you would see if you were installing NoteTab Light in Windows will appear (Figure 9-12). Go through that wizard, accepting all the defaults along the way, until the installation is complete.

Figure 9-12: A Windows installation wizard running under Wine

If the Open with Wine option does not appear, select **Save to Disk** in Firefox's what-do-I-do-with-this window, and click **OK**. When the download is complete, place the NoteTab Light EXE file in your home folder, open a Terminal window, type `wine NoteTab_Setup.exe` in that window, and press ENTER.

NOTE *If you are trying to install an application that comes in a Zip archive, you must first download the file, extract it, and then run the setup wizard yourself. You can do this via a Terminal window by using the* cd *command to move into the folder, and then typing* wine *plus the name of the setup file within the application folder, usually* wine setup.exe.

Running a Windows Application in Wine

Running NoteTab Light is quite easy because it provides you with a desktop launcher. Just double-click that launcher, and NoteTab Light will soon appear, just like a regular Linux app would. In other cases, however, you won't be as lucky because there might not be an easy-to-find launcher. In such cases you can use Wine File, which you can run via the Run Application panel applet. Just type `winefile`, press **Run**, and a Windows Explorer–like file browser will appear (Figure 9-13).

Figure 9-13: Searching your "C:" drive with Wine File

Wine File as is will show the contents of your entire hard disk, not just your fake C: drive. This can be a bit unwieldy to deal with, so it is probably best to click the **C:/** button, which will open another subwindow displaying only the content of that fake drive—your Wineland, so to speak. In that window, you can then double-click the **Program Files** directory, and from there, navigate to the app you want to run, and then double-click that app's EXE file in order to do so.

10

GUTENBIRD

Setting Up and Using Your Printer and Scanner

Two of the most common computer peripherals are printers and scanners. This only makes sense, as it is those two tools that turn a web-surfing, game-playing, music-churning, number-crunching box of chips into a meaningful production tool—a virtual publishing house, if you will. These two tools help your computer convert digital information into hard copy (in the case of printers) and hard copy into digital information (in the case of scanners). It is not surprising, therefore, that these tools often come together these days in the form of multifunction printers.

In this chapter, you will learn how to connect these useful devices to your computer, how to set them up, and how to use them. If you're more into working with your digital camera than with a scanner, you might want to sneak a peek at Chapter 14; otherwise, put on your printer's smock, and follow on. . . .

Printers

Unless the only thing you use your computer for is playing games, listening to MP3s, or stopping doors on hot, breezy days, you will no doubt want to hook up your machine to a printer. Despite the paperless office era that the personal computer was supposedly going to usher in, it seems that the computer's strength as a desktop-publishing and general work tool has made producing high-quality printed documents an even more attractive proposition than ever before.

Confirming That Your Printer Is Supported

Setting up a printer to work with your new system is a pretty easy task, but you do have to make sure that your printer is supported by Linux. Fortunately, it seems that printer support in the Linux world is getting much, much better than it once was. In general, support for Epson, Brother, Samsung, and Hewlett-Packard printers is pretty good, while support for other makers and other printer types is a bit spottier, though improving.

If you really want to make sure your printer is supported (and why wouldn't you?), the best thing to do is go to www.linuxprinting.org. On that site, you can check out the online database to see if your printer is currently supported and, if so, to what degree. Listings for supported printers also include information on what drivers are best for your purposes. If you're thinking of buying a printer, there is also a page of suggested makes and models. Read this before making your purchase decision. You might also want to consult Ubuntu's list at https://wiki.ubuntu.com/HardwareSupport-ComponentsPrinters.

Setting Up Your Printer

If you have a USB printer, get started by connecting it to your computer and then powering up the printer. If your printer connects to your computer's parallel port, you will first have to turn your computer off, connect your printer to the computer, turn on the printer, and then start your computer. Of course, if your printer was connected and on during installation, you can skip this step. Either way, your printer should be detected, though you won't get one of those immediate new-hardware-found alerts that you do in Windows.

Once your system has restarted, here is what you need to do:

1. Go to the **System** menu, and select **Administration ▸ Printing**.

2. A Printers window will appear, showing a printer icon with the name *New Printer*. Double-click that icon, after which a setup wizard will appear (Figure 10-1).

    The name of your printer should appear in the pane below the words *Use a detected printer*, due to the wonders of plug and play (which means that your printers, scanners, and other devices can tell your computer what they are). Unfortunately, just because your system knows which printer you have hooked up to it hardware-wise doesn't actually mean it can communicate with that printer in terms of printing (ditto for Windows and Mac OS X). That's what drivers are for.

Figure 10-1: The printer setup wizard

3. Continue by clicking the **Forward** button, which will take you to the second page of the wizard, shown in Figure 10-2.

Figure 10-2: Selecting the make and model of the printer in the printer setup wizard

This second page of the wizard should automatically open with the make and model of your printer selected, as well as the recommended driver for that printer. If the model chosen is not correct, scroll down the list until you find the correct model. If your model isn't listed, try the one that was selected by default.

4. Once your printer is selected, click the **Forward** button, which will bring you to the last page of the wizard.

5. On this page, type a name for your printer, and, if you want, give a description and its location. When you're finished, your window should look something like mine in Figure 10-3. You can then click **Apply**.

Figure 10-3: The final page of the printer setup wizard

The wizard should close, leaving you at the Printers window where you started this quest. An icon for your printer should now appear in that window alongside the New Printer icon that you originally found there. If you have set up more than one printer, you can choose which one you would like to be the default by right-clicking the icon for that printer and selecting **Make Default** in the menu that appears. The icon for that printer should then be emblazoned with a blue checkbox (Figure 10-4), indicating that it is the default printer for your system.

Figure 10-4: The New Printer icon in the Printers window after completion of the printer setup wizard

Your printer is now set up and ready for use. However, just to make sure that everything is hunky-dory, it is always a good idea to print a test page.

1. Right-click the icon for your printer in the Printers window, and select **Properties** in the popup menu.
2. In the Properties window that appears, click the **Print a Test Page** button.

Your system will send a test document to your printer and let you know it's done so in a small window, which you can close. The printer should print out the test document shortly.

NOTE   *If your test page didn't come out the way it should, or if your printer wasn't configured automatically or correctly by the system, check out www.linuxprinting.org, and see if there are any special requirements or caveats for your model.*

For the Driverless Among You

As I mentioned, there are some printers for which Linux does not yet have built-in support. For those of you who find yourselves with such printers, there are a few routes you can take in order to get things to work.

Checking the Connections

You'd be surprised how many times I have triumphantly solved someone's printer problems by simply wiggling or replugging their USB or parallel connectors. Loose connections are often the culprit when your printer's model name fails to appear in the first page of the printer setup wizard.

If that approach fails, browse to www.linuxprinting.org, as it is sometimes the case that Linux can only support certain printers if they are connected via the parallel port, even if they work via USB in other systems.

Third-Party Drivers

Recently, more and more Linux printing drivers are becoming available. If you don't find your printer on that second page of the printer setup wizard, just trying Googling the make and model of your printer plus the word *linux*. In my case, having a Samsung SCX4100 laser printer that did not appear at www.linuxprinting.org, I searched for *samsung+SCX4100+linux*.

This led me to www.driverstock.com, which provides free printer drivers for most operating systems, including Linux. On that site, I found not only the driver for my printer, but also the driver for its built-in scanner.

You might also want to check the website for the manufacturer of your printer, as many now provide Linux drivers for a number of their printers. Brother, Lexmark, Hewlett-Packard, and Samsung do, to name a few. Canon seems to be the main holdout as far as the big boys go. There is also a German company (www.turboprint.info) that provides Linux drivers, albeit for a fee, for machines that are really hard to deal with and for high-quality graphic solutions.

If you happen to find and download a driver for your printer that does not come with its own installer (the driver file should end in *.ppd*), go back to the printer setup wizard, click the **Install Driver** button on the second page, and then navigate to the driver file you downloaded.

Don't forget to give the Ubuntu forums (www.ubuntuforums.org) a try to see if anyone there has any experience getting the printer in question to work on their system.

Trial and Error

Finally, there is always the old trial-and-error approach, which works on occasion. When setting up your printer via the wizard window, try selecting **Generic ▸ PostScript Printer**, which works with some machines. If that fails, try choosing from one of the other models and/or drivers available for printers from your printer's manufacturer.

After you are done with the wizard, open the Preferences window for the printer you added, click the **Print a Test Page** button, and see what happens. If nothing happens, click the **Driver** tab, select a different printer model, and then press the **Print a Test Page** button again. Repeat that process until something works. With any luck, something will . . . might . . . well, just give it a try if you're desperate.

Printing Details

Now that your printer is set up, you will no doubt want to start printing. This is an easy task and not much different from how it works in the Windows and Mac worlds, so you will need little explanation in this regard. There are a few points of difference, however, so I will touch upon these.

Printing to PDF

One of the nice features of Linux is that you can save most documents as PDF files. In some cases, such as in OpenOffice.org, you do this by exporting the document to PDF. In most other applications, however, you do it via the Print dialog box, in which case you are said to be "printing to PDF." Whether you are *saving* to PDF, *exporting* to PDF, or *printing* to PDF, you are essentially doing the same thing: creating a PDF file of your document.

This is very handy, as it allows you to create documents that cannot be altered by others and yet can easily be read regardless of what word processor program or computer platform the reader is using. Best of all, this feature, which you would have to pay a pretty penny for in the Windows world, costs you nothing, as it is built in to your system.

In most GNOME applications, you can print to PDF by going to the **File** menu of the application in question and selecting **Print**. When the Print window (Figure 10-5) appears, select **Create a PDF document** in the Printer pane, and then click the **Print** button.

Figure 10-5: Printing a file to PDF in most GNOME applications

Printing Web Pages to PDF

Printing to PDF is also a very handy way of saving a web page that you would like to keep on hand in its graphical entirety for future reference. At this time, Firefox does not support this feature, though it does allow you to print a page to PostScript. As long as you are strictly using the file on your own system or giving it to someone else with a Linux system, you most likely won't notice any difference between PS and PDF files, as they look and act pretty much the same.

To print a web page to PostScript, go to the Firefox **File** menu, and select **Print**. When the Print dialog window appears, select **Print to file**, and then give your file a name, being sure to keep the *.ps* file ending. Click **Print**, and within seconds, the file will appear on your hard disk.

This is all fine and dandy, but if you want to distribute the document to a broader audience, the PostScript alternative just won't do, as most Windows users won't have any way to view the file. So what can you do? Well, one way is to create the PS document and then convert it to PDF using the `ps2pdf` command. This is very easy to do, though it doesn't always work so well. You may find, for example, that the text within your PS document vanishes in the output PDF file, or that the text appears, while the graphics vanish. Giving it a try can't hurt, though, so here's how you do it. Just type `ps2pdf` *filename.ps filename.pdf* in your Terminal, and press ENTER. Yup, that's all there is to it.

Project 10: Creating a Virtual PDF Printer

If you aren't satisfied with the results of a `ps2pdf` conversion, but you still want to be able to print web pages to PDF, there is a fairly simple solution—create a virtual PDF printer. By doing so, you will be able to print to PDF in any application that allows printing (sorry gamers).

10-1: Getting and Setting Up the Files You Need

To get started, run Synaptic, perform a search for *cups-pdf*, and install it. Once it is installed, open a Terminal window, type `sudo chmod +s /usr/lib/cups/backend/cups-pdf`, and press ENTER. When prompted for your password, type it, and press ENTER.

10-2: Setting Up Your Virtual PDF Printer

After the cups-PDF installation and preparation is complete, you can go on to setting up your printer. To do this, go to the **System** menu, and select **Administration ▸ Printing**. Provide your password when prompted, and then, when the Printers window appears, double-click the **New Printer** icon. In the Add a Printer wizard that appears, select **Local Printer** and **Use a detected printer**, and then click once on **PDF Printer** to select it. Once you're done, click **Forward**.

On the second page of the wizard, select **Generic** in the Manufacturer menu, and then select **postscript color printer rev3b** in the Model section. Your window should then look like that in Figure 10-6. If it does, click **Forward**.

Figure 10-6: Creating a virtual PDF printer

Finally, on the last page of the wizard, fill in the text boxes as you like and click **Apply** to seal the deal. You might want to shorten the name of the printer to something more manageable, such as *My PDF Printer*.

10-3: Using Your Virtual PDF Printer

Once you've set up your virtual PDF printer, you can use it quite easily. In fact, because your system views it as a real printer, all you have to do is go through the usual steps for printing any document, but just be sure to select your virtual PDF printer as the printer for the job in the Print dialog window when it appears.

Once you've printed a document using the virtual PDF printer, you can find your documents in the PDF folder that cups-PDF will create for you within your home folder the first time you use the virtual PDF printer.

Canceling a Print Job

It happens to all of us. You wanted to print just 1 page of a 57-page document, but you accidentally started printing the whole thing. What can you do to save your ink and 56 sheets of paper? Fortunately, the solution is simple.

Once you've clicked the **Print** button and the print job is sent to your printer, a small printer icon will appear somewhere at the right end of the top GNOME Panel (usually to the left of the other items there), as you can see in Figure 10-7.

Figure 10-7: A printer icon appears in the GNOME Panel while printing.

Just click that icon once, and a window showing your current and queued print jobs will appear (as shown in Figure 10-8). Your errant print job will be listed in that window, so click the name of the job to select it, and then, in the **Edit** menu, select **Cancel Jobs**. If you just want to stop things temporarily, you can select **Pause Jobs** instead.

Name	Job Number	Owner	Size	State
WhatCatsWant	7	rg	1.5 MB	Printing: job-printing
Truth by Numbers	8	rg	1.5 MB	Pending: none

Figure 10-8: Canceling a print job via the print queue window

After you do this, the print job listed in the queue window will disappear, and your printer will stop printing. You can then close the print queue window. This is a very easy process that you may well find is more effective than what you've experienced in other operating systems.

In some cases, things will be even easier, particularly if you installed your printer driver yourself by means of the installer that came packaged with the driver. In many such cases, the driver will provide its own progress window that will appear whenever you print a document. If so, you can simply click the **Cancel** button (or equivalent) in that window to cancel the printing job.

NOTE   *In some cases you may have to clear your printer after canceling a print job. You can do this by turning your printer off, waiting a few seconds, and then turning it on again.*

Scanners

Scanners are extremely useful and about as cheap a peripheral device as you can get. They allow you to take images or pages of text and input them, in digital form, into your computer—in much the same way as you would duplicate a document on a copy machine. However, even as digital cameras are rapidly overtaking traditional film cameras as the photographic device of choice for the masses, the number of people using scanners to transfer their non-digital images into digital form is slowly decreasing.

Despite this trend, scanners are not in immediate danger of extinction because there are more images around than those you photograph yourself. In some ways, you could even argue that scanners are becoming a bit more common due to the fact that they now often come as part of the increasingly popular multifunction printers.

Even though scanners have been around for a relatively long time, support for them in Linux is still a bit spotty. Fortunately, this is changing for the better with every new Linux release. The *back end*, the essentially hidden part of your system that handles scanner recognition and support in Linux, is called Sane, while the graphical interface for Sane is called XSane (shown in Figure 10-9). If you are wondering whether Linux will be able to recognize your scanner, or if you are trying to figure out what type of scanner to buy, you will probably want to go to the Sane website, www.sane-project.org/sane-mfgs.html.

Figure 10-9: Scanning with XSane

There you will be able to see whether your scanner is supported or get tips about what scanner to buy. As I have mentioned before, you can also try out the Ubuntu forums (www.ubuntuforums.org) and ask for Ubuntu-specific recommendations there.

Scanning with XSane

To run XSane, go to the **Applications** menu, and select **Graphics ▸ XSane Image scanning program**. XSane will then perform a search for an attached scanner. If it finds one, it will start up. If it doesn't, it will pop up a tiny window that says, "No devices available." You can do little else at that point other than click the **Close** button.

If you do run up against this problem, you can try running XSane as root by going to the **Applications** menu and selecting **System Tools ▸ Run as different user**. When the Run program window appears, type **xsane** in the Run box, and then press the **OK** button. If your stars are in alignment, XSane should detect your scanner, pop up a message that it is dangerous to run XSane as root, and then open up in its full multi-windowed glory. If your scanner still isn't detected, a trip to www.sane-project.org or www.ubuntuforums.org might be in order to see if there are any known workarounds for your particular scanner model.

To actually scan something, place the photo, document, or whatever it is you are planning to scan on the scanner bed, and then click the **Acquire preview** button at the bottom-left corner of the XSane Preview window (which usually opens up at the right end of your screen). Once the preview appears, use the selection tools in the same window to define the exact area you want to scan, and then choose your resolution and color depth settings in the main XSane window (which usually opens up at the top left of your screen). When everything is ready, click the **Scan** button, after which your scanned image will appear in a new Viewer window (as shown in Figure 10-10).

In that window, you can perform some minor tweaks of the scanned image using the buttons and menu items provided, and then save the image by going to the **File** menu and selecting **Save**. If you scanned a document that you want to convert to text, click the second button from the left (the one that says **ABCDEF**), and you will also be able to save the file as a text document.

NOTE *If you happened to download and install a driver for your scanner or multifunction printer from the device manufacturer's site (or elsewhere), you may find yourself with another scanning application provided within the driver package. If you prefer, you can use that application instead of XSane to perform your scanning chores.*

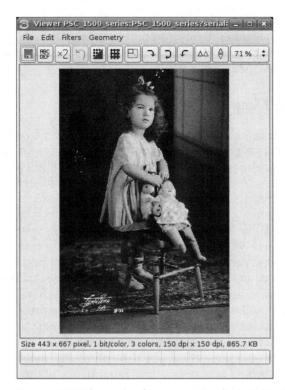

Size 443 x 667 pixel, 1 bit/color, 3 colors, 150 dpi x 150 dpi, 865.7 KB

Figure 10-10: The results of your scan are displayed in a separate Viewer window.

Why Are My Scanned Images So Big?

To wrap up this section on scanning (and, for that matter, this chapter), let me address a question that seems to confuse a lot of people. One of the first areas of confusion is that there is a general blurring of how the terms *ppi (pixels per inch)* and *dpi (dots per inch)* are used. Most applications use these terms interchangeably, and yet they aren't really the same thing. To make things simple, when you are talking about images on your screen, you are talking about *pixels* (the little squares that make up your screen image) per inch, and when you are talking about printer resolution, you are talking about *dots* (of printer ink) per inch.

Your computer screen generally has a resolution of 76ppi, while most modern inkjet and laser printers have a resolution range of 300 to 1200dpi, or sometimes even more. This means that a photo scanned at 76ppi, which looks just fine on your screen, ends up looking pretty lame when you print it out. On the other hand, when you scan a picture at 300ppi, the image will look much better in your printout but will seem gigantic on your screen. This makes sense, as the resolution of your image is more than three times that of your computer screen's resolution. The result is that your computer can accommodate the higher resolution of the image only by displaying that image at three times its original size.

As an example, have a look at Figure 10-11, where you can see an identical image scanned at three different resolutions: 76ppi, 150ppi, and 300ppi. As you can see, the 76ppi image at the far left (measuring 5 × 6 inches—about the size of the hard copy itself) is the smallest, while the other two images are proportionally bigger (about 10 × 12 inches for the 150ppi image and about 22 × 25 inches for the 300ppi image).

Figure 10-11: The same image scanned at three different resolutions

What Resolution Should I Use When Scanning?

What resolution you use when scanning really depends on a variety of factors, the most important of which is what you plan to do with the image when you're finished. When I look at Figure 10-11 on my computer screen, the smallest image looks best, the middle image looks okay, and the largest looks a bit odd, not as sharp as the other two. Basically, when scanning images for display on a computer—on web pages, for instance—it is probably best to stick with a ppi similar to typical screen resolutions or slightly larger: 76 to 150ppi.

When it comes to printing, a whole new set of considerations comes into play. First of all, there are the limitations of your scanner, since different models have different maximum resolutions. The resolution limits of your printer itself are also, naturally enough, a major consideration. For example, laser printers and inkjet printers have different characteristics; laser printers will produce better-quality images than inkjet printers, while inkjet output will be more greatly affected by the type of paper used than a laser printer will be. Of course, your printed output is not going to suffer if you scan your images at higher resolutions than those at which you plan to print them out, but you will end up with a lot of files taking up too much disk space. Remember: *The higher the resolution of a scanned image, the greater the file size in terms of disk space.* If this is of concern to you, you can simply resize the images after you're done printing using an application such as the GIMP (more on that in Chapter 14), but if you would prefer not being so cavalier with your use of disk space from the get-go, you can follow these very general guidelines:

- If you are using a laser printer, scan at the same resolution at which you are going to print.

- If you are going to use an inkjet printer with photo-quality paper, scan at about 80 percent of your target printout resolution—about 240ppi for a 300dpi printout.

- If you are using an inkjet printer with regular paper, scan at about 65 percent of your target printout resolution—about 195ppi for a 300dpi printout.

Needless to say, these are just suggestions to get you started. What works best for you and your particular scanner/printer setup may be slightly different. Nothing works better than a bit of experimentation and trial and error. In this case, you can't really go wrong. Just give yourself some time, don't get frustrated, and, most importantly, don't wait until you desperately need to scan something before trying things out—stay ahead of the game.

11

FONT FEATHERED FRENZY

Adding New Fonts to Your System

There are basically two kinds of fonts: bitmap and outline. The difference between these two is essentially the same as that between bitmap and vector graphics, which I will talk more about in Chapter 14. *Bitmap* characters are stored as a map of dots—the bitmap. The main limitation of bitmaps is that they only look good at the size and resolution they were designed for. Just like bitmap images, the more you enlarge a bitmap character, the worse it looks. This is particularly noticeable in rounded characters, such as *O* and *P*, where "the jaggies" becomes an issue.

Outline fonts, on the other hand, are similar in concept and design to vector graphics. Each character is stored as a mathematical formula, and just like vector graphics, outline characters keep their clean shape no matter how much you enlarge them. The main outline font formats are Type 1, or PostScript, which was developed by Adobe, and TrueType, which was developed by Apple. As free TrueType fonts are so readily available on the Internet and so easily handled in Ubuntu, I will focus on TrueType fonts in this chapter.

Your Ubuntu system comes with a wide variety of very usable and, at least to my eyes, rather handsome TrueType fonts. However, these tend to be a bit on the conservative side of the aesthetic spectrum, and many users will want to add a few more distinctive fonts to the system repertoire. In my own case, I had this really cool idea of writing messages to my friend in old Scandinavian runes. (Of course, my friend wet-blanketed the idea, so it all came to naught. . . .)

You probably won't be interested in sending cryptic, runic messages to your friends, but you may want to print out an award for an event using some sort of Gothic font, or you might be preparing a newsletter for the local chapter of your snail-breeders society and want to use a font that is round, bubbly, and slimy. Whatever your penchant, purpose, or desire, you will probably come to the point when you want to install some other TrueType fonts on your system.

Before you install anything, of course, you have to find some fonts. The Internet is always good source, and there are many sites that have a variety of freeware, shareware, and for-sale TrueType fonts available for download. When choosing and downloading fonts, it is best to select those designed for Windows rather than those designed for Mac. Fonts designed for the Windows world will most likely be in the form of Zip files, which will pose no problem for you, because you can extract them with File Roller. Simply double-click them, just as you have with the other archived files you have used thus far, and click the **Extract** button in the File Roller window when it appears. The font file will appear on your desktop (or wherever your Zip file happened to be) as an icon showing an upper- and lowercase sample of the first letter in that font (Figure 11-1).

Figure 11-1: Font icons display the first letter in the font.

In addition to getting a glimpse of what the fonts look like through these icons, you can also see all, or at least almost all, of the characters in a given font by double-clicking the font icon. A window, as shown in Figure 11-2, will open, showing you most of the characters in A-to-Z format and then in the traditional "The quick brown fox jumps over the lazy dog" format that you may well remember from your junior or senior high school typing classes.

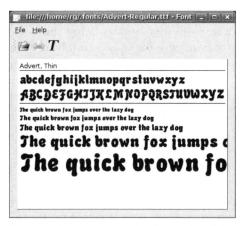

Figure 11-2: Previewing a font by double-clicking the font icon

Project 11A: Installing TrueType Fonts Locally

How you install fonts depends on who is going to use them. If you have only one user account on your machine, the easiest way is to install the fonts locally. Locally installed fonts are ones that only you or someone logged in to your user account will be able to use. On the other hand, if you have more than one user account and want the fonts to be available to all of the users on your machine, use the method described in Project 11B on page 187.

11A-1: Getting the Font Files

The Internet is awash in free fonts. For this project, I will point you to the www.fontfreak.com site, which has a very nice collection of fonts. Once you get to the FontFreak splash page, click **ENTER**, which will lead you to the main page. Then click the button on the left that says **PC Fonts**, which will bring you to the first page of PC fonts. You can browse through the various pages until you find some fonts to your liking. Which fonts you download is completely up to you.

Since you will also need fonts for Project 11B, you might as well download them now too. All in all, for the two projects, you will need at least four fonts. When you've finished downloading, drag the font files to your home folder so it's easy to follow along with my instructions. Also be sure to unzip your font files before going on to the installation steps.

11A-2: Installing the Fonts

For this project, let's use one of the fonts that you downloaded. After you've decided which font to use, follow these steps:

1. Open a new Nautilus window by going to the **Places** menu in the GNOME Panel and selecting **Home Folder**. Once you've done that, open another Nautilus window by doing the same thing.

2. In one of the Nautilus windows, go to the **Go** menu, and select **Location**. A Location input box will then appear below the button bar in that window. You can also achieve the same result by pressing CTRL-L.

3. In that Location box, type **fonts:///**, and press ENTER. Once you've done this, the window should be filled with the many icons representing the fonts you already have installed locally on your system. While you're there, it wouldn't be a bad idea to bookmark this window for future use.

4. From the other open Nautilus window (your home folder window), select the unzipped font you want to install, and drag it to the fonts:/// folder window.

You will notice that when you dragged your new font from your home folder window to the fonts:/// window, the icon for that new font file did not immediately appear. In fact, it will seem as if nothing at all happened and your installation attempt was a bust. Well, despite this lack of system acknowledgment, things were happening. The first time you install a font in this way, your system automatically creates a hidden .fonts folder in your home folder and places the font there. If you don't like this lack of immediate feedback, you can check your .fonts folder by typing **~/.fonts** in the Location box of one of the Nautilus windows. This will show you what fonts you have installed locally—at this point there should be only one.

Now that you have installed your font, you can go ahead and give it a try in one of your applications, such as OpenOffice.org Writer. (Any running applications need to be restarted before the new font will appear in that application's font menu.)

11A-3: An Alternative Approach to Installing Fonts Locally

If you prefer truly immediate feedback on your installation progress, you can try the following variation of the installation process, which yields the same results as in Project 11A-2 on page 185. However, because this installation method uses the .fonts folder that is created in step 4 of Project 11A-2, you must either go through the process in Project 11A-2 with at least one font file prior to trying this installation method, or first create the folder yourself by opening a Terminal window (**Applications ▶ Accessories ▶ Terminal**), typing **mkdir .fonts** in that window, and pressing ENTER. Now that you've got your own .fonts folder, let's use two more of the fonts you downloaded to try out the steps:

1. Assuming that you have already closed the two windows from Project 11A-2, open two new Nautilus windows.

2. In one of the open Nautilus folders, type **~/.fonts**, and press ENTER. The main pane of that Nautilus window should show only one font or, if you bypassed Project 11A-2 and created the .fonts folder yourself, nothing at all. It would definitely be useful to bookmark this location while you're there.

3. In the other open Nautilus window, which is your home folder window, highlight both of the fonts you want to install by holding down the CTRL key and then clicking the icon for each font. Then release the CTRL key, right-click either of the highlighted fonts, and select **Copy Files** in the popup menu.

4. In the .fonts window, right-click on any open space in the window, and select **Paste Files** from the popup menu. The fonts will then appear in the Nautilus window.

Of course, you can just drag the fonts from your home folder to the .fonts folder instead of going through the procedure in steps 3 and 4. It's strictly up to you. Either way, the procedure outlined in Project 11A-3 yields exactly the same results as that in Project 11A-2. The only difference is that you will immediately see that your fonts have been copied to the .fonts folder. Which method you choose in the future is, therefore, strictly a matter of personal preference.

11A-4: Uninstalling Locally Installed Fonts

Whether you used the installation method outlined in Project 11A-2 or Project 11A-3, you can uninstall any fonts installed locally by opening the .fonts folder in your home folder and then dragging the fonts you want to remove to the Trash.

Project 11B: Installing TrueType Fonts Globally

As I mentioned already, the fonts you have installed thus far can only be used by you when you log in under your usual username. If, however, you want to install fonts that can be used by you and anyone else who has an account on your computer, the process is slightly different. We'll use only one of the fonts you downloaded for this part of the project.

11B-1: Installing Individual Fonts Globally

The font folder for globally installed fonts is in root territory, so you will need to put the sudo command to use in order to install fonts in this way. Here are the steps:

1. Open a Terminal window, and then create a new folder for your fonts within the global location (let's call it MyFonts) by typing `sudo mkdir /usr/share/fonts/truetype/MyFonts` and pressing ENTER.

2. Type your password when prompted to do so, and press ENTER.

3. Copy the font you want to install globally to your newly created global font folder by typing `sudo cp fontname.ttf /usr/share/fonts/truetype/MyFonts` and pressing ENTER. Be sure to include spaces on both sides of `cp` and after `.ttf`.

Be sure to include spaces on both sides of *fontname*.ttf. Also, be sure to use the name of your font in place of the word *fontname*. For example, if your font is called arachnid, you would type `sudo cp arachnid.ttf /usr/share/fonts/truetype/MyFonts`.

You shouldn't have to enter your password after step 3 since you already provided it in step 2, so the process is now complete. That being the case, go ahead and test things out by opening OpenOffice.org and looking for the font in the font menu. Remember that you will need to restart OpenOffice.org if it was already open when you installed the font.

11B-2: Installing Multiple Fonts Globally

If you want to install several fonts globally at the same time, you can do so quite easily. The process is essentially the same as in Project 11B-1 on page 187, with a slight variation. Here's what you've got to do:

1. Create a new subfolder in your home folder window. You can call it anything you like, but I'll be using the name *fonts2go* in this project.
2. Unzip the fonts and then place the ones you want to install via this method into the new fonts2go folder.
3. Open a Terminal window, and then copy all of the fonts in your fonts2go folder to your new global font folder by typing **sudo cp fonts2go/*.ttf /usr/share/fonts/truetype/MyFonts** and pressing ENTER. Note the spaces surrounding cp and after *.ttf.
4. Type your password if prompted to do so, and press ENTER.

NOTE   *In step 3, you did not need to type the names of the fonts, as the wildcard character (*) was essentially telling your system to copy all files ending in .ttf within the fonts2go folder.*

Now that you are done, check your results in OpenOffice.org. You should also back up the font files in the fonts2go folder to CD or floppy (just in case you need to install them on another system) and then trash the files. Keep the folder, however, so that you can use it again in the future.

11B-3: Uninstalling Globally Installed Fonts

If you want to remove any fonts that you installed using either of the global installation methods introduced in this project, you can do so in the following manner:

1. Open a Terminal window, type **sudo rm /usr/share/fonts/truetype/MyFonts/*fontname*.ttf**, and press ENTER. Be sure to replace *fontname* with the name of the font you are installing.
2. Type your password, and press ENTER when prompted to do so.

Project 11C: Installing Microsoft Windows Core Fonts via Synaptic

Like it or not, the computing world is still pretty much a Microsoft world, and that means that the vast majority of users, even Mac users, are using Microsoft core fonts. That being the case, it is inevitable that you will have to deal with documents using fonts such as Georgia, Verdana, Times New Roman, and Courier, to name a few. Of course, your system can substitute the fonts it has for those used in the document, but in order for you to see things as they were intended and to allow others to see your documents the way you intended (web pages are good examples), it will probably behoove you to install those Microsoft core fonts on your own system.

Fortunately for you, there are two ways to get these fonts. One is to download and install them via Synaptic, while the other, for those of you with a dual-boot setup, is to simply copy them from your Windows partition. In this project, I will explain how to perform the first of these procedures, so if you're a Windows-less Ubuntu user (or a dual-booter who thinks the Synaptic approach is easier), here's what you need to do:

1. Run the Synaptic Package Manager (**System ▶ Administration ▶ Synaptic Package Manager**), and provide your username when prompted.
2. Click the **Search** button. In the Search window that appears, type `msttcorefonts`, and then click the **Search** button in that window.
3. The msttcorefonts package should now appear in the list pane of the main Synaptic window, so click on the package name, select **Mark for installation** in the popup menu, and then follow the standard procedures you learned in Chapter 5 for installing a package via Synaptic.

When the process is complete, your new Microsoft fonts will have been successfully installed and ready for immediate use by every user account on your machine.

Project 11D: Installing Microsoft Core Fonts from Your Windows Partition (for Dual-Booters)

If you're a dual-booter with Windows installed on another partition of your hard disk, you can take advantage of the fonts you already have on your Windows partition. This is a bit more complicated than the process described in Project 11C, but you'll end up with more fonts this way, and you will also have the choice of installing the fonts locally or globally. But first, you'll have to mount your Windows partition.

11D-1: Finding Your Windows Partition

Before you can actually mount your Windows partition, you need to find out where it is, and in what filesystem it is formatted, either File Allocation Table (FAT) or New Technology File System (NTFS). As is so common in Linux, there are a couple of ways to do this. If you are a command lover, you can check things out by opening a Terminal window, typing **sudo fdisk -l** (that's the lowercase *L* there, not a numeral *1*), and then pressing ENTER. You will be prompted for your password, so type it, and press ENTER. A list of the partitions on your hard disk will appear (Figure 11-3).

```
rg@RG-Vaio-on-Ubuntu: ~
File  Edit  View  Terminal  Tabs  Help
rg@RG-Vaio-on-Ubuntu:~$ sudo fdisk -l
Password:

Disk /dev/hda: 80.0 GB, 80026361856 bytes
255 heads, 63 sectors/track, 9729 cylinders
Units = cylinders of 16065 * 512 = 8225280 bytes

   Device Boot      Start         End      Blocks   Id  System
/dev/hda1               1         383     3076416   12  Compaq diagnostics
/dev/hda2   *         384        3571    25607610    c  W95 FAT32 (LBA)
/dev/hda3            5046        9729    37624230    f  W95 Ext'd (LBA)
/dev/hda4            3572        5045    11839905   83  Linux
/dev/hda5            5046        8935   31246393+    b  W95 FAT32
/dev/hda6   *        8936        9692     6080571   83  Linux
/dev/hda7            9693        9729      297171   82  Linux swap / Solaris

Partition table entries are not in disk order
rg@RG-Vaio-on-Ubuntu:~$ █
```

Figure 11-3: Finding your Windows partition in the fdisk table

Take a look at this seemingly incomprehensible list, and then find the location and format of the Windows partition on your hard disk by scanning the column on the right for the first entry with the words FAT32 or NTFS. In most cases, this will be the first partition, /dev/hda1, but in the list for my hard disk, shown in Figure 11-3, the first partition is taken up by some diagnostic utility that the manufacturer's Windows install disk had on it. If you're using a computer from a brand-name manufacturer, you might find yourself in a similar situation.

Once you've found the first FAT32 or NTFS partition, jot down the file-system type, and then do the same for its location at the far left of the list. In my case, that would be /dev/hda2 and FAT32.

11D-2: Mounting Your Windows Partition

Armed with the information you just gathered, you can now mount your Windows partition by doing the following:

1. Create a mount point for your Windows partition by opening a Terminal window, typing **sudo mkdir /media/windows**, and pressing ENTER. You only need to perform this step the first time you try to mount your partition. After that, you need only perform steps 2 and 3.

2. What you do in this step depends on whether your Windows partition is FAT32 or NTFS formatted. Choose the appropriate step, being sure to substitute /hda2 for /hda1 if that is what your Windows partition happens to be.

If your Windows partition is in FAT32 format, type

```
sudo /dev/hda1 /media/windows/ -t vfat -o iocharset=utf8,umask=000
```

If it is in NTFS format, type

```
sudo /dev/hda1 /media/windows/ -t ntfs -o nls=utf8,umask=0222
```

3. Once you've typed the appropriate entry, press ENTER. If asked for your password, type it, and press ENTER. The Windows partition will then be mounted. You can double-check by opening a Nautilus window and clicking the **Computer** button. You should then find a hard disk icon with the word *windows* beneath it. You can even double-click that icon to access the files you have there, but you cannot save files to the partition if it is in NTFS format.

11D-3: Installing Fonts from Your Windows Partition

Now that your Windows partition is mounted, you can copy the fonts you have there and install them for use within Linux. To get started, go back to the Terminal window, type **cd**, press the spacebar, and then type the path to your Windows font folder. Most likely, the path to your font folder will be /mnt/windows/WINDOWS/Fonts, but it might be slightly different (/mnt/windows/windows/Fonts, for example) depending on the version of Windows you are using. Once you've typed what you need to type, press ENTER.

Depending on whether you want to install your Windows fonts locally or globally, the next steps will be different.

Installing Windows Fonts Locally

To install your Windows fonts locally, just copy the font that you want to install to your .fonts folder by typing **cp *fontname*.ttf ~/.fonts/** in the still open Terminal window and pressing ENTER. Be sure to replace *fontname* with the name of the font you want to install.

If you want to go wild and copy all of the fonts in your Windows font directory (that's a lot of fonts, mind you!), you can type ***.ttf** instead of *fontname*.ttf. Be sure that you have a space between cp and *fontname*.ttf and between *fontname*.ttf and ~/.fonts/. Once you're done, you're done.

Installing Windows Fonts Globally

To install your Windows fonts so that all users on your machine can use them, just return to the still open Terminal window. Then copy the font you want to the personal system font folder you created in step 1 of Project 11B-1 on page 187 (and if you didn't perform that step then, do so now) by typing

sudo cp *fontname*.**ttf /usr/share/fonts/truetype/MyFonts**. If you want to copy and install all of the fonts in your Windows font directory, you can do so by typing **sudo cp *.ttf /usr/share/fonts/truetype/MyFonts** instead. After typing either of those strings, press ENTER, after which you will probably be prompted for your password, so type it, and press ENTER again. The job will then be done.

Unmounting Your Windows Partition

When you are done with your Windows partition, you can unmount it immediately, or you can just wait until you shut down your system, whereupon it will be automatically unmounted. Before you can unmount it yourself, you must first be certain you aren't accessing the directory, either from the Terminal window or from Nautilus. So, before issuing the unmount command, close any Nautilus windows open to that partition or, if you are using the Terminal, type **cd** to change back to your home directory. Type **sudo umount /media/windows** (that's *u-mount*, not *un-mount*), and press ENTER.

Customizing Your System Fonts

Now that you know how to get and install fonts, you might be itching to use some of them to further customize your system. To get started doing this, just select **Preferences ▸ Font** in the **System** menu, which will bring up the Font Preferences window, shown in Figure 11-4.

Figure 11-4: Setting system font preferences

As you can see, you can specify font preferences in five categories: applications, documents, desktop, window titles, and the Terminal (fixed width font).

The choices you make take effect immediately, so you will soon know whether or not you can live with them. Unlike the other aspects of customization, those choices could drive you stark raving mad. Sure, it is easy and fun to live with the gaudiest desktop imaginable, the wildest and most mismatched color scheme on the planet, and the goofiest icons ever to be seen by post-Neanderthal man, but if your font selections get too out of hand, watch out! You do have to be able to read the results, after all.

Making Things Look Better

The fonts you see on your screen generally look quite smooth and clean. If you are using an LCD monitor, however, you may find that fonts will look even better if you select **Subpixel smoothing (LCDs)** in the Font Preferences window. If you're not sure whether you need to do this, just give it a try, and see if you notice any difference. GNOME applies changes immediately upon selection, so if you keep a window with text in it open behind the preferences window, you can easily see the effect of each of your selections as you make them.

Creating Your Own Fonts with FontForge

After all this font talk, it seems only appropriate that I end this chapter by giving you the means to create your own fonts (or at least modify someone else's). FontForge (previously known as PfaEdit) allows you to create or modify TrueType, PostScript, and bitmap fonts (see Figure 11-5). The interface itself seems a bit dated, but don't let that fool you; FontForge is quite capable and easy to use.

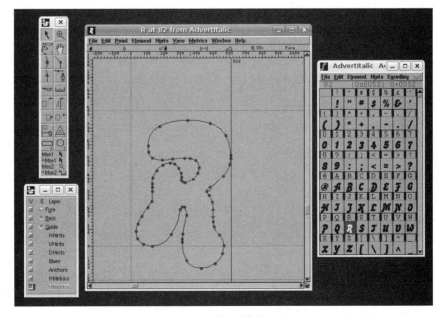

Figure 11-5: Using FontForge to create and modify fonts

Downloading, Installing, and Running FontForge

You can easily download and install FontForge via Synaptic. Just do a search for *fontforge*, mark the **fontforge** package for installation when it appears in the list of search results, and then follow the usual procedure for installing packages via Synaptic. You can run FontForge by going to the **Applications** menu and selecting **Programming ▸ FontForge**. Font creation and modification is too complex a topic for this book, but those of you already into this stuff probably just needed a pointer to the right tool and not my meager instructions.

12

POLYGLOT PENGUINS

Linux Speaks Your Language

These days, almost all operating systems are multilingual, or at least capable of becoming so. This is true of Linux as well. Just open your web browser, and, without performing any special installations, you can read pages in any European language, including those with Cyrillic alphabets, such as Russian. You can even view pages in Chinese, Japanese, Thai, Arabic, and Hebrew, to name but a few.

But the multilingual capabilities of Linux are much greater than this, and the way that GNOME-based distros, such as Ubuntu, handle multilingual matters makes it quite easy to take advantage of these capabilities. As you will soon see, you can even set up your system to give you a totally foreign language environment, allowing you to function completely in the language of your choice. Add to this the ever-expanding number of free programs available for language study, and you have a truly meaningful language-learning tool.

Read-Only Language Support

If all you want is to be able to read web pages or documents written in a foreign language, you don't need to install any additional language support except in some rare cases. From the get-go, you will be able to view documents in just about any language you happen to throw at your system—doesn't matter if it's Swedish, Italian, Chinese, Japanese, Arabic, Hebrew, Russian, Vietnamese, Armenian, or Thai. You will be able to read whatever you are linguistically capable of reading (see Figure 12-1 for an example).

Figure 12-1: A Japanese web page displayed in Firefox

Changing the Character Encoding in Firefox

Firefox usually automatically recognizes the language in which a web page is written and thus displays the page correctly. Sometimes, however, the author of the page may neglect to include the character coding for that page in the HTML, in which case Firefox, not knowing that the page is prepared in another language, will open it in the default language of your system. The result is a page in which you see nothing but odd combinations of symbols and letters that have no meaning. In this case, try changing the character coding in Firefox to the language encoding you believe the page to be in. Some languages employ more than one encoding scheme, so if you're not sure, give each one a try. You can make your choices by going to the Firefox **View** menu and selecting **Character Encoding**. From the submenu there, you can select the appropriate coding for the language of that page.

Typing Nonstandard Characters

Typing characters that are not standard in English, such as é, ç, ß, ø, æ, and å, can be done quite easily in Linux without any modifications. In most situations, you can do this by using the Character Map utility included in your system, which can be found at **Applications ▶ Accessories ▶ Character Map**. Upon running Character Map, a window like the one shown in Figure 12-2 will appear.

Figure 12-2: Inputting characters with the Character Map utility

To input the character you want, just select the language or character set in the left pane of the window, and then, in the right pane, click on the character you want to input. The character will appear in the little input box next to the words *Text to copy* at the bottom of the window. Just click the **Copy** button, and then paste the character wherever you want to place it.

In certain applications, such as the various OpenOffice.org modules, this method will not work. In these cases, the program usually offers a method of its own. In OpenOffice.org, for example, you can click **Insert** in the menu bar and then select **Special Character**. A selection window will open, and you can select the character you want there. Once you've done that, click the **OK** button, and the character will appear in your document, after which the selection window will close by itself.

Using the Compose Key Option

If you only need to type an accent or umlaut once in a while, and don't feel particularly keen on opening an application or going to a special menu to do so, using the *compose key option* for your keyboard is a good way to go. Basically what this means is that you use one of the lesser-used keys on your keyboard in conjunction with six symbols (` , ' ~ " ^) to help in the creation, so to speak, of accented characters. By default, the compose key is the right ALT key.

Let's say, for example, that you wanted to type an umlauted u (ü). While pressing the right ALT key, you would press ". Then you would release the right ALT key, press u, and . . . voilà, you'd have yourself an ü. Here are some more examples:

á	right ALT + ' then a	ñ	right ALT + ~ then n
ç	right ALT + , then c	ô	right ALT + ^ then o
è	right ALT + ` then e		

Using the Keyboard Indicator

If you often type in a particular foreign language, it might be more convenient for you to use the Keyboard Indicator GNOME Panel utility. This utility lets you switch quickly among various keyboard layouts. For example, if you often type in Swedish, and thus use the characters å, ä, and ö regularly, using the appropriate keyboard layout would be easier than repeatedly using the Character Map. Of course, you will have to familiarize yourself with the keyboard layout, or *keymap*, for each language you choose, but this is a relatively easy task.

The Keyboard Indicator is already included in your system, so there is no need to install it. To access it, simply right-click somewhere on the GNOME Panel where you would like to place a launcher for it. Then, from the popup menu select **Add to Panel**. When the Add to Panel window appears, scroll down and click **Keyboard Indicator**, and then click the **Add** button. The letters *USA* or *GBr* will then appear on the panel.

Now, this alone will give you nothing except your default keymap, so you must configure Keyboard Indicator if you want to be able to use other keymaps. To do so, just right-click the icon, and from the popup menu select **Open Keyboard Preferences**, which will open the Keyboard Preferences window.

To add a keymap, click the **Layouts** tab in that window, and then once in the new tab, click **Add**. After you do this, the Choose a Layout window will appear with a list of the keymaps available to you (Figure 12-3). In the left pane of that window, scroll down to the keymap for the country of the language you want to add, and then click it to select the standard keyboard layout for that locale (click the arrow next to the country for a list of optional layouts if you prefer). Once you've made your selection, click the **OK** button, which will bring you back to the Keyboard Preferences window, where you will find your new keymap listed along with the original. You can then click the **Close** button to complete the setup.

Figure 12-3: Adding keyboard layouts to the Keyboard Indicator

After closing the Keyboard Preferences window, the keyboard layouts can be changed by clicking the icon in the panel. You can also change between keyboard layouts by going to the **Layout Options** tab of the Keyboard Preferences window and assigning a keyboard shortcut. If you are not sure where the keys you want to type are located in your new keymap, switch to the key-map in question by clicking the panel Keyboard Indicator until it appears and then right-clicking it. In the popup menu that appears, select **Layout View**, after which a map of the new layout will appear in a separate window. The default window size is quite small, but it can be resized in the usual drag-the-corner manner.

If you just want to choose a single keyboard layout to replace your present one (such as British English instead of American English or German instead of Spanish), you can do so from the Keyboard Preferences window by adding the keyboard layout you want to use, checking the box next to the word *Default*, and then removing the original layout by clicking it once to select it and clicking the **Remove** button.

Viewing Your System in Another Language

One of the many things that originally attracted me to the Linux world was being able to install language support for languages other than English. On one of my machines, I have installed support for Chinese, Japanese, Swedish, and my default, English. With just a simple logout and a few more clicks, I can log back in with an interface in a totally different language. I can have a Chinese, Japanese, or Swedish system whenever I want.

This is very useful if you are going to be doing a lot of work in a foreign language, or if you are studying a foreign language and want to give yourself as much exposure as possible to it. It is also very handy when you have users with different native languages using the same machine. At my former uni-versity, for example, where my Japanese and Chinese students sometimes used my computer, the additional language support allowed them to log in using their own language. All in all, it is a very useful feature.

Taking advantage of this feature in the GNOME environment is very easy and, depending on the language you wish to use, requires little in terms of special installation measures. Basically all you have to do is install a group of support files for each language you want to add to your system. You can do this quite easily by going to the **System** menu and selecting **Administration ▸ Language Selector**. This will bring up the Language Support window (Figure 12-4), where you can check the boxes next to the languages for which you want to install support. Once you have made your selections, click the **Apply** button, and the Language Selector will begin downloading and then installing the support packages you specified.

Multilingual Login

Once you have installed support for any additional languages you want, you can log out of your current session and log in to a new one in a different language environment. The actual switch is made from your login screen.

Just below the text box where you would normally type your username, click the link that says **Language**, after which a window with a list of the languages you have installed will appear. Select the language you want to use in the next session by clicking once on its name and then clicking the **OK** button. The language list window will then close automatically, and you can proceed as usual by typing your login name and password (pressing the ENTER key after each, of course). A little window will then pop up asking you if you want to use the language you've chosen as your default language forever and ever. You can either click **Just for This Session** or **Make Default** depending on your personal preferences. Whatever you do end up choosing, fear not; it's no big deal to change back at a later point in time by logging out of your system, logging back in to your system under your previous default language, and clicking **Make Default**.

Figure 12-4: Installing additional language support

Your startup process will then continue, and everything will progress as it usually does. Depending on what language you've chosen, once your desktop appears you will be in another linguistic world. Your menus, applications, and even the little Tips windows that pop up when you run your mouse over a panel icon will all be in the newly selected language. (Figure 12-5 shows the System menu in a variety of languages.)

Figure 12-5: The Applications menu shown in English, Korean, Russian, Thai, and Vietnamese

Chinese, Japanese, and Korean Input

For most European languages (and many other alphabet-based non-European languages), pressing a letter on the keyboard simply prints that letter to the screen. However, Chinese, Japanese, and Korean require a kind of conversion process that is handled by a special application (actually a set of applications) called an Input Method Editor (IME). Of course, this is a Windows-world term, but I will use it here for convenience's sake. In any case, each of these languages has its own IME, and each is quite different due to the basic differences in the three writing systems.

Chinese

While most people (at least those in the linguistic know) would think that Chinese would be the most complicated system, because the writing system consists of thousands of characters, it is in fact the simplest. The Chinese IME simply takes the romanized keyboard input, known as *pinyin*, and converts it into Chinese characters, or *Hanzi*. For the IME, it is essentially a simple dictionary lookup task—big dictionary, simple IME. In the event that there is more than one character for the pinyin input, a list of possible candidates will appear, and the user can then simply select the appropriate character from that list.

Japanese

The Japanese IME has a considerably more complicated task to perform, as it has three writing systems to deal with: *Kanji* (ideographic characters borrowed long ago from China), *hiragana* (the phono-alphabetic system used mainly for tense and case endings), and *katakana* (used mainly for words borrowed from other languages). Still, the standard input method for Japanese is primarily via the standard Roman keyboard layout, plus a few extra special-function keys. Thus, typing in Japanese is a two-step process whereby the IME first converts the romanized text into hiragana as it is typed and then converts it to appropriate Kanji, katakana, or hiragana elements after the spacebar is pressed.

You can see an example of these steps in Figure 12-6. In the first line, the IME has already converted the romanized input on the fly. It has converted rinakkusdenihongonyuuryokumodekimasu (which means *You can also input Japanese in Linux*) to hiragana. The fact that line is underlined means that it has not yet been converted beyond that. In the second line, however, the user has subsequently pressed the spacebar, which caused the IME to convert the hiragana string into the appropriate Kanji, hiragana, and katakana elements. The first word, *Linux*, has been converted to katakana text, as it is a borrowed word, while *Japanese input* has been converted to Kanji; the rest stays in hiragana.

りなっくすでにほんごにゅうりょくもできます。

リナックスで日本語入力もできます。

Figure 12-6: IME conversions while typing in Japanese

Korean

The job of the Korean IME is again quite different from that of the Chinese and Japanese IMEs, as the language itself is written in a very different way. Korean is written either entirely in alphabetic letters, called *Hangul*, or in a combination of Hangul and ideographic characters borrowed from Chinese called *Hanja*. While the Hanja characters are essentially the same as their Chinese and Japanese counterparts, Hanzi and Kanji, the Korean phonetic alphabet, Hangul, has it own unique appearance, as you can see in the Korean word for Korea, *Hangug(k)*, in Figure 12-7.

H A N G U G

Figure 12-7: Korea (Hangug) written horizontally in Hangul

This seems simple; however, the representation is not quite correct, as Korean is very unique in the way that its alphabetic characters are put to the page. Unlike the usual side-by-side positioning of hiragana, katakana, and most other languages written with an alphabet, Hangul letters are grouped in pairs, triplets, or even quadruplets, which are written, as a general rule, clockwise. The IME, therefore, must take the input (usually based on a Korean alphabetical keyboard layout) while it is being typed, and it must adjust the size, spacing, and positioning of each of the letters as it puts them into appropriate clusters (see Figure 12-8).

Figure 12-8: An example of the clustering process in the Korean IME

Project 12: Installing Asian Language Input Support for SCIM

So what do you do if, for example, you want to be able to type Chinese, Japanese, Korean, Hindi, Thai, or Nepali while still in your usual English environment? What if you want to be able to type all of those languages in the same document? Can you do it?

You bet.

There are actually several ways of going about this, but the one of the most straightforward to use is Smart Common Input Method (SCIM), the base for which comes preinstalled in Ubuntu. SCIM supports most Asian languages, including Chinese, Japanese and Korean, and it provides a number of input methods for many of these.

12-1: Enabling SCIM to Work with OpenOffice.org and Firefox

Despite coming preinstalled on Ubuntu, SCIM does not yet work with OpenOffice.org, Firefox, or Thunderbird right out of the box—or to be a bit more accurate, they do not work with SCIM. Since these three applications are probably the ones an average user is most likely to use with the greatest frequency, it is a serious limitation indeed. Fortunately, there is a rather simple two-step remedy for this state of affairs.

First of all, run Synaptic, do a search for *im-switch*, and then install it. Once the installation is complete, open a Terminal window, type `im-switch -z en_US -s scim`, and press ENTER. If you get a warning message about a dependency check not working, just ignore it.

Job done.

After you log out and log back in, SCIM will be there waiting for you in whatever application you happen to need it.

12-2: Downloading and Installing SCIM Input Method Modules

You may have noticed in the previous section that I said that SCIM's "base" is already installed for you; this does not mean, however, that *CJK (Chinese/Japanese/Korean) support* is installed. As is, SCIM only allows you to type in Russian and Vietnamese. For Chinese, Japanese, Korean, and any other language support, you have to install the specific modules for those languages yourself via Synaptic. Depending on the language you want to use, you need to do a Synaptic search for *scim*, and then install one or any combination of the following:

- For simplified Chinese (pinyin) input support, install scim-pinyin.
- For traditional Chinese (zhuyin/bopomofo) input support, install scim-chewing.
- For Japanese input support, install scim-anthy.
- For Korean input support, install scim-hangul.

There are also sets of additional input methods available for each of these languages. If, for example, you type in Korean based on the standard English keyboard layout or if you need Hangul-to-Hanja conversion capabilities, you should also install scim-tables-ko. Additional Japanese methods are available in the scim-tables-ja package, while those for Chinese are available in scim-tables-zh.

You can also use SCIM as a convenient way to type in other Asian languages that do not require special conversion routines, such as Thai, Hindi, Telugu, Bengali, and Panjabi. To use SCIM for input support for these languages, install scim-tables-additional.

12-3: Typing in Asian Languages with SCIM

Once you have installed the input modules for the languages you want, using SCIM is quite simple. To get a feel for how it works, open Gedit (**Applications ▶ Accessories ▶ Text Editor**).

Once Gedit appears, click the SCIM panel applet. A list of the available languages that can be handled via SCIM will then appear in a drop-down menu (Figure 12-9). Remember, however, that the number of languages appearing in that menu will be dependent on the number of language packages you installed.

Figure 12-9: A list of the languages that can be handled by SCIM

From that list, select the language you want to use, and then, for those languages where you are given a choice, select the input method you prefer. The icon for the SCIM panel applet will reflect the change by showing the icon for the language you have chosen. You can then start typing.

At this point, a small input palette like the one in Figure 12-10 will appear at the bottom-right corner of the screen. This palette, in addition to displaying the language and input method currently in use, also allows you to easily switch between English and the current language of input, or to switch from the language in which you are currently typing to another. By clicking the red button at the far-right end of the palette, you can also find out what the hotkeys are for the input method you are currently using.

Figure 12-10: The SCIM input palette

Regardless of the input method you are dealing with, probably the most important hotkey combination you will want to use is SHIFT-spacebar, which toggles you back and forth between English and the language you currently have selected in SCIM.

13

PENGUINS BACK AT WORK

Getting Down to Business in Linux

I have to admit it: When I think about the joys of computing, I tend to think of the more hedonistic, self-indulgent areas like gaming, music, and graphics. Still, as is the case for most computer users, what I usually end up doing on my computer is work, and writing this book falls into that category.

Fortunately, Linux can get down to business and do it as well as the next OS. I think it's safe to say that you are missing nothing and are probably gaining quite a bit in terms of home and office productivity programs in the world of Linux. In this chapter, I'll walk you through the Linux offerings in this department.

OpenOffice.org

Whether they should be or not, people are quite obsessed with office suites, even though most people seldom need more than a word processor. The de facto standard among office suites is Microsoft Office, which is available in both the Windows and Macintosh worlds. Of course, as it is a Microsoft product, you can be quite sure that there is no Linux version available.

Fortunately, Linux does have an exceedingly capable office suite in the form of OpenOffice.org, which is, incidentally, also freely available (as in *free*) in Windows and Mac OS X versions. OpenOffice.org is not some lightweight sour-grapes substitute for the Microsoft Office–less Linux world; it is a full-featured contender, and in some cases, OpenOffice.org is a clear winner.

OpenOffice.org Applications

The entire OpenOffice.org office suite consists of six applications: a word processor (Writer), a spreadsheet (Calc), a presentation creator and player (Impress), a vector drawing program (Draw), a database (Base), and a mathematical formula editor (Math). Most of these can be accessed at **Applications ▶ Office**.

Since giving full and detailed instructions on how to use each of these applications would take up an entire book (and there are entire books on the subject), I will simply introduce each module to you. Being a bit of a mathematics dunce, however, I won't be venturing too deeply into what you can do with Math. That said, here goes.

Writer

As I mentioned earlier, the word processor is the office application that the majority of users turn to most often. Fortunately, OpenOffice.org Writer is a good one (see Figure 13-1). It is chock-full of features and can read and save Microsoft Word files. Like Word, it will even let you save your documents as HTML files so that you can easily change your documents into web pages.

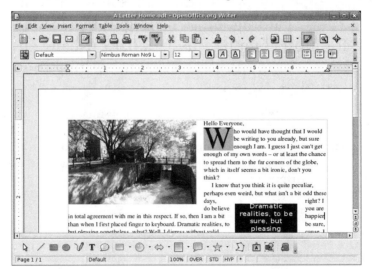

Figure 13-1: OpenOffice.org Writer

As I said, Writer is a very straightforward word processor, so I won't go on about it, but if you would like an introduction to using Writer, check out the First Steps tutorial at the OpenOffice.org website (www.openoffice.org/writerfirststeps/writerfirststeps.html).

Calc

Calc is the OpenOffice.org spreadsheet application, and it is similar to Excel in terms of capabilities and general layout (see Figure 13-2). It can also, quite importantly, read and save Microsoft Excel files.

Figure 13-2: A graph created in OpenOffice.org Calc

Since most people who use spreadsheets generally understand what they are all about and, after a bit of poking around, can figure out how to use them, I won't go into any sort of primer about using Calc. However, as there are many others who don't see any need to even try using spreadsheets, I will mention a few of the simpler things that can be done with Calc, in the hope of enticing some of you into trying it.

Most people who don't use spreadsheets think of them as a sort of giant calculators used for computing uncomfortably large sets of numbers, like payrolls (which was the original purpose of such applications). That's right, of course, but spreadsheets can be used for everyday tasks too, such as projecting household budgets, calculating grade point averages (by teachers or students), figuring out how long it will take you to save up for your trip to Hungary, or even for something as weird as comparing the seat heights for the four or five motorcycles you are trying to choose among. And when doing any of these minor mathematical tasks, you can easily create graphs in order to make all the abstract numbers speak to you visually.

If numbers are just not your thing, you can still use Calc for creating lists of information, such as birthday lists, class rosters, shopping lists, address lists . . . whatever. You can even have Calc put the lists into alphabetical order, or sort them by date of birth, and so on. Everyone eventually seems to find some use for Calc, so don't ignore it entirely.

Impress

Impress is OpenOffice.org's answer to Microsoft's PowerPoint, with which it is compatible. It allows you to create graphically attractive slides for use in presentations and also allows you to create notes or handouts to accompany them. While these features make Impress quite handy in business and education settings, you may not find as much value in it as a home user.

Draw

More useful to the home user is OpenOffice.org Draw. Although Draw isn't all that great a program for creating true graphics in the artistic sense, it is very useful for creating flowcharts, organizational diagrams (like seating arrangements for wedding receptions or conferences), or any other document in which you want a bit more control over the placement of text and graphics (especially when the two are combined), such as for fliers, awards, diagrams, and newsletters. In this sense, Draw can be used quite effectively as a simple page layout program, as you can see in Figure 13-3.

Figure 13-3: A newsletter created (and displayed) in OpenOffice.org Draw

Although Draw comes bundled with Ubuntu, it is no longer listed in the Applications menu, probably because its functions can be accessed through the other OpenOffice.org modules. Still, it is a handy application to use on its own, so if you would like to use it in its stand-alone form, you can run it either via the Run Application panel applet by typing `oooffice -draw` or by adding the launcher yourself to the Applications menu.

To add Draw to the Applications menu, open the Alacarte Menu Editor (**Applications ▸ Accessories ▸ Alacarte Menu Editor**). Once the editor window appears, click **Graphics** or **Office** (or both) in the left pane, depending on where you want the menu launcher to appear. In the right pane of the window, check the box next to the words *OpenOffice.org Drawing*. Once you're done, click the **Close** button, and the Draw launcher will then appear in the menu.

Base

New to OpenOffice.org is Base, which is a graphical front end to any databases you have on your machine, including Base's own database, called HSQL. Unfortunately, learning how to use Base is no cakewalk if you don't have any experience working with database applications, so if the database module in AppleWorks is the extent of your contact with such applications, you might want to try out a relatively easy-to-follow tutorial (with a not-so-easy-to-follow URL) at http://searchopensource.techtarget.com/tip/1,289483,sid39_gci1148271,00.html.

Math

Finally, we come to OpenOffice.org Math. As I am a bit out of it in terms of math, I can't really tell you much more about Math other than that it is a mathematics formula editor that allows you to produce complex mathematical formulae and then paste them as embedded objects into other OpenOffice.org programs. It is strictly an editor and does not calculate. I think I am safe in saying that most common folk have no need for it in their everyday lives, unless, of course, you write math textbooks for a living.

Like Draw, OpenOffice.org Math is not listed in the Applications menu, but you can access it via the Run Application panel applet by typing `oooffice -math`. Oh, and if you do happen to write math textbooks for a living, you can also add a launcher for Math to your Applications menu, just as you did for Draw, by means of the Alacarte Menu Editor. In the open editor window, just click **Office**, and then check the box next to the words *OpenOffice.org Formula*.

Microsoft Office and OpenOffice.org File Compatibility

Although I mention the point throughout this section, it is worthwhile to re-emphasize that OpenOffice.org can read and write Microsoft Office files. This compatibility is quite good, though tables sometimes prove slightly problematic.

In order to read Microsoft Office files, all you need to do is double-click the file in question, and it will open in the appropriate OpenOffice.org module. When saving files within OpenOffice.org to use within Microsoft Office, however, you must save them into the appropriate format, as

OpenOffice.org will otherwise save files into its native format (.odt for Writer documents, .ods for Calc documents, and .odp for Impress documents) by default.

To do this when saving a file, click the small arrow next to the words *File type* in the Save window, and select the appropriate Microsoft Office format from the list of available file formats listed in the pane that then appears—**Microsoft Word 97/2000/XP** for a Writer document, for example.

OpenOffice.org Features

The three main applications in OpenOffice.org (Writer, Calc, and Impress) are, respectively, quite similar to their equivalents in Microsoft Office (Word, Excel, and PowerPoint), so switching over to the OpenOffice.org applications should be relatively easy.

If you don't have any experience with Microsoft Office, you should still find it all pretty straightforward, as the basic layout is pretty intuitive. And if you are lacking in the intuition department, the built-in Help files are pretty good, too. To further help you along, the Tips system works just like tooltips in the Windows and Mac worlds. In case you aren't sure what I'm talking about, tooltips are those little yellow boxes that pop up to tell you what a button or menu item does when you place your mouse over that button or menu item.

Despite all the straightforwardness I am speaking of, there are a few interface items that will most likely be unfamiliar to you. That being the case, I will briefly discuss those items. I'll be using the word processor, Writer, as I describe these things, so if you want to run OpenOffice.org while following along, Writer might be a convenient starting point for you too.

Getting to Know the Buttons

Although you should pretty much be able to figure out what all of the buttons on the OpenOffice.org toolbars do, there are a few buttons common to all OpenOffice.org modules that most likely require, or at least deserve, a bit more explanation. I will cover the function of these buttons as shown in Figure 13-4 from left to right.

Figure 13-4: Some possibly unfamiliar buttons in OpenOffice.org

Export to PDF

This first button (Figure 13-4) is situated to the left of the two printer buttons (Print and Print Preview). You can use this button to *export*, or save, your document as a PDF file, in a manner that is similar to (albeit easier than) the one in Chapter 10.

Hyperlink

Clicking the Hyperlink button, the second button in Figure 13-4, brings up the Hyperlink window, from which you can assign links to specified documents—not only to web pages, but also to documents on an individual computer, and even targets within that document. While a hyperlink on a web page is something we have all come to take for granted, the idea of hyperlinking between text documents sounds like a pretty radical concept. It is, in fact, a rather old one that has been around since before you or I even heard of the Internet.

Navigator

The third button in Figure 13-4 (the one that looks like a starburst) is the Navigator button. Clicking this button brings up the Navigator window (see Figure 13-5), which is a pretty cool navigational feature that comes in handy when working with lengthy or otherwise complex documents.

Figure 13-5: The Navigator window

The Navigator allows you to easily bounce back and forth between pages in a document or even between elements therein, such as sections, links, and so on. Let's say that you have a document with lots of illustrations in it (like this chapter), and you want to jump directly from graphic to graphic. In this case, you would double-click the word Graphics in the main pane of the Navigator window and then click the jump buttons (the odd little buttons to the left of the page number selector) to begin jumping.

If you are dealing with a document containing various heading levels, like all of the chapters in this book, you can also use Navigator to switch among those levels. Say you've decided to add a new main heading at the last minute to a document you've been writing. All of the headings you had before thus need to be dropped down a notch; the former main heading becoming a subheading, and so on. By double-clicking the word Headings, the text of all the headings you have listed in the document would then appear. You could then select a heading in that list, and then click the Demote Level button (that's the one at the far right of the second row of buttons) to move it down a notch.

Gallery

The fourth button in Figure 13-4 is the Gallery button. By clicking this button, the Gallery, a library of graphical elements for use in your documents or web pages, will appear in a separate pane at the top of your document window (see Figure 13-6). The elements within the Gallery range from various types of lines to buttons to colored three-dimensional doughnuts, and you can even add items of your own.

Figure 13-6: The Gallery

Inserting a graphic into your document is a simple enough task even when not using the Gallery. All you need to do is go to the **Insert** menu, select **Picture ▶ From File**, and then locate the image file you want to insert. It can be handier to use the Gallery, however, when you intend to use certain graphics frequently. Once in the Gallery, your graphics are always only a click or two away and can be conveniently viewed in the Gallery browser window.

Adding your own graphics to the Gallery is also relatively easy to do. First you have to create a new category (called a *theme*) for each group of images you wish to add. To create a Gallery theme of your own, just click the **New Theme** button in the Gallery window. This will open the New Theme Properties window, where you should first click the **General** tab and give your theme a name. Once you've done that, click the **Files** tab, and then the **Find Files** button, which will bring up a Select Path window. From there you can navigate to the folder in which you are storing your clip art, photos, or other graphics. Once you have found the folder, click the **Select** button, after which a list of all the files in that folder will appear in New Theme Properties window.

You can easily add images to your new Gallery theme by clicking on the name of each image you wish to add (you might want to make sure that the box next to the word *Preview* is checked to make things a bit easier), and then clicking the **Add** button. Once you have done that, a copy of the image will immediately appear in the Gallery browser, where it will remain for future use. To use one of the images in the Gallery, just right-click the image you wish to insert into your document, and then select **Copy** or **Link** in the popup menu.

Data Source

The fifth button shown in Figure 13-4 is the Data Source button. Clicking this button opens a Data Source browser within a new pane in the top half of your document window. From that pane you can then access and edit records stored within any databases you have registered in OpenOffice.org. From a database containing personal contact information (such as Evolution's Addressbook), for example, you could simply do a search for an individual entry, and then drag the name, address, phone number, and/or email address for that entry into your document, rather than searching for the data elsewhere and then typing it in all over again.

Styles and Formatting

The last button shown in Figure 13-4 is the Styles and Formatting button. This button acts as a toggle for the Styles and Formatting window (Figure 13-7), from which you can select and then apply styles to any of the various elements within your document.

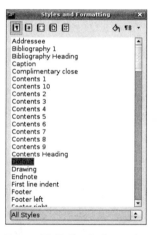

Figure 13-7: The Styles and Formatting window

To give you an example of how convenient using styles can be, imagine that you are typing a bibliography page for some document you've prepared. You typed each entry as you might any paragraph, as in:

```
Smythe, W. (2004). Reconsidering the need for speech
between non-human interlocutors beyond the age of seven. The
Journal of the Society of Elves, Faeries, and Garden Gnomes,
20 (2), 125-147.
```

Like most paragraphs you type, the entry is formatted as a first-line indent, which is fine and dandy except for the fact that you want a hanging indent, which is the norm for bibliography entries. Rather than messing around with tabs or margins to get things the way you want, all you have to do is click your mouse anywhere within the paragraph, and then double-click the **Hanging Indent** entry in the Styles and Formatting window. After that, as if by magic (though you know better), the transformation is made:

```
Smythe, W. (2004). Reconsidering the need for speech
     between non-human interlocutors beyond the age of
     seven. The Journal of the Society of Elves, Faeries,
     and Garden Gnomes, 20 (2), 125-147.
```

You could follow the same procedure for each of your other entries, or, with Hanging Indent selected, click the **paint can** button in the Styles and Formatting window, after which your mouse cursor, when placed over the document, will appear as a paint can. Place that paint-can cursor in any other paragraph in your bibliography, and that entry, too, will be formatted in the new style. The process is essentially the same when applying different styles to any other document elements.

Word Processing Done Lightly with AbiWord

If OpenOffice.org's Writer is a bit more powerful than what you need for your everyday word processing chores, and you would prefer something that pops up as soon as you click the launcher, then you might want to consider giving another word processor, AbiWord, a try (Figure 13-8).

Figure 13-8: The other Linux word processor—AbiWord

AbiWord has a very straightforward and easy-to-use interface, which you should be able to figure out without much, if any, help. It also has a couple of rather interesting features, such as its auto-resize function, which magnifies the onscreen document size (fonts, images, and everything) or shrinks it as you increase or decrease the size of the program window. And in case you're wondering, AbiWord can save and read Microsoft Word DOC files and save documents as PDF files.

You can easily install AbiWord via Synaptic by performing a search for *abiword*, and then . . . well, you know the drill by now. Once you have AbiWord installed, you can run it by going to the **Applications** menu and selecting **Office ▶ AbiWord Word Processor**.

Some Other Cool Productivity Apps

In addition to the more traditional office applications, there are a number of other applications either included with or available for your system that can be grouped together under the "productivity" label. I will introduce a few of those to you here.

Sticky Notes

Mac users will be well familiar with the digital version of the now ubiquitous little yellow Post-It–like notes called Sticky Notes (Figure 13-9) that come as part of the GNOME desktop. GNOME's Sticky Notes is a panel applet that you can add to your own panel by right-clicking on any open panel space and then selecting **Add to Panel** in the popup menu that then appears. When the Add to Panel window appears, go to the **Accessories** section, click **Sticky Notes**, and then click the **Add** button. You will then be ready for note-taking action.

Figure 13-9: GNOME's Sticky Notes

I should mention that there is one slightly annoying "feature" of Sticky Notes that makes it a bit different from what you might be used to. When you click on the desktop, all of your notes will disappear. This is as it is supposed to be, though I personally can't see the point (and wouldn't like it much even if I could). Fortunately, however, you can bring all of your notes back to view by simply clicking the Sticky Notes panel applet. In fact, if you decide to remove the panel applet and then bring it back at some later point in time, you'll be happy to know that all of the notes you created before will be back too.

Tomboy

If Sticky Notes just doesn't cut it for you and your more dramatic note-taking needs, then perhaps you will find yourself better served by an application called Tomboy (Figure 13-10). Like Sticky Notes, Tomboy also works as a panel applet, but it is a bit more full featured, albeit without making any claims to stickiness. Instead, the various notes you create can be viewed by selecting them from the menu that appears when you click the Tomboy panel applet itself. All in all, a very handy approach.

Figure 13-10: Notes taken seriously—Tomboy

What really gives Tomboy its bragging rights, however, is its search and hyperlink functions. These allow you to search for entries within your entire Tomboy note library, and create hyperlinks that connect text in one note to another linked note. In fact, Tomboy will automatically create a hyperlink whenever you type a word that matches one of your existing note headings. To make matters even more exciting (or at least more useful), Tomboy, by means of its plugins feature, allows you to export notes to HTML or print them out, either as hard copy or as PDF docs.

You can install Tomboy via Synaptic by doing a search for *tomboy*. Once installed, start it up by going to **Applications ▸ Accessories ▸ Tomboy**, after which Tomboy will appear in the top GNOME Panel.

GnuCash

If you are familiar with the personal financial management software Quicken, then you might be interested in GnuCash (shown in Figure 13-11), which is the Linux world's best-known offering in the personal finance arena. It reads Quicken and Intuit QIF files, which makes things even nicer should you be making the transition from another operating system. Unfortunately, unless you live in Germany, you cannot use GnuCash for online banking; but as the GnuCash folks themselves say, don't blame them, blame your bank.

To install GnuCash, just do a Synaptic search for *gnucash*, and then mark both **gnucash** and **gnucash-docs** for installation. Once these are installed, you can run the application via the Run Application panel applet by typing **gnucash** and then clicking **Run**.

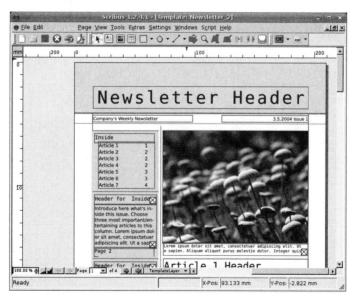

Figure 13-11: GnuCash

Scribus

To round things out, we come to the open source desktop publishing application, Scribus (shown in Figure 13-12), for those times when OpenOffice.org Writer and Draw just don't cut it. Scribus is designed to produce commercial-grade output, with support for professional publishing features, such as CMYK colors, PostScript handling, and creation of color separations, to name but a few.

Figure 13-12: Scribus

You can download and install Scribus by doing a Synaptic search for *scribus*. Once the installation is complete, you can run the application from **Applications ▸ Office ▸ Scribus**.

14

BRUSH-WIELDING PENGUINS

Linux Does Art

Now that you know that you can get down to business in Linux, it is time to don that beret of yours and address the artistic side of things. Yes, Linux does art, and as you will soon find out, there are a good number of programs on your system that allow you to create and manipulate graphic files. These days, however, there is perhaps nothing as important to most users' graphical repertoires as their digital cameras, so that is where we'll begin.

Project 14A: Digital Cameras

While scanner support for Linux is still a bit spotty, support for digital cameras is significantly better. Linux supports over 700 cameras through the bundled gPhoto2 digital camera software package, which is essentially a collection of drivers that works in the background to tell your computer how to communicate with your camera. To see if your camera is supported, go to the gPhoto2 website (www.gphoto.org), scroll down, and click **700 cameras**. On that page you will find a complete list of all the cameras supported by gPhoto2. If your camera isn't on the list, it most likely means (as the page points out) that your camera is so old that there is little demand for support for it or that it is so new that there hasn't been enough time to develop support for it. Of course, gPhoto2 is constantly being updated, so if your camera isn't on the list now, it could be in the near future. Updating gPhoto2 with Synaptic now and again should keep you as up to date as possible.

If your camera is not supported by gPhoto2, all is not lost. First of all, there are some cameras that utilize what is called the USB Mass Storage protocol. These cameras function, without the help of gPhoto2, as USB storage devices, just like a thumb drive or USB external hard disk. You can access the photos on such cameras just as you would data on any other USB storage device—just connect it to your computer, and a Nautilus window appears displaying its contents. You can then transfer files via conventional drag-and-drop procedures.

Even if your camera doesn't seem to communicate with your computer by either of these means, you can still get your images to your hard disk by removing the memory card from your camera, inserting it into a USB flash memory card reader, and plugging that reader into one of your computer's USB ports. Once you've done that, your system will mount the card reader as if it were an external drive (which is pretty much what it is), thus allowing you to use simple drag-and-drop procedures to get the images to your hard disk. Of course, you can use this method even if your camera is supported by gPhoto2 or compliant with the USB Mass Storage protocol—sometimes it is the easiest way to deal with things anyway.

14A-1: Connecting Your Camera and Starting the Import Process

If your camera is supported by gPhoto2 and you prefer to access your photos directly from your camera rather than fiddle with flash storage cards (or if you're just not sure whether your camera is supported or not), connect the USB cord supplied with your camera to the camera itself and then to one of the USB ports on your computer.

Once you've done that, turn the camera on, and set it to communicate with your computer. Switching the camera to Play mode, rather than Camera mode, usually seems to do the trick, but you should check your owner's manual just to be sure. If your camera is supported by gPhoto2, and the chances of that are quite good, a small window will appear, as shown in Figure 14-1. To view the images on your camera, click the **Import Photos** button.

Figure 14-1: Your system seeks your approval before importing photos from your digital camera.

14A-2: Setting Up and Cleaning Up Before Importing the Images

After you have clicked the **Import Photos** button in that first window, another window (Figure 14-2) will appear displaying the photos currently in your camera. In this window, you can do a little housecleaning and setup before actually saving photos to your hard disk.

Figure 14-2: Importing digital photos from a camera

If you would like to delete all of the photos on your camera after importing them, check the box next to the words *Delete imported images from the camera*. If you would like to delete only a few images before getting around to the business of importing, click on the image or images you want to delete (holding down the CTRL key if you are selecting more than one), and then click the Delete icon.

As you can see, there is also an option that allows you to keep the original filenames assigned by your camera. You no doubt understand what this means, so I'll tell you what not selecting this option means instead. When you import images from your digital camera, they will be saved in a folder and named in date-and-time format, such as 2006-02-19-19.08.13, while the images within that folder will be saved in numeric format, such as 0001.jpg, 0002.jpg, and so on. If you prefer to keep the filenames assigned by your camera (and as they appear in the Import Photos window), check the box next to *Keep original filenames*.

Finally, there is the question of where you save these date-and-time named folders. The default location is in your home folder, which is convenient enough; however, if you take a lot of photos, you will find that after some time your home folder contains so many folders full of imported images that it is difficult to find anything. Therefore, you may want to have your photos downloaded to a more specific location, such as a Photos folder.

To do this, click the drop-down menu button next to the word *Destination*, and select **Other**. This will bring up a Choose Destination Folder window. In that window, navigate to your Photos folder (or create one by clicking the **Create Folder** button in that window), and then select that folder by clicking it once. Once your selection is made, click the **Open** button, after which you will be returned to the Import Photos window with your new destination folder now listed in the Destination box at the top of the window.

14A-3: Saving the Images to Your Hard Disk

Now that everything is set up, you can save all of the photos in the Import Photos window by clicking the **Import** button. If you are in a pick-and-choose sort of mood, you can save only the images you want by holding down the CTRL key and then selecting just those images by clicking on each of them before clicking the **Import** button.

Once you have selected your photos (if you choose) and clicked the Import button, the images will be saved to your hard disk with the progress of the process indicated at the bottom of the Import Photos window. When the process is complete, the images you have just saved to your hard disk will appear in a new window, as you can see in Figure 14-3.

Figure 14-3: Imported images displayed in the gThumb image viewer

Viewing Your Images with gThumb

The images that appeared in Figure 14-3 are being displayed by an application called gThumb. As you can see, gThumb is an image viewer, but it can actually do a lot more. Although not as elegant in appearance as Apple's iPhoto, gThumb can actually perform many of the same functions, and it can even perform some functions that iPhoto can't. If you don't happen to be importing any images from your digital camera right now and would like to give gThumb a look, you can do so by going to the **Applications** menu and selecting **Graphics ▸ gThumb Image Viewer**.

Getting to Know Some of gThumb's Features

Now you know how to view images in gThumb, but so what, right? Well, as I said, gThumb does a lot more—so much, in fact, that it is a really useful tool for the digital photographer. With gThumb you can view your images as a slideshow by clicking the **Slide Show** button; view them at full-screen size (**View ▸ Full Screen**); rotate and mirror them (**Tools ▸ Rotate Image**); and convert their file formats, from JPEG to PNG, for example (**Tools ▸ Convert Format**).

If you want to adjust the actual look of things, you have still more options. To access most of these editing options, first select the image you want to tackle, and then go to the **Image** menu and select **Enhance**. Once you've done that, gThumb will have a go at making your image look its Sunday best.

If your aesthetic sense is a bit different than gThumb's, you can go the manual route, vetoing the changes gThumb made by clicking once on the image and then clicking the **Do Not Save** button. You can then go to the **Image** menu, and change the brightness, contrast, color balance, and hue saturation of your image. You can also resize and crop your images from the same menu.

If you want to print out one of your images, doing so via gThumb is extremely easy. Just click the image you want to print, and then select **Print** in the **File** menu.

Saving Photos to CD in gThumb

One of gThumb's very iPhoto-ish features is its ability to burn images to CD. To use this feature, select the images you want to save to CD (in Folder view— just click the **Folders** button to get there), and then select **Write to CD** in the **File** menu. After that, you will be asked in a separate window whether you want to save the whole shebang to disk or just those items you selected. Make your choice, and then click **OK**. A Nautilus CD/DVD Creator window will then appear showing the items you've selected. After that, it is all the same process as described in Chapter 6, so it is pretty much smooth sailing.

Project 14B: Creating Web Albums with gThumb

The gThumb features I've mentioned so far are pretty much the same as those found in Apple's iPhoto. Now, however, we come to one feature that isn't: gThumb's ability to create web albums of your photo collection. These albums can be used on your computer itself, distributed on CDs, or uploaded to your website for the whole world to see . . . and they look pretty nice.

14B-1: Selecting Images

To create a web album of your own, select the images you would like to add to your album (while holding down the CTRL key), go to the **Tools** menu, and select **Create Web Album**. A new window, Web Album (shown in Figure 14-4), will appear.

Figure 14-4: Creating a web album in gPhoto

14B-2: Selecting a Destination Folder

In the Web Album window, select a folder other than your home folder in which to place your web album (you'll end up with a mess in your home folder if you don't). After that, select the new folder you've created as the destination folder by clicking the drop-down menu button next to the word *Destination* and then selecting **Other**. In the Choose destination folder window that appears, navigate to the new target folder, select it by clicking its name once, and then click **Open**.

14B-3: Copying Images and Page Layout Options

Once you've set the destination folder for your web album, you can decide whether or not to copy the images in your album to the destination folder. In the same window, check the box next to *Copy originals to destination* if you plan to upload the web page to your website or distribute it as an archive or on CD. If you just plan to view the album on your own computer, leave the box blank.

Once you've done that, decide how many images you want to appear on each page of your album by adjusting the numbers in the Index Layout section of the window. For most screen resolutions, 2 or 3 rows by 4 columns works very nicely.

14B-4: Adding Headers and Footers

While still in the same window, give your album a title by typing that title in the Header text box. You can also type a string of text to appear at the bottom of the page by typing text in the Footer text box.

14B-5: Choosing a Theme

Finally, choose a theme for your album by clicking the **...** button to the right of the Theme text box. As you can see in Figure 14-5, there are six themes available. Click on each of the themes once to see a preview of that theme in the right half of the window. Once you have made your selection, click the **Select** button. For my part, I will be using the Classic Clips theme.

Figure 14-5: Selecting a theme for your web album

14B-6: Creating and Viewing a Web Album

Once your selections are made, you can create your web album by clicking the **Save** button. If you chose to create a web folder, a small window will appear, telling you that there is no such folder and asking you if you want to create it. Of course you do, so click **Create** in that window. After a few seconds, your web album will ready for viewing.

To see your new creation, open a Nautilus window, navigate to the target folder you created for your web album, double-click it, and then look for the file index.html within that folder. Once you've found it, double-click it. Firefox will then open to your new album. You can see mine in Figure 14-6.

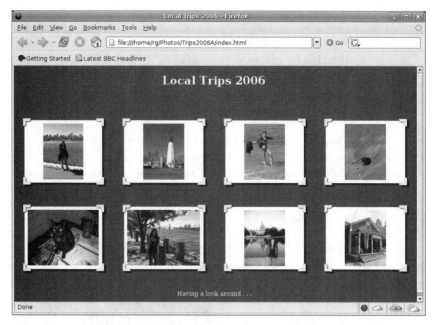

Figure 14-6: Viewing thumbnail images in a web album

As you can see, the web album presents your photos as a set of thumbnails in a photo or slide motif (depending on the theme you choose), with buttons there to connect you to whatever other pages your album happens to have. Click any one of the thumbnails in your web album, and that image will appear in enlarged form within the same window, as you can see in Figure 14-7.

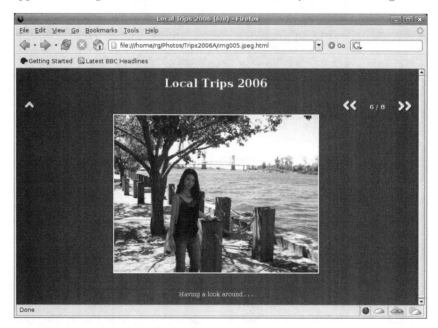

Figure 14-7: Viewing enlarged images in a web album

Project 14C: Emblems Again! (Creating Your Own)

One of the first things my mother asked me after she got Linux up and running was how to create her own emblems. You already learned how to deal with emblems in Chapter 7, but now that I have introduced many of the graphics tools at your disposal, it might be a good time to address my mother's question as well.

14C-1: Using an Existing Icon as an Emblem

You can use any image as the basis of an emblem, but the easiest way to get started creating emblems is to use one of the icons on your system as the base. The only problem with that idea is that most of your system icons are 48 by 48 pixels in size, while emblems are 36 by 36 pixels. If you don't want your new emblem to look weirdly oversized and out of place, it is best to resize it.

As I mentioned in the previous section, the gThumb application is very handy for resizing images. For this project, we will use the gnome-tigert icon, so in the left pane of the gThumb window, navigate to /usr/share/pixmaps. Once there, look for the **gnome-tigert.png** file (it looks like an orange cartoon character), double-click it, and then go to the **Image** menu and select **Resize**. This will bring up the Scale Image window (see Figure 14-8), where you can change the width of the icon to 36 pixels (the height will change automatically, as long as the box next to the words *Keep aspect ratio* is checked). Once you are done, click **Scale**.

Now you need to save the newly sized icon to your home folder, while keeping the original as it was. To do this, go to the **File** menu and select **Save As**, which will bring up the Save Image window. Save the file as gnome-tigert_emblem.png in your home folder. You can do this by clicking the drop-down menu button next to the words *Save in folder* and navigating your way home. Once that's done, click **Save**.

14C-2: Adding the Newly Sized Image to the Emblem Collection

Now that you have an image of the appropriate size, it is time to add it to your system's collection of emblems. To do this, open a Nautilus window, go to the **Edit** menu, and then select **Backgrounds and Emblems**. Once the Backgrounds and Emblems window opens, click the **Emblems** button on the left side of the window, and then click the **Add a New Emblem** button at the bottom of that window. This will bring up a small Create a New Emblem window (see Figure 14-9).

In that window, start out by giving your emblem a name. As the image is that of a tiger, I called mine *Kitten Stuff*, but you can call it something else if you'd like. Just type the name in the Keyword box.

Figure 14-8: Scaling an image in gThumb

Figure 14-9: Adding a new emblem to your collection

After you have done that, it is time to work on adding your new emblem to your system's emblem collection. To do this, just click the big button next to the word *Image*. This will open a window from which you can select the image. In the text box at the top of that window, type **~/gnome-tigert_emblem.png**, and click **OK**. Your new Kitten Stuff emblem should now appear in the Create a New Emblem window. If so, click **OK**.

That window should now disappear, and your new Kitten Stuff emblem (or whatever you called it) will appear in the Emblems window (see Figure 14-10). Now you can use your new emblem as you would any other.

Figure 14-10: A new emblem (Kitten Stuff) in the Emblems window

Getting Arty with the GIMP

The Windows and Mac worlds may have Photoshop, but the Linux world has the GIMP. While arguably not as powerful as Photoshop, the GIMP is a capable contender, which may explain why it has been ported over to both

Mac and Windows. The GIMP allows you to create bitmap graphics and, quite importantly, retouch or completely doctor image files. With the GIMP you can get rid of red-eye in your digital photos, airbrush out unwanted shadows (or even facial blemishes), give your image a canvas texture, change a photo into an oil painting, and even add a bell pepper here and there—and with drop shadows no less (see Figure 14-11). To run the GIMP, go to the **Applications** menu, and select **Graphics ▸ GIMP Image Editor**.

Figure 14-11: Manipulating a digital image in the GIMP

Using the GIMP to Resize Images and Convert File Formats

Like gThumb, the GIMP is also a very handy tool for resizing images. This can be done by simply right-clicking an image opened in the GIMP and then selecting **Image ▸ Scale Image** in the popup menu. This will bring up the Scale Image window, where you can set the new size of the image.

The GIMP is also an excellent tool for converting images from one file format to another. You can, for example, open a bitmap (.bmp) file and save it as a PNG (.png) file, or save a JPEG (.jpg) file as a GIF (.gif) file, and so on. While this can also be done with gThumb, the GIMP supports an extremely wide variety of file formats, and it even lets you save an image file as a compressed tarball, which makes it a true file-conversion king.

To perform a file conversion, just right-click an image opened within the GIMP and then select **File ▸ Save As** in the popup menu. You can make the same selection from the **File** menu if you prefer. Either way, the Save Image window will then appear. In that window you can specify the new file format by replacing the original file extension in the Name box at the top of that window with the extension for the format you want to convert the image to. If you're not sure what formats are available to you, click the small arrow to the left of the words *Select File Type*, and then choose from the options in the pane that appears below. To save a work in progress, use the GIMP-native XCF format, so that you can continue working on the image later.

Dialogs

The GIMP interface, as you might have noticed, is based on a series of dialogs, two of which appear when you first run the application. You can, however, open still others, and, more importantly, you can dock those together to form larger single dialogs. While this is quite easy to do, figuring out how to do it is something that leaves many GIMP newbies at a loss.

The various dialogs available to you in the GIMP can be found by going to the **File** menu in the main GIMP window (that's the one that usually appears at the left of your screen, as in Figure 14-11), and selecting **Dialogs**. From the submenu that appears, make your choice from the list of dialogs shown.

After you've opened a couple of dialogs, you can dock them together by clicking and then holding the name of the dialog, located just below the title bar, and dragging that name to the bottom of the dialog you wish to dock it to. The name of the dialog will appear as a floating icon/name tab as you do your dragging (Figure 14-12).

Figure 14-12: Docking dialogs in the GIMP

When the thin, gray band near the bottom of the target dialog turns brown (compare the bottom of the two dialogs in Figure 14-12 to see the difference), release the mouse button, and the dialogs will be joined as one, as you can see in Figure 14-13.

Figure 14-13: Docked dialogs
in the GIMP

Learning More

It is lots of fun to learn to use the GIMP by just playing around with it for a while. Most of the fun stuff, to get you started, is located in the Filters and Script-Fu menus of any image window. Of course, you should make a backup copy of any file you are planning to experiment with before altering it.

If you prefer working through manuals and tutorials to just finding things out by goofing around, you can download and install the GIMP User Manual via Synaptic by searching for *gimp* and then marking **gimp-help-en** for installation. Once it is installed, you can access the manual from within the GIMP from the Help menu. If you prefer, you can just view the manual online at http://docs.gimp.org/en. You can also find a series of skill-level-based tutorials at www.gimp.org/tutorials.

XPaint

If the GIMP comes across as a bit overwhelming for you, or if it seems to be overkill for your simpler tasks, you might want to try out an application known as XPaint, which you can download and install via Synaptic (search for *xpaint*). XPaint is similar to Windows Paint and MacPaint.

Even if you are a satisfied GIMP user, there is still good reason to download and install XPaint, because in addition to its simple paint tools, it can take screenshots of regions (Figure 14-14) rather than just of a particular window or of the full screen. If you have ever used the Mac OS X application Grab, you may well be familiar with this feature.

By the way, once installation is complete, there will be no launcher for XPaint in the Applications menu, so you will have to run from the Run Application panel applet or from a Terminal window by typing xpaint.

Figure 14-14: Taking screenshots of screen regions with XPaint

Sodipodi

The GIMP, like other so-called *paint programs*, creates bitmap images in various file formats. These are images in which the location and color of every single pixel is recorded. The image is essentially a collection of dots, or *bits*. The file you create is a rather hefty map of these bits (hence its name), and this map tells your system where everything in your image is supposed to go when it is displayed or printed.

Drawing programs, on the other hand, create vector images, or drawings. The vector image file is a collection of mathematical formulae representing the various shapes in your image. This may sound rather unimportant to you, but such drawings have advantages in certain cases. One of these advantages is that vector image files take up less space on your hard disk than bitmaps. Another, and perhaps the most important, advantage is that shapes in vector images retain their smooth edges when the images are enlarged. A smooth circle created as a bitmap, for example, would begin to show jagged edges ("the jaggies") when enlarged to any extent, while the same circle in a vector image would remain smooth and round no matter how much you increased its size.

If you're interested in giving a drawing program a go, then my pick for creating true graphics is Sodipodi—the name is Estonian for *mishmash* (see Figure 14-15).

To download and install Sodipodi, do a Synaptic search for *sodipodi*, and then mark the file for installation. Once it is installed, you can run it from the **Applications** menu by selecting **Graphics ▸ Sodipodi**.

If you would like to learn how to use Sodipodi, go to the Sodipodi home page at www.sodipodi.com. Be sure to click the **Galleries** link at the top of that page to see examples of what you can do with the program.

Figure 14-15: Sodipodi

Project 14D: Installing Picasa via the GDebi Package Installer

It wouldn't be right to dedicate a whole chapter to Linux's graphical capabilities without mentioning one of the newest entries in the Linux application arena—Picasa. Those of you coming from the Windows world are no doubt familiar with this very popular image viewing, organizing, and editing application from Google, and you will no doubt be pleased to discover that it is now available for Linux. Picasa is not an open source application, which may cause some Linux diehards to turn away, but it is free, feature rich, nice to look at, and decidedly cool (Figure 14-16). It also gives you easy access to various online photo blogs, photo finishers, and product providers, such as PhotoStamps, Shutterfly, Kodak, and even Walgreens.

Picasa is not available via Synaptic, but it is available from Google as a DEB package. Rather than install that package via the command line, as you learned to do in Chapter 9, in this chapter you will learn to install Picasa (or any other DEB package) by means of the graphical GDebi package installer.

NOTE   *You may notice on the Picasa site that the Linux version uses Wine, which you learned about in Chapter 9. You do not, however, have to have Wine installed in order to use Picasa. Whatever bits of Wine it uses are included in the DEB package.*

14D-1: Downloading the Picasa Package

To get Picasa, go to http://picasa.google.com/linux/download.html. On that page, click the link for the Debian/Ubuntu version of the Picasa package. In a separate window, Firefox will ask you what you want to do with the file. Select **Save to Disk**, and then click **OK**, after which the download will begin.

Figure 14-16: Picasa

Once the picasa_2.2.2820-5_i386.deb (or newer) package is on your hard disk, make sure all package management software (such as Synaptic, the Add/Remove Programs utility, and Update Manager) is closed, and then double-click the Picasa package itself. This will bring up the package installer, GDebi (Figure 14-17).

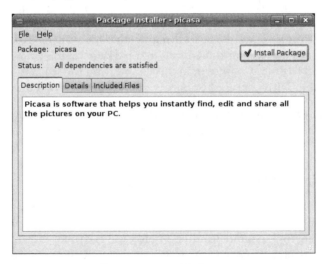

Figure 14-17: Installing Picasa via GDebi

As you can see, the GDebi package installer looks as if it were a piece cut out of the Synaptic window. It provides a description of the application, details about the file you are attempting to install, and a list of what's included in the package. To get down to the actual installation, just click the **Install Package** button. A small window will appear, telling you that you need administrative rights in order to proceed. Click **Grant**, and you will be prompted for your password. Type that, and click **OK** to begin the installation. GDebi will show the progress of the installation and let you know when it is done.

14D-2: Running and Setting Up Picasa

Once Picasa is installed, you can run it by going to the **Applications** menu and selecting **Graphics ▶ Picasa**. The first time you do this, Picasa will ask you if you want it to scan your entire computer for images (the default selection) or just your desktop. Do not, I repeat, do not accept the default (*Completely scan my computer and all network directories for pictures*).

The reason for this warning is that even though you may have yet to add a single image to your computer, your system is already chock-full of them. If you were to accept the default, Picasa would be filled with all sorts of stuff that you really wouldn't want there. It is supposed to be an organizer for *your* photos, after all. With that in mind, select **Only scan the Desktop**, and then click the **Continue** button. Picasa will then scan your desktop for images and add any images it finds to its library.

Working with Picasa should be very straightforward, but if you want to find out more, check out http://picasa.google.com/linux. On that page, you will find a basic overview, links to more Linux-specific information (including FAQ and forum pages), and a Picasa tour.

A Few Other Graphics Apps to Consider

In addition to the graphics applications I have covered in this chapter, there are still more available via Synaptic (or for some easy browsing, via the Add Applications tool). While you can experiment with what's available, I will point out a few others worth noting. If nothing else, these applications will give you an idea of the breadth of stuff out there waiting for you.

Blender

Perhaps one of the most impressive open source applications available today is Blender. Blender (Figure 14-18) is a professional-level 3D modeling, animation, and rendering program. It is rather complex, but that is the source of its power and popularity (it comes in versions for just about every operating system out there). If you would like to find out a bit more about Blender before taking the time (and disk space) to install it, go to www.blender3d.org. Find it via Synaptic by searching for *blender*; once the program is installed, you can run it from **Applications ▶ Graphics ▶ Blender 3D modeller**.

Figure 14-18: Blender

QCad

Another open source application that has found its way into almost all operating systems is QCad (Figure 14-19). QCad is a 2D computer-aided design (CAD) program with which you can create technical drawings such as room interiors, machine parts, or even musical instruments (I've seen a plan for a Nyckelharpa done on QCad!). To find out more, go to the project home page at www.ribbonsoft.com/qcad.html. Search Synaptic for *qcad*, and install the application. Once it is installed, you can run it from **Applications ▶ Graphics ▶ QCad**.

Figure 14-19: QCad

Tux Paint

To wrap things up, let's turn to an application for the kids (or the kids within us) and have a look at Tux Paint. With its big colorful buttons and fun and funky tools, Tux Paint, shown in Figure 14-20, is an app that your children can handle and enjoy. The best of Tux Paint's features (at least in my opinion) are its stamps, of which there is a good variety—everything from apples to seahorses, and euro coins to boot! Search Synaptic for *tuxpaint*; launch it from **Applications ▸ Graphics ▸ Tux Paint**.

Figure 14-20: Tux Paint

15

TUX ROCKS
Music à la Linux

It's now time to move on to the audio side of things. Yes, Linux does indeed rock, and in this chapter you will find out about those musical talents that your system possesses. The size of this chapter alone should be some indication of how much there is to offer. You will learn how to rip CDs, create MP3 and Ogg Vorbis files (files which you can recognize by their .mp3 and .ogg filename extensions), add album cover art, change file tags, play music files, and burn files onto audio CDs that you can play in any CD player. You'll also learn how to play a variety of audio streams. If you're interested in learning how to work with your iPod in Linux, how to deal with podcasts, and how to convert audio files from one format to another . . . well, you'll have to wait until Chapter 16.

Audio File Formats

Before we go any further, it is probably best to discuss the various formats in which audio data can be stored on your computer. For the longest time, the de facto standards have been WAV (created by Microsoft/IBM and using the

.wav extension), AU (from Sun/Unix and using the .au extension), and AIFF (from Apple and using the .aiff extension), all of which are uncompressed formats. Files saved in these formats are, therefore, exceedingly large, with an average WAV file of CD-quality music weighing in at about 10MB per minute. To put that in perspective, my first Macintosh back in 1988 had a 40MB hard disk—more space than I thought I would ever need, but not enough space to store a WAV file of Nirvana's "Come as You Are."

As computers underwent their evolution into the multimedia machines they are today, it became clear that something was going to have to be done about those disk-space-devouring audio files. Audio compression formats were thus developed. These compression formats worked, to oversimplify things a bit, by cutting out the portions of a sound signal that the human ear cannot hear—sort of a dog-whistle approach. The most widely known and embraced of these audio compression formats is MP3. Audio files encoded in MP3 format can end up being as little as one-twelfth the size of the original WAV file without any noticeable loss in quality.

Another audio compression format that was developed was Ogg Vorbis. Ogg Vorbis was a product of the open source community, so, unlike MP3, which has always been used under the shadow of yet-to-be-exercised patent rights, it was free of patent and licensing worries from the get-go. Because of that, and the fact that it was the equal of MP3 in terms of quality and performance (if not, as many claim, better), Ogg Vorbis became the darling of the Linux community.

As you work with the audio rippers mentioned in this chapter, you are sure to notice yet another encoding option—FLAC. *Free Lossless Audio Codec (FLAC)* is an encoding format that, unlike MP3 or Ogg Vorbis formats, does not remove any audio information from the audio file during the encoding process. The downside of this is that FLAC only provides space savings of 30 to 50 percent, which is much less than the 80 percent neighborhood achieved by MP3 or Ogg Vorbis formats. The upside, of course, is that the FLAC files should be equivalent to CDs in terms of quality.

Given that retention of audio quality, FLAC becomes an ideal choice if you are not satisfied with the audio quality provided by Ogg Vorbis or MP3 files. It is also a good choice if you might want to create both Ogg Vorbis and MP3 files . . . or if you just don't know which one you want to work with yet. In such cases, you can just rip the file and encode it in FLAC format. You can convert the FLAC file later, when you know what you want or need. You'll learn how to easily convert audio files from one format to another in Chapter 16.

Project 15A: Installing MP3 Support for Audio Apps

All that talk about Ogg Vorbis and FLAC aside, there are still many people who like or need to deal with MP3 files. You may, for example, already have numerous MP3 files ripped from your music collection, or you may enjoy listening to one of the many Internet radio streams that are broadcast in MP3 format. Unfortunately, MP3 playback and encoding support is not included in Ubuntu due to licensing concerns. Even if you plan on using

Ogg Vorbis format in your future ripping and encoding endeavors, installing MP3 support is a good idea so as to cover all your audio bases. It's also a very easy process.

To install MP3 playback and encoding support for most of the applications I will be discussing in this chapter (and MP3, Ogg Vorbis, and FLAC support for some other add-on apps), run Synaptic (**System ▸ Administration ▸ Synaptic Package Manager**), and then install the following items using the procedures you learned in Chapter 5:

- gstreamer0.10-plugins
- gstreamer0.10-plugins-ugly
- gstreamer0.10-plugins-ugly-multiverse
- gstreamer0.10-plugins-bad
- gstreamer0.10-plugins-bad-multiverse
- gstreamer0.10-ffmpeg
- gstreamer0.8-flac
- gstreamer0.8-ogg
- gstreamer0.8-lame
- gstreamer0.8-mad
- gstreamer0.8-misc
- lame
- libxine-extracodecs

You can find these items by doing Synaptic searches for three terms: *gstreamer*, *lame*, and *libxine*. After the installation is complete, open a Terminal window, type `gst-register-0.8` (don't use `sudo`), and press ENTER. After you close Synaptic and the Terminal window, you will be ready to start ripping CDs and encoding tunes at your will.

Audio Rippers and Encoders

The application you use to rip audio files from CD and encode them into space-saving MP3 or Ogg Vorbis formats is commonly referred to as a *ripper*. For some time now, the most commonly used non–command-line ripper was Grip, which still has its dedicated following. Other simpler-to-use rippers, however, have surfaced more recently, such as RipperX, Goobox, and the one that comes bundled with Ubuntu: Sound Juicer.

Sound Juicer

Sound Juicer (Figure 15-1) is a relatively new program that is pretty straightforward to use and quite capable in terms of what it does. It isn't perfect, though, and it still can be a bit quirky. In addition, unlike many of its ripping cousins, Sound Juicer does not automatically create a playlist for the songs you rip and encode, and it lacks a simple means by which to adjust the encoding bitrate.

Figure 15-1: Ubuntu's default ripping and encoding application—Sound Juicer

Despite these limitations, there are still many people who prefer Sound Juicer to the competition, so you might as well give it a try to see how you like it. To get started, just place the CD you want to rip in your drive; Sound Juicer will start up automatically and display the title of your CD, the artist's name, and titles of all the tracks in the application window.

NOTE *It is important to mention at this point that if you are not connected to the Internet, these bits of album information will not appear because album and track data are not embedded in the CD itself. What happens instead is that the audio ripper or player on your machine sends the digital ID of the CD you're playing to an online database, such as freedb.org or CD DataBase (CDDB), which is now officially known as Gracenote. In turn, the online database sends the album information for that CD back to the player or ripper.*

You can go about things another way by going to **Applications ▸ Sound & Video ▸ Sound Juicer CD Ripper** and then placing your CD in the drive. In this case, however, you might have to go to the Sound Juicer **Disc** menu and select **Re-read** before your album and track information will appear.

Setting the Default Folder for Ripped Files in Sound Juicer

By default, Sound Juicer is set up to rip your CDs and encode audio tracks in Ogg Vorbis format, and the default location in which Sound Juicer saves these files is your home folder. Because Sound Juicer, like all other rippers, will create an artist folder for each CD you rip, you will end up with a lot of folders in your home folder if you rip albums from a large number of artists. It is best to create a *Music* folder within your home folder, as you did for your graphika account, and then make that folder your default location for ripped music.

To set the default from Sound Juicer, go to the **Edit** menu, and select **Preferences**. This will open the Preferences window where you can change the output path by clicking the menu button next to the word *Folder* (the button itself should say *Home* at this point) and then selecting **Other** in the menu that appears. After that, browse to your **Music** folder, click it once in the list to select it, and then click the **Open** button.

Adding an MP3 Encoding Option for Sound Juicer

Although you've installed the files necessary to allow you to encode ripped tracks in MP3 format, you can't actually start doing so in Sound Juicer without performing a few extra steps. Here's what you need to do:

1. Go to the **Edit** menu, and select **Preferences**.

2. In the Preferences window, click the **Edit Profiles** button.

3. In the Edit GNOME Audio Properties window, click the **New** button.

4. Type **MP3** in the text box in the New Profile window that appears, and click **Create**.

5. Once you are back in the Edit GNOME Audio Profiles window, click **MP3** in the Profiles list to select it, and then click **Edit**.

6. In the Editing Profile "MP3" window (Figure 15-2), type the following in the GStreamer Pipeline text box:

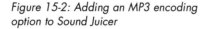

```
audio/x-raw-int,rate=44100,channels=2 ! lame name=enc ! id3mux
```

Figure 15-2: Adding an MP3 encoding option to Sound Juicer

NOTE   *There are no spaces before or after the commas in the preceding line of code. If you prefer, you can just copy this line from the Sound Juicer Help files. To do this, select **Help ▶ Contents** to bring up the Sound Juicer Manual window, click **Preferences** in the left pane of that window, and then scroll down in the right pane to the very end of the page, where you will find the line in a pink box.*

7. In the File Extension box in the same window, type **mp3**, and then check the box next to the word *Active?*.

8. Close all windows, and then restart Sound Juicer.

Ripping and Encoding Sound Files in Sound Juicer

To start ripping the audio tracks from the CD you have in your drive, you first need to select the format in which you wish to encode the tracks. To do this go to **Edit ▸ Preferences**, and then select either **MP3 (MP3 audio)** or **CD Quality, Lossy (Ogg Vorbis audio)** in the Output menu. Once you've done so, click **Close**.

After that, all you need to do is click the **Extract** button at the bottom of the Sound Juicer window to rip and encode all of the tracks on the CD. If there are certain tracks you do not care to rip and encode, just uncheck the checkboxes next to the names of those songs before you click Extract. If you only want to rip and encode a few of the songs in the list, it might be better to first go to the Edit menu, select Deselect All, and then check the checkboxes next to the songs you do want to rip before clicking Extract.

While the songs are being ripped and encoded, Sound Juicer will show you its progress at the bottom-left corner of the window, and when it's all done, it will tell you so in a small window. Once you get that message, click **Close**. You can eject the CD by going to the **File** menu and selecting **Eject**. If you want to rip and encode another CD, pop it into the drive; just as with the first CD, the album, artist, and song titles will all appear in the program window, and you can rip away yet again.

Goobox

Another ripper with a fair-sized following is Goobox (Figure 15-3). Despite having the simplest interface of all the rippers, it is rich in features, and those features are easy to understand and use. Not only does Goobox provide an easy means by which to switch encoding formats and adjust encoding bitrates for the tracks you want to rip and encode, but it is also fast. And unlike Sound Juicer, Goobox has no problem adding genre tags to the songs you rip.

Figure 15-3: The CD player and ripper Goobox

Goobox also works quite well as a CD player. Sound Juicer can serve in the same role, but Goobox looks as if it were made for the job. In fact, it looks more like a CD player that can rip and encode CD tracks than the other way around. It even allows you to easily download and display the album covers for the CDs you are playing. Because of its ripping and playback strengths, I changed my own system settings so that Goobox automatically appears when I insert an audio CD instead of the default Sound Juicer.

Downloading, Installing, and Using Goobox

You can easily download and install Goobox with Synaptic (just search for *goobox*). Once the installation is complete, you can run Goobox by going to the **Applications** menu and selecting **Sound & Video ▶ CD Player**.

NOTE *At the time of this writing, the current version of Goobox available on the Ubuntu repositories (0.9.91-1build1) does not download album track information, which significantly limits its functionality. Hopefully, by the time this book reaches your hands, a new version correcting that bug will be available. For now, I'll describe how things are done when everything works as it should.*

To get down to ripping and encoding with Goobox, just insert your CD in the drive, and the tracks, with artist and titles, will soon appear in the Goobox window. Before ripping and encoding your CD, you might want to check the information that is going to be encoded in the tags for the various tracks you rip. These tags include the artist name, album title, track titles, year the CD was released, and musical genre. It is much easier to do this before the tracks are ripped and encoded to MP3 or Ogg Vorbis format, so it isn't a bad idea to check first.

To do so, just go to the **Edit** menu, and select **CD Properties**. In the CDDB Track Editor window that appears (Figure 15-4), you can check things out and make any changes you feel are necessary. I often change the Genre section to make things more meaningful for me (I use *Latin Pop* or *Latin Alternative*, rather than just *Latin*, for example). You can also edit the tag information for privately released CDs that are not listed in online CD databases, CDs for which you have to input all of the information yourself.

If you want to rip only a few tracks, rather than the whole album, make your selections by clicking on the song titles, holding down the CTRL key while doing so if you want to select more than one song. If you want to adjust the encoding bitrate for file size or sound quality reasons, you can do so by going to the **Edit** menu, selecting **Preferences**, and then clicking the **Encoding** tab in the Preferences window. You can make your adjustments using the simple sliders in that tab.

Once you're ready to rip, go to the **CD** menu, and select **Extract Tracks**. A small window, shown on the left in Figure 15-5, will appear. In that window you can choose whether to extract just the tracks you've selected or to rip the whole album. If you click the small arrow next to the words *Advanced Options*, the window will expand (see the right side of Figure 15-5), and you can choose the encoding format you want to use.

Figure 15-4: Editing track information before ripping in Goobox

As I mentioned in "Setting the Default Folder for Ripped Files in Sound Juicer" on page 242, it is also a good idea to have Goobox save your encoded files in your Music folder. You can do this by clicking the menu button beneath the words *Destination Folder* and navigating to and selecting your Music folder. You only need to perform this step the first time out.

Figure 15-5: Extracting tracks in Goobox

Once your decisions are made, click the **Extract** button in the Extract Tracks window, and the ripping and encoding will begin. Goobox will show its progress in a separate window, where it will also let you know when it is done.

Goobox as a CD Player

As I mentioned before, Goobox works very well as a CD player. Using it in that capacity is straightforward enough; all you have to do is click the Play, Pause, Stop, Next, and Eject buttons, as you would in any other player. Also, like other CD players, it places a small control applet in the top panel, which you can click to hide and show the main player window, or right-click to access the playback controls while the main player window is hidden.

To add album art for the CD you are playing, click the CD icon just below the Play button, and select **Search on internet** in the popup menu that appears. Goobox will display a window filled with album covers (most of which are seemingly identical) for you to choose from (Figure 15-6). Click your choice, click **Apply**, and then click **Close**.

Figure 15-6: Downloading and selecting album cover art in Goobox

Making Goobox the Default CD Playback Application

If you would like to change your system settings so that Goobox instead of Sound Juicer automatically starts up every time you insert a CD, you can do so by following these steps:

1. Go to the **System** menu, and select **Preferences ▸ Removable Drives and Media**.
2. In the Preferences window that appears, click the **Multimedia** tab.
3. In the Audio CD Discs section of that tab, change the command from `sound-juicer -d %d` to **goobox**, and click the **Close** button.

Audio Players

Now that you know how to rip your audio CDs and encode them to space-saving MP3 and Ogg Vorbis files, you need to use another application to play them. Fortunately, this is an area where Linux shines, as there is quite a selection of audio players available, two of which I will discuss here.

Rhythmbox

The default audio player in Ubuntu is called Rhythmbox (see Figure 15-7). Rhythmbox, using Sound Juicer as its ripper/encoder, seems to function pretty much like a simplified version of Apple's iTunes application, though, for better or worse, iTunes it is not. It is, however, a relatively easy-to-use audio player which, despite some quirkiness in its early stages, has developed quite a following in the Linux world.

Figure 15-7: The Rhythmbox sound player

Running and Setting Up Rhythmbox

To run Rhythmbox, just go to the **Applications** menu, and select **Sound and Video ▸ Rhythmbox Music Player**. The first time you run Rhythmbox, you are greeted with a three-step setup wizard. To get through the first introduction screen, click **Forward**. In the second screen, you should tell Rhythmbox where it is you keep (or plan to keep) your music files. Use the Music folder you created in "Setting the Default Folder for Ripped Files in Sound Juicer" on page 242. Just click the **Browse** button to locate the folder graphically, and then click **Forward** in the wizard window. In the third and final screen, click **Apply**, and Rhythmbox will scan your Music folder and add any songs it finds there to its library.

Adding Songs and Albums to the Rhythmbox Library

If you are familiar with Apple's iTunes, then you should understand the Library in Rhythmbox too, as it is essentially the same concept, though it does not physically move your files as iTunes does.

To add new albums to your Rhythmbox library, go to the **Music** menu, select **Import Folder**, and then navigate to the folder for the new album you want to add. If you want to add a number of albums by the same artist, just navigate to and select the folder for that artist instead. If you just want to add a single audio file, you can also do that—just select **Music ▸ Import File**, and then navigate to the song in question.

If you are not the navigating type, you can also add files and folders by other means. The simplest way is to drag the folder or song you want to add to the Library into the right pane of the Rhythmbox window. You can also add a song to the Library directly by right-clicking the file and selecting **Open With ▸ Open with "Rhythmbox Music Player"** in the popup menu that appears.

Rhythmbox, in conjunction with Sound Juicer, also allows you to add songs to the Library directly from a CD, albeit it in a somewhat indirect way. To do this, select **Music ▸ Import Audio CD**, and Sound Juicer will appear and display the contents of the CD you currently have in your drive. After that, you can rip and encode the songs as you normally would in Sound Juicer. Once you're done, the songs will automatically appear in the Rhythmbox Library.

Browsing the Rhythmbox Library

The Rhythmbox Library is a collection of all of the music you add to it, which can prove to be a bit unwieldy as your collection grows. Fortunately Rhythmbox has a nice browser function, like the one in iTunes, that allows you to see lists of the artists and albums in the Library. If you click a specific artist in the Artist pane, a list of albums by that artist will appear in the right pane. You can then double-click one of the albums in that right pane to play it. If you want to play all of the albums you have by that artist, just double-click the artist's name in the left pane. All in all, a very handy feature.

If you would like to add an additional layer of categorization to the browser, you can do so by adding a Genre pane to the browser. To do this, just go to the **Edit** menu, select **Preferences**, and then click the **Library** tab in the window that appears. After that, select **Genres, artists and albums**, and you will have a three-pane browser in the Rhythmbox window (Figure 15-8).

Figure 15-8: The Rhythmbox browser

Creating Playlists in Rhythmbox

Of course, you can tailor things even further so as to match every situation and your every mood. There are days, after all, when you're feeling a bit too ethereal for Britney (and thank goodness for that). To prepare for such moments, you can create *playlists*, which are lists of songs to be played in a predetermined order. Just think of each playlist as an all-request radio station . . . where all the requests are your own.

To create a playlist in Rhythmbox, go to the **Music** menu, and select **Playlist ▸ New Playlist**. When the Playlist icon appears in the left pane of the Rhythmbox window, type a name for the list, and then add the songs you want by simply dragging them from the Library pane to the Playlist icon. The songs themselves will remain in the Library, so you aren't really moving anything—just creating aliases.

You can also create *automatic playlists*, which are lists that automatically scan the Library for songs that match your creation criteria. You could choose to create a list for the all the songs in your Library by a particular artist or of a specific genre. To do this, just select **Music ▸ Playlist ▸ New Automatic Playlist**. A window will appear in which you can specify what the list is to contain. You can even specify how many songs you want in the list.

Once you've created your lists, you can play one by clicking the list once and then clicking the Play button near the top of the window. You can do the same thing by just double-clicking the list.

Streaming Media with Rhythmbox

In addition to allowing you to play the music you have on your hard disk, Rhythmbox also allows you to play Internet radio streams in either MP3 or Ogg Vorbis format. To add a stream, click the **Radio** icon in the left pane of the Rhythmbox window, and you will come face to face with . . . well, actually nothing the first time around. To cure this state of emptiness, you can add new streams by going to the **Music** menu and selecting **New Internet Radio Station**. When the New Internet Radio Station window appears, type a title for the stream, select the genre, and then type the URL. Once you're done, click **Add**, and the stream will appear in the right pane of the Rhythmbox window.

But where do I find these radio streams, you ask? For the largest collection of MP3 streams, just go to www.shoutcast.com, find a stream that seems interesting to you, right-click the **Tune In!** button for that stream, and then select **Copy Link Location** in the popup menu. After that, paste the URL in the URL box of Rhythmbox's New Internet Radio Station window, and click **Add**. You can then double-click the stream in the right pane of the Rhythmbox window to play it.

Internet radio streams are also available in Ogg Vorbis format. Compared to the number of MP3 streams out there, however, the number of Ogg Vorbis broadcast streams is still rather limited. Things seem to be changing, though, and the number of Internet broadcasters who are experimenting with Ogg Vorbis seems to be increasing, albeit very slowly.

Radio France is a good example of one of these Ogg Vorbis broadcasters. Radio France has a number of program streams for Internet listeners in Windows Media Player format, but it also provides Ogg Vorbis streams for all of its broadcast programs. The stream I recommend you try out is Fip, which is an exceedingly cool collection of music of all genres; you will be constantly surprised by what they play. If you are worried about language, don't be; there is very little talk, and roughly 80 percent of the music played is in English. I don't speak any French other than *je suis fatigué*, but I have no problems at all.

If you want to give streaming media in general (and Radio France in particular) a try, type `http://ogg.tv-radio.fr:1441/encoderfip.ogg` in the URL box of Rhythmbox's New Internet Radio Station window, and then click **Add**. Assuming you are already connected to the Internet, Fip should start playing after a few seconds of pre-buffering.

If you would like to try any of the other Radio France broadcast streams, go to www.radiofrance.fr/services/aide/difflive.php#ogg, and you will find a list of addresses. If, on the other hand, the more traditional variety of pop and rock is your cup of tea, another broadcaster offering Ogg Vorbis streams is Virgin Radio. Virgin Radio has both standard pop/rock and classic rock broadcast streams. To listen to Virgin Radio, go to the Virgin Radio site at www.virginradio.co.uk/thestation/listen/ogg.html. Once there, click the appropriate link (modem or broadband) for the program stream you'd like to hear.

amaroK

Another somewhat recent entry into the Linux audio player arena is amaroK. Although actually a KDE app, amaroK (Figure 15-9) has such an attractive interface and such interesting and useful features that it has won over many converts, even within the GNOME world. Although figuring out all of its features can be a bit confusing at first, it will become second nature in no time.

Figure 15-9: amaroK

In case you are wondering, the name *amaroK* comes from the title of an old Mike Oldfield album of the same name. The word itself is derived from the Inunkitut word for *wolf*, which explains the logo for the application—a blue wolf.

Installing and Using amaroK

To install amaroK, you need to download and install two files via Synaptic: amarok and amarok-gstreamer. Once you perform a search for *amarok* and mark it for installation, Synaptic will automatically mark amarok-gstreamer for installation as well, so you don't really have to worry about installing it separately.

Once all the necessary files have been marked, applied, and installed, you can run amaroK from the **Applications** menu by selecting **Sound & Video ▶ amaroK**. The amaroK First-Run Wizard will then appear.

The first page of the wizard is just an introduction, so the only thing you have to do is click **Next**. On the second page, you will be asked to select the interface you wish to use. To enjoy the full effect of amaroK (and to follow along with my descriptions in this chapter), accept the single-window default by clicking **Next**.

The next page of the wizard is important because it is there that you tell amaroK where you are keeping your music files. Doing this allows amaroK to add the albums, songs, and/or playlists it finds there to its Collection list and to update that list whenever you add or delete files from that location. Assuming you followed my earlier directions to create a Music folder, navigate your way to that folder in the wizard window, and check the box next to its name. The wizard page should then look like mine in Figure 15-10. Once it does, click **Next**.

The rest of the wizard is essentially a no-brainer. Just click **Next** on the Database page, and then click **Finish** on the congratulatory final page. After that, the main amaroK player and its small panel controller applet will appear.

Figure 15-10: Telling amaroK where to find your music folder

Playing Songs, Building Your Collection, and Creating Playlists in amaroK

If you click the **Collection** tab on the left side of the amaroK window, you will see entries for all of the artists that amaroK found in your Music folder. AmaroK will automatically check the folder from time to time and make changes to the Collection list whenever you make changes to the Music folder itself. If you've just added something and it isn't showing up yet, go to the **Tools** menu and select **Rescan Collection**. Occasionally, amaroK seems to be on a bender of sorts and places things where they should not be in the Collection pane. If this should happen, just go the **Tools ▶ Rescan Collection** route again, and things will be as they should.

To get down to the business of playing music, drag an artist, album, or individual song to the right pane of the amaroK window, and click the **Play** button. This is also essentially the first step in building a playlist. For example, if you would like to create a playlist of songs you like to listen to while working, you would create the list using the drag-and-drop method I've just described (as I have done in Figure 15-11) and then save the list by going to the **Playlist** menu and selecting **Save Playlist As**.

Figure 15-11: Creating playlists in amaroK

Once the playlist is saved, the Playlists pane will appear at the left side of the window in place of the Collection pane, showing your new playlist in addition to any playlists amaroK found while scanning your Music folder. Remember that if you are using Goobox for your ripping and encoding needs, playlists are automatically created for each album that you rip.

While looking at the Playlists pane, you will notice that amaroK has a lot of other playlists there, much like those found in iTunes, such as Favorite Tracks, Genres, Most Played, Newest Tracks, Random Mix, and on and on.

Streaming Media with amaroK

Another one of amaroK's capabilities is acting as a streaming media player. As you probably noticed when looking at the Playlist pane of the amaroK window, there is an entry there called Radio Streams. Clicking the + next to that list and the + next to the Cool Streams folder within that reveals a list of preset radio broadcast streams that you can listen to with amaroK. If you would like to add other streams to the list, you can do so by clicking the **Add** button directly above the Playlists pane and selecting **Radio Stream**. When the Add Radio Stream window appears, type a name for the stream and the URL, and then click **OK**. The stream will then appear in the Radio Streams section of the Playlists pane.

Displaying and Downloading Album Cover Art in amaroK

AmaroK has a lot of other cool features worth mentioning. One of these is its ability to download and display the album cover art for the album you are playing. To get the cover for an album, just play any song from that album, and then click the **Current** tab. In that tab, click the icon that looks like a book with a question mark on it (Figure 15-12, left), and amaroK will search Amazon.com for the appropriate cover. Once it has found the right cover, it will display it in a separate window (Figure 15-12, top). If the cover is the correct one, click **Save**, after which the cover art will appear in the Current tab for every song you play from that album (Figure 15-12, right).

Figure 15-12: Fetching album cover art in amaroK

If amaroK cannot find the correct cover for the album in question, you have a couple of options. If the the album is a foreign one, you can try opening the Cover Manager (shown in Figure 15-13) by going to the **Tools** menu and selecting **Cover Manager**. In that window, click the **Amazon Locale** button, and then select the locale you want. There are six choices available: International, Canada, France, Germany, Japan, and United Kingdom. Once you've made your choice, click the square for the missing album cover, and see if that does the trick.

Figure 15-13: The amaroK Cover Manager

If that doesn't work, there's still hope, though you will have to do most of the work yourself. Just search the Internet for the album cover (Google's Image Search is a good bet), and then download the cover to your hard disk. Once you've done that, right-click the empty cover icon for the album in question, select **Set Custom Image** in the popup menu, and then navigate to the image you just downloaded.

Other Cool Features in amaroK

AmaroK has still more cool features worth noting. The one that you can't help but notice is that it provides an onscreen display of the track or stream that is playing, showing not only the title and artist of the track, but the album cover art as well (Figure 15-14). This is especially handy when using amaroK in hidden mode, which you can accomplish by using the amaroK panel applet as a toggle.

Figure 15-14: amaroK's onscreen display

AmaroK can also display the lyrics to the song you are playing, though to be quite honest, it's unlikely to retrieve lyrics for less popular music. To see, or at least try to see, the lyrics to the song you are playing, click the **Lyrics** tab (directly to the right of the Current tab) at the top of the left panel. AmaroK will immediately do an online search and then display its results.

If you use the right arrow button to the right of those tabs at the top of the left pane, you also navigate your way over to the **Artist** tab. If you click that tab, amaroK will do a Wikipedia search for information on the artist currently playing (Figure 15-15). Of course, this is not foolproof. When I tried it for the British band Sing-Sing, for example, I got a Wikipedia page on Sing Sing prison in New York. Interesting enough, I suppose. . . .

Figure 15-15: Artist information from Wikipedia in amaroK

Creating Audio CDs

All this talk about encoding and listening to MP3 and Ogg Vorbis files on your computer is fine and dandy, but there are no doubt times when you would like to have your songs on a plain audio CD that you can play while you slog your way to work on the New Jersey Turnpike or the Ventura Freeway. Luckily, this is easy enough to do with the bundled application Serpentine.

To create an audio CD, go to the **Applications** menu, and select **Sound & Video ▶ Serpentine Audio CD Creator**. When Serpentine appears, add songs to the main pane by clicking the **Add** button and navigating to the songs you want to add. You can add any mix of songs, in any mix of audio formats. You can also add songs you have saved to a playlist by going to the **File** menu and selecting **Open Playlist** or **Open Rhythmbox Playlist**, depending on the type of playlist in question.

As you add songs to the Serpentine window, the CD image in the bottom of the window will show you how much more space you have available on the disk (Figure 15-16). The default disk size is 74 minutes, which would be the norm for a 650MB blank CD, so if you are using a 700MB CD, change the setting to 80 minutes by clicking the drop-down menu button next to the words *Disc Capacity* and making the appropriate selection.

Figure 15-16: Preparing to burn an audio CD with Serpentine

When you have added all the songs you want to burn to the CD, click the **Write to Disc** button. Serpentine will then begin preparing the tracks to burn to disk. When it is ready, it will prompt you in a new window to insert a blank CD into your drive, so do that, and once the LED on your drive stops blinking, click the **OK** button. Serpentine will then begin burning the disk, and when it is done, it will automatically eject your disk and let you know in yet another window that the job is done. You can then take the disk, plop it in your car stereo or wherever else you want to play it, and enjoy the results.

Project 15B: Listening to RealMedia Streams with RealPlayer

Now that you know how to play Ogg Vorbis and MP3 files and Internet broadcast streams, it is time to help your system go a bit more mainstream by installing RealPlayer 10 (Figure 15-17). RealMedia streams are widely available on the Internet and are provided by many mainstream broadcasters, both local and international. You can also play RealVideo streams, when they're available.

Linux users familiar with earlier versions of RealPlayer will be happy to know that RealPlayer 10 is much improved over previous Linux offerings. One of the big advantages is that RealPlayer 10 now has a working Firefox-compatible plugin, which means that you can now listen to RealMedia streams that were previously unavailable because they could only be accessed through browser-embedded players. If you don't know what I'm talking about, take a look at the example from the Radio Sweden site in Figure 15-18.

Figure 15-17: RealPlayer 10

The Radio Sweden site (www.sr.se), like many others, uses an embedded player for the broadcast streams it provides; however, without installing the proper plugin, the player cannot be used (Figure 15-18, left). But once the RealPlayer plugin is installed, its controls automatically appear (Figure 15-18, right), allowing you to use the embedded player just as you would the stand-alone version (shown in Figure 15-17).

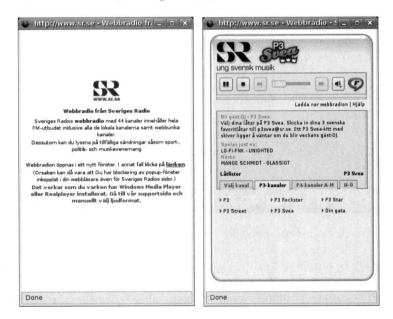

Figure 15-18: Embedded media players in Firefox before and after installing the RealPlayer plugin

While on the topic of changes, I should also mention that RealPlayer 10 is now theme compatible. This means that if you change your system theme from Human to Crux, for example, those effects take place in RealPlayer 10 too. This means you are no longer stuck with the look that the Real folks provide. Yes, things just keep getting better.

Now that you know what is store for you with RealPlayer 10, it's time to get down to installing it. Before we begin, however, I should mention that there are actually three ways to install RealPlayer. In this project, I am going to focus on the one that, albeit seemingly more cumbersome, is less likely to create problems for you down the road. It is also the standard way of doing it and, without question, the most legal.

15B-1: Getting Ready to Install RealPlayer

The first phase of the installation process involves getting the RealPlayer file itself. Here are the steps:

1. Open your web browser, and go to www.real.com/linux. On that page, click the **Download RealPlayer** button.
2. When the download is complete, be sure to place the downloaded file in your home folder.

15B-2: Installing RealPlayer

Once the RealPlayer file is snug in your home folder, quit Firefox, open a Terminal window, and then follow these really easy steps:

1. Make the RealPlayer installation file executable (aka *runnable*) by typing `chmod a+x RealPlayer10GOLD.bin` and pressing ENTER.
2. Type `sudo ./RealPlayer10GOLD.bin`, and press ENTER.
3. Type your user password when prompted to do so, and press ENTER.
4. When prompted to press ENTER to continue, press ENTER.
5. When asked to complete the path where you want to install RealPlayer, type `/opt/RealPlayer`, and press ENTER.
6. In the next window, to begin copying files, simply accept the default by pressing ENTER.
7. When you are asked whether to allow the installer to configure system-wide symbolic links, type `Y`, and press ENTER.
8. You will now be asked to specify the prefix for symbolic links. Just press ENTER.

After a very short while, the installer tells you that it's finished, and you will be returned to your user prompt. You can then close the Terminal window. You can also delete the RealPlayer binary file that you downloaded.

15B-3: Setting Up RealPlayer and Testing Your Installation

Now that Real Player 10 is installed on your machine, it is time to go through the final setup steps and then test it all out. You can start by going to the **Applications** menu and selecting **Sound & Video ▸ RealPlayer 10**. A simple setup wizard will appear, which you will have no trouble with on your own, as all you really have to do is click the button at the bottom-right corner of the window four times. Once you have completed the wizard, the RealPlayer window will appear. Firefox will also appear at this point, opened to the Helix Community page and most likely informing you that your player is up to date. To test the installation, close the RealPlayer window, but leave Firefox open.

The next step is to check whether Real Player will automatically run when you click a link for a RealMedia stream in Firefox. To do this, go to www.npr.org, and click the **NPR Program Stream** link in the middle of the page. When the NPR Audio Player Preference window appears, click the **Real** link on the left. A small Firefox window will then appear, asking you what it should do with the file. The default should be *Open with: /usr/share/ realplay.* If so, click **OK**, but don't check the box next to the words *Do this automatically for files like this from now on* until you know that everything is working as it should (a good rule of thumb regardless of what you're doing). If all is as it should be, the RealPlayer window will soon appear, and the NPR stream will begin playing.

Now let's check and see if the RealPlayer plugin is working right in terms of embedded players. Point your browser to www.sr.se/p3/svea, and click the **Lyssna på Svea** (Listen to Svea) button. A new window will appear. If the window looks like the one on the right in Figure 15-18 you have a total success on your hands. Congratulations.

MP3 and Ogg Vorbis Streams with RealPlayer

An interesting and not unwelcome result of installing RealPlayer with the Firefox plugin is that you can now play MP3 and Ogg Vorbis Internet broadcast streams with a single click of your mouse. Go to www.shoutcast.com, and click the **Tune In!** button next to one of the streams to see what I mean. All very handy, you've got to admit.

Going to Town with RealPlayer

Now that you are all set up, you probably want some more streams to try out. There are plenty of sites with RealMedia streams, but let me steer you to some of my favorites to get you started (you may already know some of these):

- Car Talk (car talk)
  www.cartalk.com/Radio/Show

- Michael Feldman's Whad'Ya Know? (comedy/game)
  www.notmuch.com/Show

- A Prairie Home Companion (Garrison Keillor, et al.)
  www.prairiehome.org

- Radio Netherlands (pop music)
  www.rnw.nl

- Sounds Eclectic (alternative/world music)
  www.soundseclectic.com

Other Cool Audio Apps

The applications I have covered so far are only a taste of what Ubuntu has in store for you via its repositories. You can start out by browsing though the offerings listed in the Add Applications tool. You can also perform searches in Synaptic for other applications you hear about on the Internet or that I mention in this section. Try them out, keep them if you like them, or remove them if you don't. After all, it doesn't cost you anything in Linux.

To give you a starting point, I will mention a few applications that I think might be worth investigating.

XMMS

The X MultiMedia System (XMMS) was the original king of Linux audio players. Set up to look like a component stereo (with movable components!), XMMS (shown in Figure 15-19) is skinnable, takes up little desktop space, and has a variety of features beneath its simple surface. It also works quite well in conjunction with other audio apps. To find out more, check out my article at www.linuxdevcenter.com/pub/a/linux/2004/04/15/xmms_tips .html. Search Synaptic for *xmms*, install it, and find it under **Applications ▶ Sound & Video**.

Figure 15-19: Different faces of the versatile audio player XMMS

Streamtuner

If you are an Internet radio junkie, there is probably no application as useful to you as Streamtuner (Figure 15-20). Streamtuner is, as its name implies, an online radio stream tuner. It works by downloading lists of available streams from a variety of sources, which you can then easily browse. When you find something you like, just select the stream, click the **Play** button, and the stream will open in the player of your choice, though it works best with RealPlayer or XMMS. Search for *streamtuner*, install it, and run the command streamtuner.

Figure 15-20: Browsing Internet radio streams with Streamtuner

Streamripper

If you installed Streamtuner, you might also want to install Streamripper, which is a sort of Internet audio stream recorder. It works in conjunction with Streamtuner, allowing you to rip the streams you are listening to (and even those you aren't listening to) and save them as MP3 files. To record a stream from within Streamtuner, just right-click the target stream, and then select **Record** in the popup menu. To get Streamripper, do a Synaptic search for *streamripper* (not *kstreamripper*) and install it.

EasyTag and Audio Tag Tool

For the true audio geek, these two applications allow you to alter the tags of your MP3 and Ogg Vorbis music files. EasyTag is the more full featured of the two, but Audio Tag Tool (Figure 15-21) has a friendlier user interface. Give 'em both a try and see what you think. Search Synaptic for *easytag* or *tagtool*, install one, and locate it under **Applications ▶ Sound & Video**.

LMMS

Linux MultiMedia Studio (LMMS) is a hybrid tracker/sequencer/synthesizer/sampler that is easy to use—at least that's what the LMMS home page suggests when it promises "easy music-production for everyone." I can't swear to that fact myself, as I don't know much about apps in this genre, but there is a lot of hoopla about it out there in the Linux world, and it sure looks cool, as you can see in Figure 15-22. It sounds really cool too (try out the demos once you install it). Search Synaptic for *lmms*, install it, and run the command lmms.

Figure 15-21: Editing MP3 and Ogg Vorbis file tags in Audio Tag Tool

Figure 15-22: Creating music with LMMS

16

PLUGGIN' IN THE PENGUIN
Ubuntu and Your iPod

With all the talk in the previous chapter about ripping, encoding, and playing back audio files, you may be wondering whether or not you'll be able to transfer any of those files to your iPod using Linux.

Well, you will be happy to know that Ubuntu does iPods, even Nanos. You will also be happy to know that using your iPod on your Ubuntu system is quite easy. All you have to do is plug your iPod into one of your computer's USB ports, after which Ubuntu will automatically mount it and place an iPod icon on your desktop (Figure 16-1). Yes, no longer do you have to mess around with mount and unmount commands or editing system tables. Just plug in your pod, and Ubuntu will do the rest.

Figure 16-1: A desktop icon for a mounted iPod

Knowing Your Limits

Although you can use your iPod in Ubuntu, you should remember that support for such devices is still rather new. Because of that, there is likely to be the occasional odd moment while working with your iPod. I have been using mine without problems, but a friend did lose all his data when he managed to freeze his system doing something bizarre. The same thing happened to me on a Mac, so I guess that's just the life of the pod. Anyway, if you do happen to lose all the data on your iPod or somehow corrupt its system, you can just use Apple's iPod Updater while in Windows to bring it back to normal and repopulate its song library from your hard disk.

If your iPod already has songs on it that you ripped using iTunes, you will be happy to know that such MP3s pose no problem. They are MP3s, after all. If, however, you have files encoded in iTunes' default AAC format, you should be aware that Linux does not have much in the way of playback support. Only XMMS, installed along with the XMMS-MP4 plugin, seems to provide an easy way for you to play such files. As for the protected AAC files you might have bought from the iTunes store—well, forget about playing those back on Linux. Nevertheless, these playback support limits shouldn't prove to be a problem—you can still add regular or protected AAC files to playlists, copy them to your hard disk, and delete them from your iPod in Linux.

For a Linux diehard, however, there is one big problem with regard to encoded audio formats (and it isn't a limitation only in Linux): iPods do not support Ogg Vorbis files. There is talk that Apple might include support in future iPods, but I wouldn't hold my breath. In the meantime, you can quite simply convert your Ogg Vorbis files to MP3 format for use on your iPod, though there will be a bit of a loss in quality. (This is understandable, considering both formats have their own, incompatible methods of compression which require the throwing out of actual music data.) Of course, if you originally encoded your audio files in FLAC format, this quality issue will be moot. You'll learn more about this in "Converting Audio File Formats" on page 278.

iPod Filesystem Formats

Regardless of which iPod you're talking about, all iPods have a formatted filesystem, just like your hard disk. In fact, with the exception of the Shuffle and the Nano, they actually have hard disks inside them. The filesystem format that is in place on your iPod depends on which system you originally used it on. If you first used it on a Mac, it will be in Apple's HFS+ file format. If you first used it on your Windows machine, it will be in Microsoft's FAT32 format.

Actually, in the short term, it doesn't matter which filesystem your iPod was formatted by; Ubuntu will usually mount either one, allowing you to browse through all the files on your little white beastie. If your iPod is HFS+ formatted, however, browsing and exporting tracks is just about all you will be able to dependably do, assuming your system does mount it. It is important that your iPod be FAT32 formatted if you want to really use it as you would in Windows or, ironically, Mac OS.

Determining Your iPod's Format

How do you know whether your iPod is HFS+ or FAT32 formatted? Well, as I said, it is basically a matter of knowing which system you've been using your iPod with up until now. When you first plugged your fresh, out-of-the-box iPod into your computer, it really couldn't do anything yet. At that time, your Windows or Mac system popped up some wizard asking you to run the iPod Updater tool. That tool is primarily a formatter, which formats your device in FAT32 if you're running it in Windows and HFS+ if you're running it on a Mac.

If you've been a two-OS sort of person up until now and have been happily using your iPod on both a Mac and a Winbox, then you can be sure that your iPod was formatted using FAT32, because Windows spews out chalk spittle when it tries to deal with anything that Microsoft itself didn't create. In other words, Windows can't read drives formatted by HFS+, while Mac OS can read both HFS+ and FAT32 drives. If you are using an iPod Shuffle, you can also be sure that it is FAT32 formatted, because all iPod Shuffles are—period.

Of course, if you're a prove-it-to-me kind of person, you can seek truth from facts by going to the **Applications** menu, selecting **Accessories ▸ Text Editor**, and then opening the file /etc/mtab in the text editor to reveal the format of your iPod. Just look for a line that says something like /dev/sda2 /media/ipod or /dev/sdb2 /media/ipod and see what is listed to the right of that. If it says vfat, then you know your device is FAT32 formatted. If not, well . . . you're just going to have to change it.

Reformatting Your iPod

And how do you change your iPod from HFS+ to FAT32 format? First you're going to have to find a machine running Windows XP (preferably Service Pack 2 for more recent iPods) and a recent edition of iTunes. Once you've found your machine, you need to go to www.apple.com/ipod/download and download the most recent Windows version of the iPod Updater you can find there. Once you've downloaded and installed the updater, you will be asked if you would like to restart your machine (because the updater requires you to do so). Just say no for the time being, and plug your powered-up iPod into one of the machine's USB ports. Windows will go through one of its found-new-hardware scenarios and then ask you to restart the machine. This time you can agree to it, so go ahead.

When the machine starts up again, the iPod Updater will automatically detect that you have an iPod in a non-Microsoft format connected to the machine and ask you if want to update it. You do, so click **Yes**, after which the iPod Updater will appear (Figure 16-2).

Before you go any further, make sure that you have everything on that iPod backed up somewhere, because the updater is going to reformat your iPod, and that means that it is going to wipe it clean. Of course, if the iPod is sort of a backup of what you've got on your computer already, this shouldn't really be an issue. Once you are ready to roll, just click the **Restore** button in the Updater window, and then click **Restore** again in the confirmation window that appears.

Figure 16-2: The iPod Updater in Windows

When the process is complete, run iTunes to perform the final setup steps. If your iPod does not soon appear in the left pane of the iTunes window, close all your applications, restart the system, and run iTunes again. Your iPod should appear in iTunes this time around. When it does, iTunes will present you with a brief wizard that you can pretty much handle on your own. The only direction I will give here is that when you come to the wizard page that asks you if you want iTunes to automatically update your iPod with your photo and music collections, deselect the two checkboxes; doing otherwise could lead to unwanted weirdness down the line.

Once the process is done, you will have a properly configured, FAT32-formatted, and all but empty iPod that is ready for use in Linux, Windows, and Mac OS. You can even use your iPod now on all three systems interchangeably, though I would only do so if the auto-update function is disabled.

Auto-Updating Your iPod

When you enable auto-update on your iPod via iTunes, the function is set up within your iPod itself. With a FAT32-formatted iPod, you can use your iPod on a Winbox, Mac, or Linuxbox—or all of them interchangeably. If you set up your iPod to auto-update songs and playlists, however, you are leaving yourself open for trouble unless you have exactly the same music collection on your Linux, Mac, and Windows machines.

The reason for this is simple. While iTunes allows you to add files to your iPod, it does not allow you to copy files from it. The auto-update feature is thus strictly a one-way street. This means that when you hook up your auto-update–enabled iPod to an iTunes-enabled computer, iTunes will automatically add the tracks in its library to your iPod, and, more frighteningly, it will remove any tracks from your iPod that are not present in its library. I learned this the hard way when I took my wife's loaded iPod to work and plugged it into my office Winbox with its completely empty iTunes library. When I brought the little podster back home to her with nothing at all on it, what ensued wasn't pretty.

If you have an iPod that is already in FAT32 format, it is best for you to disable the auto-update function on your iPod while it is connected to your Winbox, before bringing your iPod into the Linux world. To do this in Windows, just go to the **iTunes Preferences** (while your iPod is connected), click the **iPod** tab, and then select **Manually manage songs and playlists** (Figure 16-3).

Figure 16-3: Disabling the auto-update function on your iPod via iTunes in Windows

Managing Your iPod in Ubuntu

Normally in Windows and Mac OS, you load files to your iPod via iTunes, but, of course, since Apple has not created a Linux version of that popular application (and I doubt it ever will), you will have to find some other way to go about things. Fortunately, there are a few Linux applications that can work to various degrees with your iPod, including two you learned about in Chapter 15: amaroK and Rhythmbox.

In fact, Rhythmbox is set as the default application for iPods in Ubuntu, and as such it will automatically appear once your iPod is connected to your machine and mounted by your system. All you have to do then is click the IPOD icon in the left pane of the Rhythmbox window, and you can see the contents of your iPod. Click the small arrow to the right of the IPOD icon in the left pane, and you can also see your collection of playlists. But other than all that seeing, there isn't much more you can do with your iPod via Rhythmbox.

However, there are a few other applications, specifically designed for use with your iPod, that are arguably a bit more useful. These are the de facto Linux standards (in the GNOME world, anyway): gtkpod and YamiPod, a freeware entry, available in Linux, Windows, and Mac versions.

Managing Your iPod's Audio Files in gtkpod

The most commonly used Linux application for iPod file handling is gtkpod, which is shown in Figure 16-4. It is a pretty straightforward application with a fairly large user base, which means you should be able to get a lot of questions answered in Ubuntu and other Linux online forums should you have any. It also handles most of the functions that one uses when dealing with an iPod, including album cover art (but it does not handle photos other than that).

Figure 16-4: Managing your iPod with gtkpod

Downloading, Installing, and Running gtkpod

Of course, in order to use gtkpod, you first have to download and install it. You can do this via Synaptic by doing a search for *gtkpod* and then installing gtkpod-aac following the installation steps in Chapter 5. If you didn't install the list of files mentioned in Project 15A on page 240, now would be a good time to do so. After that, plug your iPod into one of your computer's USB ports, if you haven't already. Once your iPod is mounted (once the desktop icon appears and Rhythmbox opens) go to the **Applications** menu, and select **Sound & Video ▶ gtkpod**. You can close Rhythmbox if you like.

Using gtkpod

When the gtkpod window opens, you should see two entries in the left pane: one called Local and another with the name of your iPod. Sometimes there will be some other name there instead. Mine read amaroK, for some unknown reason. If you find yourself facing a similar naming mismatch, just change the name for the top entry so that it matches that of your iPod.

Once you've come to grips with the name thing, display the contents of your iPod by clicking the entry for your iPod in the left pane and then clicking the **Read** button. The contents of your iPod will appear in the right pane. If you have any playlists on your iPod, you can also click the small arrow to the left of your iPod's name in the left pane of the window, which will reveal the lists you have created.

You can add new songs or folders full of songs by clicking the **+File** or **+Dirs** buttons below the menu bar and then navigating to the items you want to add. You can also create playlists either by clicking **+Playlists** to create a playlist of the contents of a particular folder, or by clicking the **New PL** button to build your own playlist.

In the case of the latter method, a new list will appear in the Playlists pane at the left side of the window, after which you just drag the songs you want from the right pane in order to build your list. Just be sure to drag the files directly onto the playlist icon, as gtkpod can be a bit finicky in this department. You can also add songs to existing lists in the same way.

While on the topic of dragging and dropping, it is worth noting that you can add songs to your iPod library by simply dragging them from your Music folder (or any other folder) and then dropping them in the right pane of the gtkpod window. If you want to add a song to both your iPod's library and a specific playlist, drag a file or directory from your Music folder to the icon of the playlist in question. Pretty cool.

Album Art and Tag Handling

Tag editing, including album cover images, is another area in which gtkpod can prove quite useful. Click any track in the playlist, select **Edit Details**, and the Details window for that track will appear (Figure 16-5). In that window you can edit all of the tag entries (artist, album, track title, genre, and so on), and, very importantly, you can set the album cover art for the track. Once you have finished making your changes, click the **Apply** button, and then click **OK**.

Figure 16-5: Editing tags in gtkpod

Copying Files from Your iPod to Your Hard Disk

A handy feature of gtkpod that isn't available in iTunes (at least not without a special freeware plugin) is the ability to copy songs from your iPod to your hard disk. To do this, select the tracks or playlists you want to export (hold the CTRL key to make multiple selections or use the tabs to select whole artists or genres if you like), click the **File** menu, and select **Export Tracks from Database**. A submenu will then appear, showing three choices: *Selected Playlist, Selected Tab Entry,* or *Selected Tracks.* Choose the entry that matches your selections.

This approach works well enough, but it doesn't seem to work for AAC files. In that case, just drag the file in question from the gtkpod window to your desktop, and the file will automatically be copied there. That file, however, will not have its original filename. It will have an odd name, such as *INEI.m4a* or *OSPO.m4a*. The files exported in this manner are themselves fine; all you need to do is rename them as you would rename any other file (right-click the file, and then select **Rename**—in case you forgot).

Playing Tracks on Your iPod with gtkpod

It is possible to use gtkpod in order to play the tracks on your iPod, though gtkpod must use a helper application to do this, as it has no playback capabilities of its own. The default helper app for this purpose is XMMS, which isn't a bad choice—especially if you want to have headache-free AAC file support. Of course, if you haven't installed XMMS, the default setup won't do you any good. You must, therefore, either choose a different helper app, such as Rhythmbox or amaroK, or run Synaptic, doing a search for *xmms* and installing xmms and xmms-mp4 (if you want AAC playback support).

If you decide to change the audio helper application for gtkpod, open the gtkpod Preferences window by going to the **Edit** menu and selecting **Edit Preferences**. Once in the Preferences window, click the **Tools** tab, and then click the uppermost **Browse** button. In the window that appears, scroll up and select **rhythmbox** or **amarok** (depending on which you prefer). Once your choice is made, click the **OK** button, and then once back to the Preferences window, repeat the process, this time clicking the second **Browse** button. Click **Apply** and then **OK** to record your changes and close the Preferences window.

Finishing Up the Job with gtkpod

Once you've done all you want to do with gtkpod, click the **Sync** button to record the changes to your iPod. You can then quit gtkpod. After that, right-click the desktop icon for your iPod, and select **Unmount Volume**. When the desktop icon disappears, you can disconnect your iPod from your computer.

Using YamiPod for Your iPod File Management Needs

A relative newcomer to the iPod file management arena is YamiPod. YamiPod, which also comes in Mac and Windows versions, looks like a cleaned-up version of gtkpod; YamiPod's layout is more straightforward, making it easier to use in many ways. It also allows audio-direct, helper-less playback (which gtkpod doesn't), and it is easier to deal with in terms of playlist creation and handling.

Downloading, Installing, and Running YamiPod

To get YamiPod, you'll need to download it yourself from the project's website at www.yamipod.com. Just go the site's Downloads page, and then download YamiPod to your hard disk. The file will appear on your disk as a tarball, so first extract the tarball, and then move the yam-linux folder, which is the product of that extraction, to your home folder. Once you've done that, there is one small chore you need to perform before you can run the application: copying the libfmodex file within the yam-linux folder to the /usr/lib folder. Since /usr/lib is in protected territory, you will have to use the sudo command to perform the copy procedure.

Here are the steps:

1. Open a Terminal window, type **cd yam-linux**, and press ENTER.
2. In the same Terminal window, type the following command, and press ENTER (and make sure to leave a space on either side of cp and between so.* and /usr):

```
sudo cp libfmodex.so.* /usr/lib
```

3. When prompted for your password, type it, and press ENTER. When your user prompt reappears, you can close the Terminal window.

As YamiPod itself is an executable binary file, you don't have to install it to put it to work, and you are now ready to step into action. To get things under way, plug your iPod into one of your USB ports, and then double-click the YamiPod file within the yam-linux folder. YamiPod will appear as a small window until it reads the contents of your iPod, after which the window should expand into something like the window in Figure 16-6.

Figure 16-6: Managing your iPod with YamiPod

Using YamiPod

Working with YamiPod is very simple. To add songs to your iPod, just drag tracks or folders from your Music folder to the bottom pane of the YamiPod interface or to any open playlist in the playlist pane. An Add To Ipod window (Figure 16-7) will appear, showing the tag information for each of the songs you've just dragged over. In that window you can edit the tags for each of the songs, if you'd like to, before adding them to the library. When you've finished making your changes, just click the **Add All** button, and the songs will be immediately added to your iPod's library.

Figure 16-7: Adding songs to your iPod with YamiPod

To create a playlist, click the + button near the top-right corner of the window, and name your list in the New Playlist window that appears. Once you've made your choice, click **OK**. You can then drag the tracks you want to add to the list from the main library pane in the bottom half of the window. You can also drag files directly from your Music folder to the Playlist pane, thereby adding those tracks to the playlist and your iPod's library at the same time.

If you would like to remove a track from the library, just right-click the track in question, and then select **Delete song** in the popup menu. To remove a playlist, just select the targeted list from the drop-down menu button at the right-top corner of the window, and then click the – button to the right of that.

Finishing Up Your YamiPod Session

Since YamiPod performs changes to your iPod in real time as you perform those changes within the YamiPod window, wrapping things up is quite simple. Just click the small, circular eject button at the very bottom-right corner of the YamiPod window. YamiPod will then close, and your iPod will be automatically unmounted.

Exporting Files from Your iPod with YamiPod

Like gtkpod, YamiPod allows you to export files from your iPod to your hard disk. To copy songs from the library in YamiPod, select the tracks you want to copy in the main library pane (and hold down the CTRL key while doing so if you are making multiple selections), right-click any one of the selected files, and then select **Copy song to** in the popup menu.

Podcasts

Although both YamiPod and gtkpod allow you to copy podcasts to your iPod, neither application provides you with a list of available podcast feeds. YamiPod does have a feature by which it can download the feeds you want if you provide the URL, but I don't recommend doing that, as it seems to crash the program.

The result of these facts is that if you want to look for podcasts and add them to your iPod's library, you will have to do a little more work than you're used to. One application that can help is iPodder (Figure 16-8), which you can download and install via Synaptic by doing a search for *ipodder*, and then . . . well, you know the steps by now.

Figure 16-8: iPodder podcast browser and receiver

Once you select and download your podcasts, iPodder will place them in the downloads subfolder of the iPodderData folder that it creates for you in your home folder. To add these podcasts to your iPod in gtkpod, create a playlist called Podcasts (if there isn't one there already), and then add the podcast file to the playlist, as you would any audio file, by simply dragging it onto that playlist.

You can add podcasts to your iPod via YamiPod in almost the same way. Just select the **Podcasts** playlist from the drop-down menu button at the top-right corner of the YamiPod window, and then drag the file to the top-right pane of the window.

Setting Up Your System to Automatically Launch YamiPod or gtkpod

If you like, you can set up your system so that YamiPod or gtkpod automatically launches when you plug your iPod into one of your USB ports. To do this, go to the **System** menu, and select **Preferences ▸ Removable Drives and Media**. When the Preferences window appears, click the **Multimedia** tab, and then check the box next to the words *Play music files when connected* in the iPod section of that tab. In the Command box, type **gtkpod** if you want to use that application, or if you prefer YamiPod, click the **Browse** button and navigate your way to the YamiPod binary file within your home folder. Once you're done, the Preferences window should look something like Figure 16-9. If so, click **Close**.

Figure 16-9: Setting up your system to run YamiPod when you plug in your iPod

Photo Transfer with GPixPod

Ever since the iPod Photo appeared in 2004, iPods have been able to display photos. Unfortunately, until recently there was no simple way to transfer photos from your computer to your iPod in Linux. Things have, quite fortunately, changed since the appearance of a handy application called GPixPod. GPixPod (Figure 16-10) is, admittedly, an application still in development. Nevertheless, it should work on all color iPods, though it is not yet fully compatible with the original iPod Photo. Since version 0.4.1, it also seems to work with the Nano.

You can get GPixPod from its project page at http://sourceforge.net/projects/gpixpod. Click the **Download GPixPod** button, and then on the next page that appears, click the **Download** button. On the next page, click the **gpixpod-0.4.4_all.deb** (or newer) link, which will bring you to a list of mirrors. Select the one closest to you, and then wait for the GPixPod download to complete.

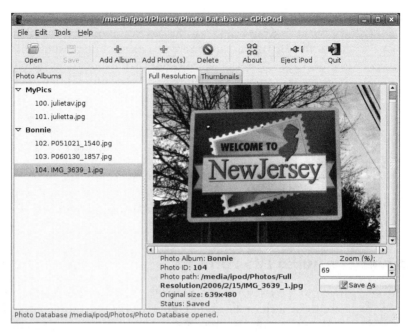

Figure 16-10: Adding photos to your iPod with GPixPod

Once the gpixpod-0.4.4_all.deb package is on your hard disk, you have to install it. Rather than resort to the command line, as you did when installing DEB packages back in Chapter 9, let's go the easy route by just double-clicking the package itself. This will bring up the package installer, gdebi (Figure 16-11).

NOTE   *Make sure that neither Synaptic nor the Add/Remove Applications utility are open when running gdebi, as only one package management tool can run at a time.*

Figure 16-11: Installing GPixPod via gdebi

As you can see, the gdebi package installer looks like a piece cut out of the Synaptic window. It provides a description of the application, details about the file you are attempting to install, and a list of what's included in the package. To get down to the actual installation, just click the **Install Package** button. A small window will appear, telling you that you need administrative rights in order to proceed. Click **Grant** in that window (the equivalent of typing your password when using Synaptic), after which the installation will begin. Once GPixPod is installed, you can run it by going to the **Applications** menu and selecting **Graphics ▸ GPixPod**.

NOTE *You cannot add photos to the GPixPod interface without first connecting your iPod to your system. You should also note that you can not view images added to GPixPod's database in the right pane of the application window until you save your changes by clicking the Save button.*

Converting Audio File Formats

If you would like to convert MP3 to Ogg Vorbis format or vice versa, SoundConverter (shown in Figure 16-12) is an application that makes it all quite simple. Because SoundConverter does not come bundled with Ubuntu, you will have to install it yourself (if you didn't install it in Chapter 5). To do so, just run Synaptic, search for *soundconverter*, and install it.

All you have to do to use SoundConverter after that is add the songs you want to convert to the main pane by clicking either the **Add File** or **Add Folder** buttons. If you prefer, you can also drag files from your Music folder (or wherever else you store your audio files).

Figure 16-12: Converting audio file formats with SoundConverter

Once you've chosen the files to convert, you need to choose which format to convert them to. You can do this by clicking the **Preferences** button and then making your choice in the Preferences window (Figure 16-13). While you're there, it is also a good idea to tell SoundConverter to place your converted files in a location other than the folder where the original files are stored. Doing this prevents having to deal with duplicates in Linux audio playback applications that automatically scan your Music folder, such as amaroK. This is not an issue in either gtkpod or YamiPod, as they will not allow you to add Ogg Vorbis files to their library lists. You might also want to check the box next to the words *Create subfolders* in order to keep things organized. Once you have set things up and are ready to convert, click **Close** in the Preferences window, and then click **Convert** in the main window. SoundConverter will then begin doing its stuff.

Figure 16-13: Setting conversion preferences in SoundConverter

17

COUCH PENGUINS
Video and DVD Playback in Ubuntu

Now that we've covered much of what Ubuntu can do in terms of audio, let's turn our attention to what is arguably the second most important of its talents in our CNN/MTV–era world: video. Ubuntu is quite capable in terms of video playback, allowing you to view video files you download from the Internet or from your digital movie camera, video CDs (VCDs), unencrypted DVDs (encrypted ones, too, with a little more work up front), and some Internet video streams. It even allows you to download movies from your digital video camera and then edit them.

Playing Video Streams with RealPlayer

In Chapter 15, we covered RealPlayer's role as an audio application that allows you to play Internet audio streams. Audio streams are not the only thing that RealPlayer can handle, however; you can use it to play video streams as well. If you would like to try out RealPlayer's capabilities for playing video streams, or if you just happen to be a fan of Katie Holmes, point your web browser to www.katieholmespictures.com/movies.shtml, scroll down to the

Videos section, and then try out one of the many clips available there. Once you have made your selection, RealPlayer will pop up and begin playing the stream in a slightly enlarged window.

If the Beatles are more your cup of tea, try "The Birth of Beatlemania" at NPR's All Songs Considered site (www.npr.org/programs/asc/archives/ beatles40). Be sure to click the **Real Video** link on that page. Firefox will then pop up one of its what-should-I-do-with-this-thing windows with Movie Player listed as the default player. Movie Player doesn't do as good a job with RealMedia streams, so you definitely want to change things. In that window, click the drop-down menu button, which at this point says *Movie Player*, and select **Other**. When the Choose Helper Application window appears, double-click **File System** in the left pane of the window, navigate your way to /opt/RealPlayer in the right pane, and then scroll down until you find the file realplay. When you find it, click it once to select it, and then click **Open**. Once back in that original what-should-I-do window, check the box next to the words *Do this automatically for files like this from now on*. Your window should look like that in Figure 17-1. If so, click the **OK** button, after which RealPlayer will start up and play the stream.

Figure 17-1: Telling Firefox what to do with the RealAudio document

If you would like to view the video at an enlarged size, you have two ways of going about it. The first and easiest way is to drag one of the bottom corners of the RealPlayer window until it is the size you prefer. The other way is to go to the **View** menu and select **Fullscreen** or **Zoom ▶ Double Size**.

DVDs

Your system also allows you to play DVDs; however, due to licensing concerns, playback is limited to unencrypted disks. Unfortunately, this rules out a vast majority of the DVD movies you buy or rent at your local video shop and leaves you with a rather limited choice of movies that you can play on your computer. Of course, DVDs created on personal computers (such as the DVD slideshows that people create these days with applications such as iDVD on the Mac) pose no problem. Given the limited offerings in the unencrypted DVD world, you will no doubt want to enable your system to play back the encrypted variety, so you will learn to do so later in this chapter.

Can I Play Foreign DVDs?

Your computer can play DVDs of any broadcast standard (NTSC, PAL, or SECAM) and of any regional encoding. This is a better setup than that DVD player you have hooked up to your TV, because the vast majority of stand-alone DVD players in the United States (and I would venture to guess that the size of that majority is 99.9 percent) do not allow you to play anything other than Region 1 NTSC disks (NTSC being the broadcast standard in the United States and what its televisions are designed to display, while the DVD region is 1). This information is usually provided on the back of DVD packages (see examples in Figure 17-2), though the packaging for most disks produced for the US market does not include it.

Figure 17-2: Examples of regional encoding labels on DVD packages

Despite the wonderful everything-goes nature of your computer in terms of DVD playback, there is a serious caveat to bear in mind. Depending on the manufacturer of your DVD drive, you will only be able to switch back and forth between DVDs of differing regional encodings four or five times. After that, the drive will be locked into the regional encoding of the disk you were playing at that time . . . *forever*. This is unrelated to your operating system—it is strictly a hardware matter. The only exception to this region-lock rule are those DVDs labeled *Region Free* or *ALL* (sometimes inaccurately labeled as *Region 0*), which can be played on any DVD player in any region, and thus do not register as a regional encoding switch when you plop one of them in your computer's DVD drive.

If your drive does eventually lock into one regional encoding, especially one for which you have few DVDs, there is some good news. That news comes in the form of Videolan's libdvdcss2, the library you will install in the following project which will allow you to play back encrypted DVDs. In addition to that primary function, libdvdcss2 also, in theory, allows you to play back DVDs from multiple regions even if your DVD drive is already locked into one region. It does this by performing a *cryptic attack* (to use Videolan's term for it) on your drive until it can find the disk key for that drive. Of course, this process of cryptic bombardment can take several minutes, so it is not the optimal way of going about things. Better than being stuck, though. Whether or not this process of bypassing regional encodings is legal remains a subject of debate, so if you are concerned about such things, you should do a little research.

Project 17: Installing Support for Encrypted DVDs

As I already mentioned, Ubuntu does not allow you to play encrypted DVDs from the start. In order for you watch such DVDs (and that would be the vast majority of them), you need to install a whole bunch of stuff, with the package libdvdcss2 being the most crucial of all. Fortunately, if you installed all of the files I mentioned back in Project 15A on page 240, you are almost there—all you need is libdvdcss2. Of course, if you didn't install those files back in Project 15A, you'd better do so now, because you won't be able to go on without them.

You can get the libdvdcss2 file by running a script that is included in one of those packages I was just nagging you about—gstreamer0.10-plugins, to be exact. That script will download, install, and set up the libdvdcss2 file for you. To run the script, close all open package-management software windows (Synaptic, the Add/Remove Programs utility, or Update Manager), open a Terminal window, and then type the following line:

```
sudo /usr/share/doc/libdvdread3/examples/install-css.sh
```

Once you've typed that line and pressed ENTER, you will be prompted for your password. Type it, press ENTER, and the script will begin its job of downloading, installing, and then setting up libdvdcss2, with the progress of each of these steps shown in the Terminal window. You will know the installation and setup are complete when your cursor is once again blinking at your user prompt. You are then ready for some real DVD viewing.

Totem Movie Player

The default video player in Ubuntu is Totem, and now that you have installed libdvdcss2 in Project 17, you can actually put it to some good use. Totem, as you can see in Figure 17-3, has a very simple interface, which makes using it equally simple. You can run Totem by going to the **Applications** menu and selecting **Sound & Video ▸ Movie Player**. You can also run it by simply placing a DVD in your drive, because Ubuntu is set up to run Totem any time you do so. If you don't happen to have a DVD on hand but you want to see Totem in action, you can also bring it up by double-clicking that Ubuntu video that comes with your system in the Examples folder (Experience Ubuntu.ogg).

Switching Totems

Before going on any further, I should mention that Totem, despite all that simplicity I talked about, can be an absolute pain in the proverbial posterior. You may be one of the lucky ones, but for me and many others, Totem is as cooperative as a crocodile in your local swimming hole. The problem is not actually Totem itself, but rather the gstreamer back end that performs its video processing.

Figure 17-3: Totem Movie Player

Totem, you see, is merely a graphical *front end* that provides you with an easy way to use software that works in the background—a *back end*, which in this case is gstreamer. All is not lost, though, because there is a version of Totem that utilizes the Xine video-processing back end instead of gstreamer. That much more cooperative version is available via Synaptic.

If you find yourself having problems with Totem as is, I strongly recommend installing the Xine version. To do this, run Synaptic, search for *totem-xine*, and install the back end. Once you're done, you won't notice any changes up front. You will have the exact same Totem interface in the exact same menu location, but you'll be a much happier camper because Totem will then work as it's supposed to. You will experience, among other things, superior sound (or at least better volume), more dependable DVD playback, and less quirky playback of Windows Media Video (WMV) files.

Using Totem to Play DVDs, VCDs, and Other Multimedia Files

As I already mentioned, you can play a DVD in Totem by simply placing your DVD in the drive, after which Totem will open and begin playing your movie. If you've got a copy of *Red Detachment of Women* on VCD that you're aching to watch, you can do so in the same way. Just pop the VCD in your drive; Totem will start up and begin playing it.

Totem not only plays DVDs and VCDs, but it can also play MPEG files and, because you installed that big cocktail of packages I keep going on about, it can play WMV files too. You can play such files by either double-clicking them directly or going to the Totem **Movie** menu, selecting **Open**, and then navigating to the video file you want to view.

Making Things Look a Bit Better in Totem

One thing you may notice when using the Xine version of Totem is that videos seem to look a bit washed out. This can be easily fixed by going to the Totem **Edit** menu and selecting **Preferences**. In the Totem Preferences window, click the **Display** tab, and then lower the **Brightness** and **Contrast** sliders to points similar to those shown in Figure 17-4. You can, of course, change things to suit your own tastes. Once you're done, click **Close**.

Figure 17-4: Adjusting brightness and contrast settings in Totem

Totem as an Audio Player?

You may have noticed while in the Display tab of the Preferences window that there was a Visual Effects section. Well, those visual effects aren't for the videos you play, but rather are visualizations to accompany your audio files when played via Totem (Figure 17-5). Yes, Totem not only does video, it does audio as well. In fact, it is, somewhat oddly, the default audio player for Ogg Vorbis and MP3 files in Ubuntu. Just double-click one of those files, and sure enough, Totem will be the application that pops up, blasting your ears out with your favorite melodies. Of course, you can also play such files from the Totem **Movie** menu, by selecting **Open** and then navigating to the songs you want to play. If you have a CD in your disk drive, you can even use Totem as a CD player by going to the **Movie** menu and selecting **Play Disc 'Audio Disc'**.

Figure 17-5: Totem as an audio player

A Couple of Other Cool Totem Features

There are a couple of other cool features in Totem that you might like to know about. One is its ability to perform screen captures of whatever video you happen to be viewing at the time. Just go to the **Edit** menu, select **Take Screenshot**, and you've got yourself a screen capture—a still image taken from a video file.

Another feature worth mentioning is Totem's Sidebar. As you no doubt noticed, at the bottom-right corner of the Totem window, there is a Sidebar button. If you click that button, a new pane will open at the right side of the Totem window. In that pane you can load, create, and save playlists. Such lists can consist of any combination of supported video or audio files, thus providing you with the whole multimedia banana. Any time you play a file in Totem, that file appears in the Playlist pane, but you can also add items to the list by simply dragging the files there from your desktop or any Nautilus window.

Using Your Digital Video Camera

Although they haven't achieved the ubiquitous status of digital still cameras, digital video cameras have become increasingly common in recent years. Likewise, while Linux support for still digital cameras is quite good, its support for DV cameras can be called . . . well, let's just say it's "progressing."

Don't be discouraged by my tone in that last sentence, though. You should have no trouble downloading video from your camera to your computer, editing those video files, and adding effects and even subtitles. To be honest, there are still some problems, especially in the area of file format conversions, but, as with all things Linux, it will only be a matter of time until the wrinkles are ironed out. There are also a couple of cool video editing apps that, while not quite ready for prime time, seem promising and are well worth keeping an eye on: PiTiVi and Diva.

For the time being, however, the application of choice for the digital video camera user is Kino. Kino, shown in Figure 17-6, is an iMovie-like application with which you can capture video from your camera and then edit it. To install Kino, open Synaptic and perform a Name and Description search for *kino*. In the list of results that appears, mark and then install **dvdgrab**, **kino**, and **kinoplus**. Once it's installed, you can run Kino by going to the **Applications** menu and selecting **Sound & Video ▸ Kino**.

Setting Up Your System to Capture Digital Video

When you want to transfer a digital image from your digital still camera to your computer, you basically just download it. When you want to transfer a video clip from your DV camera to your computer, however, you have to capture the video stream while you play it; probably the easiest way to go about doing this is by using Kino. Before you can begin capturing video with Kino, however, there are a few steps you must first perform the first time around.

Figure 17-6: Using your digital video camera with Kino

These are the steps:

1. Connect your camera to your computer using the FireWire (IEEE 1394) cable that came with (or you were forced to buy for) your camera.

2. Turn on your DV camera in play mode. Once you've done this, the raw1394 module will appear in your system's /dev directory (if it hasn't already).

3. After a couple of seconds, turn off your camera. You can leave the cable connected.

4. Open a Terminal window, type **cd /dev**, and press ENTER.

5. In the same Terminal window, change the permissions of the raw1394 module, so that everyone on your machine can read and write to it, by typing **sudo chmod a+rw raw1394** and pressing ENTER.

6. You will then be prompted for your password, so type it, and press ENTER.

If all goes without a hitch, you will be returned to your user prompt without any other messages appearing in the Terminal.

Capturing and Editing Digital Video with Kino

Once you have gone through the preparatory steps I've just mentioned, you are ready to capture video from your camera. To do this, connect your camera to your computer by FireWire cable (if it isn't still connected), turn on your camera to Play mode, and then start up Kino. Once Kino is open, click the **Capture** tab to the right of the playback pane.

To get started capturing video, you can use the playback controls located below the playback pane. These control buttons actually control the functions of your camera itself. Start out by clicking the rewind button until you get to the beginning of the video segment you want to capture. Once you get there, click the play button, after which the video on your camera will play back within the Kino window. When you reach the point at which you want to start capturing, click the **Capture** button just above the play back controls in the Kino window. Kino will then start capturing your video to disk (in your home folder by default). To keep things easy to manage, the captured video stream will be split into several files, the number of which depends on the length of the video played.

You will notice that after you click the Capture button, the video playback in the playback pane will stop moving. This being the case, you will need to view the action in your camera's viewer in order to know where you are in the capture process. When you get to the point where you'd like to stop capturing, click the **stop** button. You can then view the captured video by clicking the **Edit** button and then using the playback controls at the bottom of the playback pane. You can also view the video in Timeline view (as shown in Figure 17-7) in order to navigate between the various segments of the video; click the **Timeline** tab, click the segment you wish to view, and then use the playback controls below the playback pane.

Figure 17-7: Kino's Timeline view

If you feel like getting a bit arty, you can also try out the effects available in Kino (some examples of which are shown in Figure 17-8) by clicking the **FX** tab and then playing around with the various effects in the drop-down menu below the words *Video Filter*. Make your choice, specify the segment you'd like to convert (or at least experiment with) by typing the beginning and ending frame numbers in the boxes below the word *Overwrite*, and then click the **Preview** button to see the results without saving the changes to disk. If you do want to convert the segment so as to keep the effect, click the **Render** button, and Kino will create a new file of just that segment. Those files, as well as the original captures, can all be viewed in Totem, which is a better application to use for video viewing, by simply double-clicking the files.

Figure 17-8: Examples of Kino's video effects, before and after

Other Video Apps

I've covered the main video applications in Ubuntu, but there are still others available that you might want to consider. A very popular alternative video/ DVD player, for example, is MPlayer (Figure 17-9), which you can download and install by performing a Synaptic search for *mplayer*. Be sure to download not only mplayer itself, but also mplayer-fonts so as to avoid annoying error messages.

Another video/DVD player you might want to consider is gxine, which is similar in several ways to Totem, but it gives you a bit more control over things. Again, you can download and install gxine via Synaptic by performing a search for *gxine*.

Figure 17-9: The popular video player MPlayer

If you are not only a video watcher but also a budding video artist, then you might want to consider a handy pair of video/DVD authoring and editing tools: QDVD-Author, which is a DVD creator application in the iDVD vein (albeit without the superficial polish of Apple's offering); and DVD::Rip, which, as you might imagine, allows you to rip the contents of a DVD to your hard disk. These applications are available via Synaptic by performing searches for *qdvdauthor* and *dvdrip*.

18

DEFENDING THE NEST
Security

Many a Windows user has entered the Linux fold after a host of bad experiences with *malware* in the Windows world—viruses, spyware, and all sorts of other malicious bits of software code, too numerous to imagine. Windows is also plagued by a seemingly endless array of security vulnerabilities, leaving the system easy prey to invaders with less than noble intentions. Every trip out into cyberspace thus becomes something like a run through the infectious diseases ward of a hospital. For a Windows user, it can sometimes seem that more time is spent ridding the system of viral pests and defending it from invaders than is actually spent getting things done.

Fortunately, Linux does not suffer greatly from such problems, leading to the much-touted claim that Linux is practically virus free and quite secure. There are numerous lines of reasoning proffered to explain Linux's malware- and exploit-resistant nature. One reason is simply popularity—or lack thereof. As Linux is not as widespread a system as Windows is, it is also a much less attractive target of digital evil-doers, who very often seem to be motivated by the challenge and headline-catching glory that comes with creating a truly global virus or finding a theretofore unknown back door.

Another reason is that Linux users, as a general rule, work on their computers in a non-privilege mode, one in which the user does not have the right to install software without a password. This is not the case, at least not by default, in Windows. A virus or other form of malware attached to an email or piggybacked upon another file or application cannot, therefore, install itself in your Linux system without that password . . . well, theoretically, at least. Of course, now that Windows uses its own privilege structure, this point is a bit less of an issue.

There is also the matter of structural design. Every system out there has security holes that can be exploited by digital and human foe alike. Windows might well be called the Swiss cheese of operating systems in this regard. Of course, Linux has its holes too, though far fewer of them than Windows does; and Linux plugs them up through downloadable updates faster, once they are found.

Finally, there is the defensive edge that Ubuntu's pre-configured security policy brings—there are no open incoming ports in Ubuntu desktop systems. This means that your Ubuntu Linux system is even less susceptible to unwanted intrusions.

Does My System Need Protection?

So with all this talk about Linux's great security, you may wonder whether you need to bother worrying about it at all. Well, if you take a look at the Ubuntu forums, you might find yourself a bit confused. When asked whether Linux users need to install antivirus software or firewalls, most users answer with an emphatic *no*. On the other hand, you'll find that there are an awful lot of people out there who have installed or are trying to install that software. Hmmm.

So what's a Linux user to do?

If you are on a network where you transfer a lot of files among a lot of Windows machines, you might want to think about installing some antivirus software, if for nothing more than the good of the Windows systems involved and the users of those systems—your unenlightened (i.e., Windows-using) email pals, for example. You might also want to give it a go if you are, by nature, on the cautious side of the spectrum. Basically, if it makes you feel safer to install some protection, go ahead. If it makes you feel safer to go whole hog and install the full line of defense mechanisms I cover in this chapter, go ahead. After all, either way you go, it isn't going to cost you anything, and it certainly isn't going to hurt you any.

The First Line of Defense

Regardless of the system you happen to be using (though I am assuming that you have become a Linux devotee by now), the first line of defense for any computer permanently hooked up to the Internet is a *router*—an electronic device that allows a number of computers on a local network (such as in your home or at your office) to connect to and share a single connection from your Internet service provider (ISP). While the router is connected to your modem via cable, the connection from the router to the computers on your local network can be wired, wireless, or both.

What has a router got to do with the defense of your computer? Well, most routers include a *firewall*, which essentially functions to keep all of the bad stuff out there on the Web away from your computer, much in the way that the firewall in your car keeps the heat, fumes, and noise from your engine out of the passenger compartment. This built-in firewall is one reason that even people with only one computer, who could just as easily connect their computer directly to their cable or DSL modem, use a router. Of course, just how much security the firewall in your router provides depends on which filters you select in the firewall setup software. For example, a very common and useful filter (particularly for those with a wireless network) limits Internet access to those machines specified on the firewall's access list. This prevents your next-door neighbors from hitching a wireless ride via your ISP connection. They aren't paying the bill, after all.

The setup software for a router is built in to the router itself, so you don't have to worry about software installation and system compatibility. Using your router with Linux is no different than using it with Windows. You can access the software and modify your settings via a simple web browser, as you can see in Figure 18-1. Just type the IP address of the router (usually provided in the owner's manual) in the browser's location bar, press ENTER, and you'll be ready to go.

Figure 18-1: Setting up a router

Software Firewalls

If you don't have a router and don't plan on getting one, or if you have one, but you are bordering on paranoia, you might want to consider using a software firewall, in particular one of the most popular software firewalls available for Linux, Firestarter.

You can download and install Firestarter via Synaptic by doing a search for *firestarter* and then installing it. Once it is installed, run Firestarter by going to the **Applications** menu and selecting **Internet ▶ Firestarter.** You will then be prompted for your password, so type that, and click the **OK** button.

The first time out, Firestarter will open with a pretty self-explanatory setup wizard. If the wizard doesn't seem all that self-explanatory to you, and you're not sure what to do, just accept the default settings by clicking the **Forward** button in each of the wizard screens until you get to the last one (shown in Figure 18-2). In that screen, make sure that the box next to *Start firewall now* is checked, click the **Save** button, and then click **Quit**. When the wizard is finished, the main Firestarter window will appear and, assuming the correct network device was detected and selected, the firewall will be up and running.

Figure 18-2: The last screen of the Firestarter setup wizard

If the wrong network device was selected, a warning window will appear telling you so. In that case, you can do a bit of trial-and-error manipulation by clicking the **Preferences** button in the main Firestarter window and then clicking **Network Settings** in the Preferences window that appears (Figure 18-3). In that window, select one of the other devices listed in the dropdown menu next to the words *Detected device(s)*, and then click the **Accept** button. Once back at the main Firestarter window, click the **Start Firewall** button, and see what happens. If you still can't start the firewall, repeat the process I've just described, this time selecting a different network device.

Figure 18-3: Selecting network devices in Firestarter

Once your firewall is up and running, there is nothing more that you really need to do. You can simply look at the Firestarter window (Figure 18-4) to see what is going on network-wise on your computer—what active connections you have, how much information has been coming and going, and if there have been any events in which, for example, the firewall has blocked an intruder. If you click the **Events** tab, you can then see the details of those events, such as what connection attempts were blocked, where they came from, and when they happened.

Figure 18-4: Firestarter in action

Taking Control of Firestarter

You can control how Firestarter deals with various network events by creating your own *policies*. The default policy set in Firestarter allows you to basically do whatever you normally do via the Internet, while it blocks new connections to your computer from the Internet or any other computer on your network.

To make things a bit more draconian, you can click the **Policy** tab, select **Outbound traffic policy** in the drop-down menu next to the word *Editing*, and then select **Restrictive by default, whitelist traffic**. If you just want to deny anyone working on your computer access to a specific website, for instance, simply click the **Deny connections to host** field to select it, and then click the **Add Rule** button. In the Add New Outbound Rule window, enter the URL for the targeted site, click **Add**, and then click the **Apply Policy** button in the main Firestarter window.

Confirming That Firestarter Runs Automatically

After you run Firestarter the first time, it will set itself to automatically start up whenever you start up your system. Don't be concerned when you don't see the graphical interface you saw when you first started it up; Firestarter will be running in the background, silently protecting your computer.

If you are the doubting type, you can check to see whether or not Firestarter actually is running in the background by opening a Terminal window, typing `sudo /etc/init.d/firestarter status`, and then pressing ENTER. If Firestarter is running, you will see the message `* Firestarter is running. . .` in the Terminal window. Worries over.

Finding Out More

If the world of firewalls is new to you, you can check out the Firestarter home page to learn a bit more. To check out the online manual, just to go to the Firestarter **Help** menu, and select **Online Users' Manual**, which will bring up the page in your web browser. If you prefer to check out the manual before installing Firestarter, point your browser to www.fs-security.com/docs. You will also find a pretty good quick tutorial there.

ClamAV: Antivirus Software, Linux Style

Despite the lack of viruses out there that can wreak havoc upon your Linux system, your computer could still act as a transmitter of Windows viruses. As a result, there are a number of free antivirus scanners out there for Linux users interested in helping to protect Windows users from viruses. These include Aegis (available via Synaptic), Panda Antivirus (www.pandasoftware.com/download/linux.htm), f-Prot (www.f-prot.com), and numerous others. For most Linux users, however, the virus scanner of choice is the open source contender—ClamAV.

Although it can be used on a number of operating systems, ClamAV is considered to be *the* Linux antivirus software package. It is open source, totally free, and you don't have to worry about licenses or suffer the bother of renewing them. Unfortunately, on its own, ClamAV is a command-driven application, which makes it a bit less user-friendly. Fortunately for all involved, there is also a graphical interface available, albeit a simple one, by the name of ClamTk. Both ClamAV and ClamTk are available via Synaptic, so if you want to give them a try, just do a search for *clamtk*, mark it for installation, and then install it. Synaptic will download it, ClamAV, and any other packages needed to make the whole thing work.

Using the ClamAV/ClamTk Duo

Once installed, just click the Run Application panel applet, type `clamtk` in the Run Application window, and then click the **Run** button. This will bring up the Clam Tk Virus Scanner window (Figure 18-5). After it appears, you should set up ClamAV so that it will automatically quarantine any viruses it finds. To do this, go to the **Actions** menu, and select **Quarantine Infected Files**. Then go to the **File** menu, select **Scan Directory**, and, in the left pane of that window, double-click the icon for the folder or disk you want to scan. Once you've done that, click the **OK** button, and ClamAV will start scanning your system. ClamTk will let you know what it (or, rather, ClamAV) is scanning at any given moment in the empty space just below the button bar. If it finds anything suspicious, it will list that item in the main pane of the window.

Figure 18-5: ClamTk—the graphical interface for ClamAV

As I mentioned before, the only viruses you are likely to encounter during a virus scan are those designed for Windows systems, and because those viruses cannot affect your Linux system, focusing your efforts where they are likely to do the most good seems a sound way of doing things. Although it won't hurt you any to scan your entire system for viruses, especially if doing so makes you feel better, it is probably better to focus your virus scanning activities on your Windows partition, if you have one, and on any files that you will be sending as email attachments, particularly to Windows users.

Project 18: Virus Scanning with avast!

While ClamAV may be the virus scanner of choice in the Linux world, my personal favorite is still avast!, which defended me during my Windows years. I think it is easier to use and, for what it's worth, nicer to look at. On the downside, it does require you to register every year so that you can get a license key, but that is hardly a monumental task, and it is still free—at least for home and noncommercial use, which, if my target audience for this book was correctly predicted, should include you. If nothing else, it is worth a try, so just go for it.

18-1: Downloading the avast! RPM and License Key

First you have to get the avast! 4 file and license key. You can do this by opening your web browser and going to www.avast.com/eng/avast-for-linux-workstation.html. Once there, click the **Download** icon on the right side of the page. On the download page, click the **Download** button for the RPM of the avast! Linux Home Edition, and then download the file to your home folder. Once you've done that, click the **registration form** link, and fill out and submit that form. You should receive your license key by email a few minutes later.

18-2: Converting the avast! RPM to a DEB Package

Once the avast! RPM is safely downloaded to your home folder, you need to convert it to an Ubuntu-friendly DEB package using the application Alien, which you installed and learned to use in Chapter 9. Assuming you have Alien installed, just type `sudo alien -d avast*.rpm`, and press ENTER.

After that, type your password when prompted to do so, and then just wait until you get the message `avast4workstation_1.0.4.2_i386.deb generated` (your version number may be different) in the Terminal window. The newly generated DEB package will appear in your home folder along with the original RPM.

18-3: Installing the avast! DEB Package

Now that you've created the avast! DEB package, you can install it using the `dpkg` command, as you did in Chapter 9. Just type `sudo dpkg -i avast*.deb`, and press ENTER. When the Terminal displays your usual user prompt, you will know that you have successfully installed avast! and are ready to move on.

18-4: Running and Using avast!

Once avast! is installed, you can run it by clicking the Run Application panel applet (or pressing ALT-F2), typing **avastgui** in that window, and then clicking the **Run** button. The first time you run avast!, a small window (Figure 18-6) will appear asking you to input your license code. Assuming you registered your free copy of avast! at the beginning of the project as I instructed you to do, your registration key should already be waiting for you in your emailer's inbox. Go have a look, copy the key, and paste it into the text field in the Registration window (you'll have to use the CTRL-V key combination to do this). Once the license key is in place, click the **OK** button.

Figure 18-6: Entering your avast!
license key

The main avast! window (Figure 18-7) will now appear, but before you get started scanning away, it is a good idea to check if there are any new virus watches to be added to your present database. New viruses are constantly appearing in cyberspace, and it is thus necessary to keep avast!'s virus database up to date so that it recognizes any viral newcomers. To perform the update, just click the **Update database** button, and let avast! do its thing.

Figure 18-7: avast! virus scanner

When avast! is done updating the virus database, you can get on to the work of virus scanning by first deciding whether you want to scan just your

Home directory, the entire system, or selected folders. You can also decide how thorough a scan you wish to perform via the three choices available in the middle of the window: Quick, Standard, or Thorough.

Which one of these sensitivity modes you choose depends on how thorough you want the scan to be. The Quick scan just scans files that end in certain extensions (.exe, .scr, .com, .doc, etc.), because these are the file types that are most often virus carriers. The Standard scan targets more files, ignoring extensions, but still limiting the scan to those file types that are usually associated with viruses. Finally, the Thorough scan scans everything and searches for every type of virus.

Once you have made your selections, click the **Start scan** button, and avast! will start doing exactly that—showing its progress within the same window, no less. When the scan is complete, a small window will pop up telling you, hopefully, that no viruses were found. When was the last time you got a message like that on your Windows machine?

A

UBUNTU DESKTOP CDs FOR AMD64 AND POWERPC USERS

 As I mentioned in Chapter 1, the version of the Ubuntu Desktop CD that comes with this book is designed to work with i386 processors. It will also work with AMD64 processors, albeit not in 64-bit mode. In order to use Ubuntu with AMD64 processors in 64-bit mode, or on PowerPC machines you must get a different disk on your own. There are several ways of doing this: downloading an ISO (disk image) and then burning it to CD yourself, ordering the CD (for free) from Ubuntu, or ordering it from an online Linux CD provider (for a nominal cost).

Downloading and Burning Ubuntu Desktop CD ISOs to CD

To download an ISO of the Ubuntu Desktop CD, go to the Ubuntu download page at www.ubuntu.com/download. On that page, click one of the links for the region in which you happen to be.

On the next page, go to the Desktop CD section at the top of the page, and click either **64-bit PC (AMD64) desktop CD** or **Mac (PowerPC) desktop CD**, depending on the type of machine you have, on the page that appears.

The download will begin immediately after that. Remember that the ISO file you will be downloading is a heavyweight, weighing in at over 600MB, so the download will take a bit of time. Don't count on getting it all down and done before dinner . . . or, if you happen to be using a dial-up Internet connection, before dinner tomorrow. Yikes!

Burning the ISO to CD in Windows

Once the Desktop CD ISO has been downloaded and checked, you need to burn it to CD before you can use it. Although Windows has built-in CD writing capabilities, it does not have the ability to burn ISOs. To burn an ISO to CD in Windows, therefore, you must use a third-party commercial application, such as Nero. If you don't have a commercial disk-burning utility installed on your system, you can instead download the free and handy ISO Recorder, which only works with Windows XP, though a beta version for the new Windows Vista is also available.

To get ISO Recorder for Windows XP, Gold or SP1 (Service Pack 1), go to http://isorecorder.alexfeinman.com/v1.htm, and scroll to the Download section. Once there, click the link at the end of the sentence *ISO Recorder can be downloaded here*. To get ISO Recorder for Windows XP SP2 (Service Pack 2), go to http://isorecorder.alexfeinman.com/v2.htm, and click the **Here is the current build** link near the top of the page. Once the download is complete, double-click the **ISORecorderSetup.msi** file on your hard disk to install it.

After the installation is complete, you can get down to burning your ISO to disk by double-clicking the **ubuntu-*x.xx*-live-amd64.iso** file on your disk (*x.xx* represents the version of the ISO you've downloaded), and selecting **Copy image to CD** in the popup menu. A CD Recording Wizard window, like that in Figure A-1, will then appear.

Figure A-1: Burning an ISO to CD in Windows using ISO Recorder

It is generally considered best if you burn installation or live CDs at a lower speed than the maximum speed allowed by your drive, with 2X to 4X speeds considered optimal. To do so, click the **Recorder Properties** button in the CD Recording Wizard window, and then drag the slider in the properties window that appears down to about 4X. After that, pop a blank CD into the drive, if you don't have one there already, and click the **Next** button. The CD burning process will begin. Once it's done, the CD will pop out of the drive, and you'll have yourself an AMD64-compatible live CD. You can then use it by following the same directions found at the beginning of Chapter 2 for using the live CD that comes with this book.

NOTE *If your CD does not seem to work, there could be a problem with the ISO file you down-loaded. You can check this out by doing an integrity check as explained in Appendix B. Instructions for both Mac and Windows systems are provided.*

Burning the ISO to CD in OS X

To burn an ISO file to CD in OS X, first check to make sure the ISO image is not mounted by opening a Finder window and checking the disk area at the top of the left pane. If it is mounted, a white drive icon will appear in that location. If the drive icon is there, click the arrow next to that entry to eject, or *unmount*, it.

After that, click **Applications** in the same Finder window, and then look for and open the **Utilities** folder. In that folder, find and then double-click **Disk Utility**. If the ISO is not listed in the left pane of the Disk Utility window when it opens, go back to the Finder window, locate the Ubuntu Live CD ISO you just downloaded, and then drag it to the left pane of the Disk Utility window, just below the listings for your current drives. Once the ISO file appears in that list, click it once to highlight it. Your Disk Utility window should then look something like that in Figure A-2.

Figure A-2: Burning the Ubuntu Desktop CD ISO to CD in Mac OS X

To complete the process, click the **Burn** icon in the Disk Utility toolbar, and then insert a blank CD in your drive when prompted to do so in the window that appears. Once the blank disk is inserted and recognized, you will be able to adjust the burn speed by clicking the drop-down menu button next to the word *Speed*. Select as low a speed as your hardware will allow, which, depending on the age of your Mac, will probably be 4X to 8X. Once you've done that, click the **Burn** button in that same window, after which the burning process will begin.

Getting an Install Disk from Ubuntu

The easiest and most foolproof way of getting an Ubuntu Desktop CD is by simply ordering one (or more) for free from Ubuntu—you don't even have to pay shipping or handling. They will not only send you one install CD for your particular machine architecture, but they will actually send you one for each of the architectures they support: i386, AMD64, and PowerPC. In fact, you don't even get a choice of which you want—it's basically an all-or-nothing deal, which in this case isn't such a bad thing. Of course, the only downside of this approach is time. It can take four to six weeks for you to get the CDs in this manner, so if you are the impatient type, you might want to opt for one of the other methods.

To order your install CDs from Ubuntu, go to https://shipit.ubuntu.com, click the **create a new account** link, fill out the simple registration form (you don't have to enter any sensitive information, basically just your name and address), and then select the number of CDs you want. It's all very easy.

Ordering an Install Disk from Other Online Sources

If you are in a hurry to get your install CD, you can also order a copy from one of the many online sources that specialize in copying and selling install CDs for a variety of Linux distributions at very low prices. For example, you can get an Ubuntu install CD from LinuxCD (www.linuxcd.org) for a penny shy of two dollars. CheapBytes (www.cheapbytes.com) and UseLinux (www.uselinux.net) are two other well-known sources you might want to try.

Mac Users: Booting Your Mac from the Ubuntu Desktop CD

Most Mac users are probably aware of this already, but I thought I'd better explain how to boot your machine from the Ubuntu Desktop CD just in case. Insert the CD in your drive, restart the machine, and then after the machine shuts down and before it begins starting up again, press and hold the C key. Once Ubuntu starts booting, you can release the key and follow the onscreen directions. From then on out, the procedures are the same as those for the i386 version mentioned at the beginning of Chapter 2. If you have any problems, check out the Ubuntu forums at www.ubuntuforums.org.

B

CHECKING THE INTEGRITY OF DOWNLOADED ISOs

When you download ISOs, or disk images, via the Internet, it is always a good idea to check the integrity of the download to make sure that all is as it should be. The cautious do this before burning the image to disk. The more impatient or reckless, such as myself, do it only after burning an image to disk and finding out it doesn't work. Since blank CDs are cheap these days, this latter approach really doesn't cost you much more than a bit of time, so the choice is strictly up to you. If you do find yourself wanting or needing to check the integrity of the ISOs you've downloaded, I will provide you with the details for doing so in Windows, Mac, and Linux systems.

Checking the Integrity of an ISO File in Windows

To check the integrity of an ISO in Windows, you need a tiny little DOS program called md5sum, which is also common in the Linux world. This program is not included with Windows, so you'll have to get it and install it yourself.

Fortunately, this is very easy to do. Just go to www.etree.org/md5com.html, and click the **md5sum.exe** link in the top half of the page, after which the md5sum.exe file will soon appear on your hard disk. Once it's there, here are the steps you need to follow in order to check your ISO:

1. Drag the md5sum.exe file to C:\Windows\system32 if you're running Windows XP; C:\winnt\system32 if you're running Windows 2000; or C:\windows\command if you're running Windows 95, 98, or the absolutely dreadful Windows Me.

2. Go to the site from which you downloaded the Ubuntu Desktop CD ISO (www.releases.ubuntu.com/6.06), and scroll down to the bottom of the page, where you will find a list of files in link form. Right-click the **MD5SUMS** link near the top of the list. In the popup menu that appears, select **Save link as** in order to save the file. Once you're done, you should have an MD5SUMS file on your hard disk.

3. Place the MD5SUMS file in the same directory as the Ubuntu Desktop or Install CD ISO, making sure there are no other MD5SUMS files in that directory. To make it easier to follow along with my directions, create a folder named ISO on your desktop, and place both the MD5SUMS file and the ISO in that folder.

4. Open the Command Prompt by going to the Start menu and selecting **All Programs ▶ Accessories ▶ Command Prompt**.

5. In the Command Prompt window, type `cd Desktop\ISO`. After you've done that, press ENTER. Your command prompt should then read something to the effect of `C:\Documents and Settings\rg\cd Desktop\ISO`, though your username will no doubt be different than my *rg*.

6. In the Command Prompt window, now type `md5sum -c MD5SUMS`, and then press ENTER. As the MD5SUMS file contains checksums for all Ubuntu ISOs, you will almost immediately be greeted by a list of ISO files followed by the word `FAILED`. You will notice, however, that your command prompt has not yet returned, meaning that your system is still busy reading what is indeed there. When the checking is all done, your command prompt will return, and the entry for the disk ISO you've downloaded, such as desktop-amd64.iso, should be followed by an `OK`, as in Figure B-1. If so, then you are ready to burn. If not, you'll need to download the file again, this time from a different mirror perhaps. Oh, and don't worry about the `9 out of 10 listed files could not be read` warning near the bottom of the Command Prompt window; you only had one ISO file in the ISO folder, so that explains that.

Figure B-1: Viewing the results of an ISO integrity check in Windows

Checking the Integrity of an ISO File in Mac OS X

Checking the integrity of an ISO in Mac OS X is a bit different from what I've described for Windows, in that OS X does not include md5sum, and there isn't a similar utility that is easy to install. Thus, you will have to go about things in a slightly different, and decidedly un-Maclike, manner. Here are the steps:

1. Go to the site from which you downloaded the Ubuntu Desktop ISO, and scroll down to the bottom of the page, where you will find a list of filenames in link form. Click the **MD5SUMS** link near the top of the list, after which a new page filled with seemingly meaningless text will open. Keep this window open, as you'll need the information on that last line (Figure B-2) in a short while.

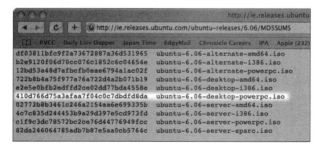

Figure B-2: Viewing the checksum for the Ubuntu Desktop CD for Mac

2. Determine the path to your ISO file by right-clicking the file and selecting **Get Info**. The path to your ISO file will be listed next to the word *Where* in the Get Info window.

3. Now comes the un-Maclike bit. Open a Finder window, click **Applications** in the left panel, and then scroll down and open the **Utilities** folder. Once in that folder, find and then double-click **Terminal**, after which the Terminal application will appear.

4. In the Terminal window type **openssl md5**, plus the path to the ISO file that you found in the Get Info window in step 2, plus the name of the file itself. When you're done, it should all look something like this, although your username (mine is *rg*) and ISO path might be different:

```
openssl md5 /Users/rg/Desktop/Ubuntu-6.06-desktop-powerpc.iso
```

5. Assuming everything looks as it should, press ENTER.

6. The openssl md5 program will then scan the file, which might take a little while, and then it will produce an odd string of numbers, such as that shown in Figure B-3. Compare that string of numbers with those you found on the Ubuntu download site in step 1, and if they match, your ISO is fine and ready for burning. If not, you've got a stinker on your hands and will have to download the file again, perhaps from a different download mirror.

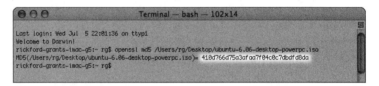

Figure B-3: Viewing the results of the ISO integrity check in OS X

Checking the Integrity of an ISO File in Linux

As a new Ubuntu user, you may not be at the stage where you find yourself downloading ISOs, but that time will no doubt come. For that reason, I am also including instructions on how to check the integrity of an ISO via Linux. Fortunately, the process is quite simple—similar in fact to that mentioned in the Windows section on page 307, though the md5sum application is already included with Ubuntu, so things are even easier. Here's all you need to do:

1. Go to the site from which you downloaded the Ubuntu Desktop CD ISO, and scroll down to the bottom of the page, where you will find a list of files in link form. Right-click the **MD5SUMS** link near the top of the list. In the popup menu that appears, select **Save Link As** in order to save the file. Once you're done, you should have an MD5SUMS file on your hard disk.

2. Place the MD5SUMS file in the same directory as the downloaded ISO, making sure there are no other MD5SUMS files in that directory. To make it easier to follow along with my directions, create an ISO folder on your desktop, and place both the MD5SUMS file and the ISO in that folder.

3. Open a Terminal window (**Applications ▸ Accessories ▸ Terminal**), type **cd Desktop/ISO**, and press ENTER.

4. In the Terminal window, now type **md5sum -c MD5SUMS**, and then press ENTER. As the MD5SUMS file contains checksums for all Ubuntu ISOs, you will almost immediately be greeted by a list of ISO files followed by the word FAILED. You will notice, however, that your command prompt has not yet returned, meaning that your system is still busy reading what is indeed there. When the checking is all done, your command prompt will return, and the entry for the disk ISO you've downloaded should be followed by an OK, as in Figure B-4. If so, then you are ready to burn. If not, you'll need to download the file again, this time from a different mirror perhaps.

```
rg@ubuntuVaio: ~/Desktop/ISO
File  Edit  View  Terminal  Tabs  Help
md5sum: ubuntu-6.06-alternate-i386.iso: No such file or directory
ubuntu-6.06-alternate-i386.iso: FAILED open or read
md5sum: ubuntu-6.06-alternate-powerpc.iso: No such file or directory
ubuntu-6.06-alternate-powerpc.iso: FAILED open or read
md5sum: ubuntu-6.06-desktop-amd64.iso: No such file or directory
ubuntu-6.06-desktop-amd64.iso: FAILED open or read
ubuntu-6.06-desktop-i386.iso: OK  <<<
md5sum: ubuntu-6.06-desktop-powerpc.iso: No such file or directory
ubuntu-6.06-desktop-powerpc.iso: FAILED open or read
md5sum: ubuntu-6.06-server-amd64.iso: No such file or directory
ubuntu-6.06-server-amd64.iso: FAILED open or read
md5sum: ubuntu-6.06-server-i386.iso: No such file or directory
ubuntu-6.06-server-i386.iso: FAILED open or read
md5sum: ubuntu-6.06-server-powerpc.iso: No such file or directory
ubuntu-6.06-server-powerpc.iso: FAILED open or read
md5sum: ubuntu-6.06-server-sparc.iso: No such file or directory
ubuntu-6.06-server-sparc.iso: FAILED open or read
md5sum: WARNING: 9 of 10 listed files could not be read
rg@ubuntuVaio:~/Desktop/ISO$ █
```

Figure B-4: Viewing the results of an ISO integrity check in Linux

RESOURCES

As Linux owes much of its growth and development to the Internet, it should come as no surprise that there is a wealth of information available to you online. In addition to the usual news, how-to, and download sites, you will also find a variety of tutorials, forums, blogs, and other sources of useful information—all of which you can turn to as you use and learn more about your system.

Forums

When you are looking for advice, trying to solve a particular problem, or just looking for some general tips, online forums are the way to go. Fortunately, Ubuntu has a forum all its own, and since Ubuntu is primarily a desktop-oriented Linux distro, you are likely to find many fellow newbies and newbie-friendly posters there, rather than the hard-core geekiness you might find on some other sites. There are, of course, other newbie-friendly forums, which, although not Ubuntu-specific, should also be able to provide you with lots of helpful information.

Regardless of which forum you are posting in, just be sure to mention that you are using Ubuntu, which version you have (Dapper Drake, in case you forgot), and that you are new to Linux. And remember to always seek clarification when you get an answer you don't understand. The same poster will usually come back and clarify things for you. You should feel right at home at most of these sites.

Ubuntu Forums   www.ubuntuforums.org

Ubuntux   www.ubuntux.org/forum

JustLinux   www.justlinux.com

Linux Forum   www.linuxforum.com

LinuxQuestions.org   www.linuxquestions.org

Kubuntu Forums   www.kubuntuforums.net

Linux Reference

These are sites, many of which are geared towards newbies, where you can learn more about using Ubuntu or Linux in general.

Ubuntu Guide   http://ubuntuguide.org/wiki/Dapper

Ubuntu Documentation   https://help.ubuntu.com

tuXfiles   www.tuxfiles.org

LinuxCommand.org   www.linuxcommand.org

Linux Online   www.linux.org

Blogs

A lot of great information can also be found in blogs. In these, you can discover the findings of fellow users as they try new things, share tips, and offer solutions to problems.

Ubuntu Blog   http://ubuntu.wordpress.com

Ubuntux Blog   www.ubuntux.org/blog

linux.blogs   www.linuxblogs.net

Hardware Compatibility Issues

If you want to find out whether or not your hardware is compatible with Linux, or if you want to read up on other matters related to hardware support, take a look at the following sites:

Ubuntu Hardware Support   https://wiki.ubuntu.com/HardwareSupport

Linux Compatible.org   www.linuxcompatible.org/compatibility.html

LinuxPrinting.org   www.linuxprinting.org

Linmodems.org   www.linmodems.org

SANE Project (Scanners)   www.sane-project.org

Linux on Laptops   www.linux-laptop.net

TuxMobil   www.tuxmobil.org

Wireless Connections

If you use a wireless card to connect to the Internet and have trouble getting your card to work or just want to know where all the free wireless hotspots happen to be, the following sites should help.

Wireless LAN Resources for Linux   www.hpl.hp.com/personal/ Jean_Tourrilhes/Linux

EZ Goal WiFi HotSpots   www.ezgoal.com/hotspots/wireless

Free Downloads

If you find yourself looking for more goodies to play around with, you should be able to find plenty of free stuff to download at one of these sites.

Applications and Other Packages

SourceForge.net   http://sourceforge.net

FreshMeat.net   http://freshmeat.net

GnomeFiles   www.gnomefiles.org

Free Fonts

Font Freak   www.fontfreak.com

Font Paradise   www.fontparadise.com

Divide by Zero Fonts   http://fonts.tom7.com

News and Information

These sites are mainly informational, keeping you abreast of what's going on in the Linux world. DistroWatch focuses on the various distributions available out there, whereas Linux Today and LinuxPlanet fit better in the online magazine/newspaper genre.

DistroWatch   www.distrowatch.com

Linux Today   www.linuxtoday.com

LinuxPlanet   www.linuxplanet.com

Magazines

If you are more of a tactile type who enjoys the feel of paper pressed between your fingers, then you might like to turn to some of the Linux magazines available at most major newsstands. (*TUX* comes in PDF form only, so you'll have to get that one online.)

As you will notice, there are two unrelated magazines sharing the same name: *Linux Magazine*. One of these is from the United States, one from Europe. The newbie who wants some pizzazz in his or her reading materials, useful tips, and some things to play around with should go for the Euro version. The US version is targeted toward business users and power geeks, not newbies.

TUX   www.tuxmagazine.com

Linux Magazine (**Euro**)   www.linux-magazine.com

Linux Magazine (**US**)   www.linuxmagazine.com

Linux Journal   www.linuxjournal.com

Books

Once you've finished working through this book, you should be able to do just about whatever you want in Ubuntu. Still, your interest may have been piqued enough that you would like to get deeper into things and find out a bit more about Linux. Here are some books that might help in that quest.

How Linux Works   www.nostarch.com

The Debian System   www.nostarch.com

The Linux Cookbook   www.nostarch.com

Running Linux   www.oreilly.com

Linux Multimedia Hacks   www.oreilly.com

Linux Pocket Guide   www.oreilly.com

OpenOffice.org 2.x Resource Kit   www.phptr.com

Ubuntu CDs

If you would like to order PowerPC or AMD64 versions of the Ubuntu Desktop CD, get a replacement for the i386 version that comes with this book, or get the next version of Ubuntu when it comes out (if you don't want to or can't download it), you can place an order with any of the following sites. Remember that those from Ubuntu will be free, while those from other suppliers will cost you a little ($5 to $12) but will be delivered much faster.

Ubuntu   https://shipit.ubuntu.com

CheapBytes   www.cheapbytes.com

LinuxCD   www.linuxcd.org

INDEX

Mahjongg. *See* Xmahjongg
make clean command, 151, 155
make command, 151, 155
make uninstall command, 155
makefile, 154
malware, 293
Mandrake, 2
Mandriva, 2
master partition, resizing for dual-boot system, 26
Math, 209
md5sum, 307–308
memory card reader, for photo transfers, 220
memory, Linux minimum requirements, 17
menus on GNOME desktop
  adding contents to panel, 39
  manipulation, 40–42
    changing icon order, 42, *42*
    changing icons, 40–42
microphone, for Skype, 160
Microsoft Office, 206
  OpenOffice.org file compatibility with, 209–210
Microsoft Windows. *See* Windows (Microsoft)
mirroring photos in gThumb, 223
mkdir command, 130, 186
modems, 53–54
  compatibility issues, 55–56
  external dial-up, 56
monitor, identifying, 16
Monkey Bubble, 69–70, *70*
motherboard, identifying, 16
mounting Windows partition, 190–191
move (mv) command, 130
  to change filename, 143
MP3 file format, 240
  adding encoding option for Sound Juicer, 243, *243*
  converting to/from Ogg Vorbis format, 278–279, *278*
  installing support, 240–241
  RealPlayer for, 260
  ripper for, 241
MPEG file format, using Totem to play, 285

MSN/Windows Instant Messenger, 63
msttcorefonts package, 189
multilingual environment, 12, 195. *See also* language
  login screen, 199–200
multisession CD, burning, 91–92
  adding additional session, 92
multiverse repositories, 67
mv (move) command, 130
  to change filename, 143

N

names
  for files during CD burn, Windows compatibility, 89
  for folders in Nautilus, 80
Napster, 63
Nautilus, 78–79, *78*
  copying files and folders, 81
  creating, naming and renaming folders, 80
  file and folder permissions within, 85–87
    changing, 86–87
  as FTP client, 85
  moving files and folders, 81
  navigating through folders, 81–83
    bookmarks for, 82–83
    with tabbed browsing, 81–82, *82*
    typing paths, 82
  as network browser, 83–87, *83*
  opening window, 185
  side pane, 78–79, *79*
    customization, 105–106, *106*
    hiding, 79, *80*
Navigator window, 211, *211*
network
  browser, Nautilus as, 83–87, *83*
  interface card for laptop, 50, *50*
  shares, 83
Network icon, 32
network interface card (NIC) 50–52
Network Settings window
  Ethernet connection, 48, *49*
  Modem connection, 54
news and information, web resources, 315
NIC (network interface card), 50–52

Electronic Frontier Foundation
Defending Freedom in the Digital World

Free Speech. Privacy. Innovation. Fair Use. Reverse Engineering. If you care about these rights in the digital world, then you should join the Electronic Frontier Foundation (EFF). EFF was founded in 1990 to protect the rights of users and developers of technology. EFF is the first to identify threats to basic rights online and to advocate on behalf of free expression in the digital age.

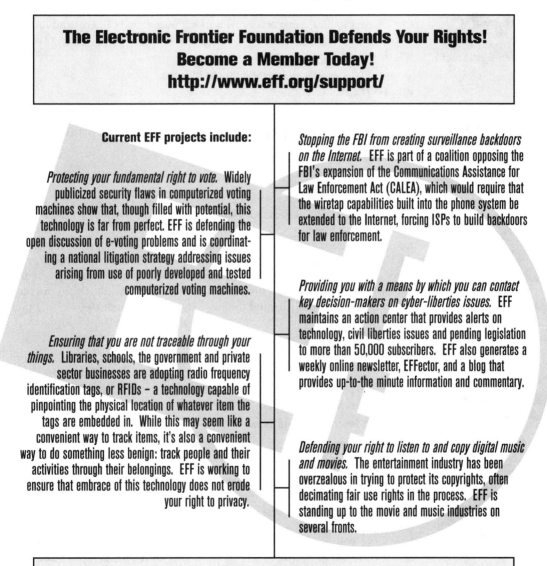

The Electronic Frontier Foundation Defends Your Rights!
Become a Member Today!
http://www.eff.org/support/

Current EFF projects include:

Protecting your fundamental right to vote. Widely publicized security flaws in computerized voting machines show that, though filled with potential, this technology is far from perfect. EFF is defending the open discussion of e-voting problems and is coordinating a national litigation strategy addressing issues arising from use of poorly developed and tested computerized voting machines.

Ensuring that you are not traceable through your things. Libraries, schools, the government and private sector businesses are adopting radio frequency identification tags, or RFIDs – a technology capable of pinpointing the physical location of whatever item the tags are embedded in. While this may seem like a convenient way to track items, it's also a convenient way to do something less benign: track people and their activities through their belongings. EFF is working to ensure that embrace of this technology does not erode your right to privacy.

Stopping the FBI from creating surveillance backdoors on the Internet. EFF is part of a coalition opposing the FBI's expansion of the Communications Assistance for Law Enforcement Act (CALEA), which would require that the wiretap capabilities built into the phone system be extended to the Internet, forcing ISPs to build backdoors for law enforcement.

Providing you with a means by which you can contact key decision-makers on cyber-liberties issues. EFF maintains an action center that provides alerts on technology, civil liberties issues and pending legislation to more than 50,000 subscribers. EFF also generates a weekly online newsletter, EFFector, and a blog that provides up-to-the minute information and commentary.

Defending your right to listen to and copy digital music and movies. The entertainment industry has been overzealous in trying to protect its copyrights, often decimating fair use rights in the process. EFF is standing up to the movie and music industries on several fronts.

Check out all of the things we're working on at http://www.eff.org and join today or make a donation to support the fight to defend freedom online.

ELECTRONIC FRONTIER FOUNDATION · 454 SHOTWELL STREET · SAN FRANCISCO, CA 94110 · 415.436.9333

LINUX MADE EASY
The Official Guide to Xandros 3 for Everyday Users

by RICKFORD GRANT

Based on Xandros 3, arguably one of the most user-friendly versions of Linux available today, *Linux Made Easy* concentrates on the subjects of most interest to the average home user or hobbyist: installation, using the Internet, playing CDs and audio files, using scanners, working with digital cameras and images, games, downloading software and fonts, USB storage devices, PDAs, printing, Internet telephony, and more.

AUGUST 2005, 496 PP. W/CD, $34.95 ($47.95 CDN)
ISBN 1-59327-057-7

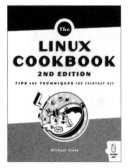

THE LINUX COOKBOOK, 2ND EDITION
Tips and Techniques for Everyday Use

by MICHAEL STUTZ

Linux is cool, but it's not always well documented. There are tons of inconsistent HOWTO files, out-of-date FAQs, and programs scattered everywhere. Whenever you want to do anything with Linux, you usually have to read every piece of documentation out there and basically reverse engineer a solution. Many Linux books for non-geeks are organized by major system, with a chapter on installation, one for video, one for sound, one for networking, and so on. But what if you want to write a book? Or record an album? If you can't dig around on the Web to find someone else doing the same thing, you are out of luck. Unless, that is, you have *The Linux Cookbook.*

AUGUST 2004, 824 PP., $39.95 ($55.95 CDN)
ISBN 1-59327-031-3

HOW LINUX WORKS
What Every Superuser Should Know

by BRIAN WARD

How Linux Works describes the inside of the Linux system for systems administrators, whether they maintain an extensive network in the office or one Linux box at home. After a guided tour of filesystems, the boot sequence, system management basics, and networking, author Brian Ward delves into topics such as development tools, custom kernels, and buying hardware. With a mixture of background theory and real-world examples, this book shows both how to administer Linux, and why each particular technique works, so that you will know how to make Linux work for you.

MAY 2004, 368 PP., $37.95 ($55.95 CDN)
ISBN 1-59327-035-6

THE eBAY PRICE GUIDE
What Sells for What (in Every Category!)

by JULIA L. WILKINSON

More than 140 million people are registered eBay users, creating a vast community of sellers and buyers all looking for the right price. No one wants to pay too much and everyone wants to get what they think they deserve for whatever they're selling. *The eBay Price Guide* is a one-stop shop for pricing information and tips for successful buying and selling on eBay, provided in the book's pages and via the Hammertap software on the included CD. The author has done extensive research to compile this exhaustive guide, which helps readers determine which items will fetch big bucks and which will go for rock-bottom prices. Fun stories, statistics, lists and eBay trivia round out the book. A must-have for the serious eBayer.

JUNE 2006, 608 PP. W/CD, $29.95 ($37.95 CDN)
ISBN 1-59327-055-0

STEAL THIS® COMPUTER BOOK 4.0
What They Won't Tell You About the Internet

by WALLACE WANG

This offbeat, nontechnical book examines what hackers do, how they do it, and how readers can protect themselves. Informative, irreverent, and entertaining, the completely revised fourth edition of *Steal This Computer Book* contains new chapters that discuss the hacker mentality, lock picking, exploiting P2P filesharing networks, and how people manipulate search engines and pop-up ads. Includes a CD with hundreds of megabytes of hacking and security-related programs that tie in to each chapter of the book.

MAY 2006, 384 PP. W/CD, $29.95 ($38.95 CDN)
ISBN 1-59327-105-0

PHONE:
800.420.7240 OR
415.863.9900
MONDAY THROUGH FRIDAY,
9 A.M. TO 5 P.M. (PST)

FAX:
415.863.9950
24 HOURS A DAY,
7 DAYS A WEEK

EMAIL:
SALES@NOSTARCH.COM

WEB:
WWW.NOSTARCH.COM

MAIL:
NO STARCH PRESS
555 DE HARO ST, SUITE 250
SAN FRANCISCO, CA 94107
USA

COLOPHON

Ubuntu Linux for Non-Geeks was laid out in Adobe FrameMaker. The font families used are New Baskerville for body text, Futura for headings and tables, and Dogma for titles.

The book was printed and bound at Malloy Incorporated in Ann Arbor, Michigan. The paper is Glatfelter Thor 50# Antique, which is made from 50 percent recycled materials, including 30 percent postconsumer content. The book uses a RepKover binding, which allows it to lay flat when open.

UPDATES

Visit **www.nostarch.com/ubuntu.htm** for updates, errata, and other information.

For updates to the software and links mentioned in this book, visit **www.edgy-penguins.org/ULFNG**.

ABOUT THE CD

This software is released for free public use under several open source licenses. It is provided without any warranty, without even the implied warranty of merchantability or fitness for a particular purpose. See the license text included with each program for details. Source code for Ubuntu can be downloaded from http://archive.ubuntu.com or can be ordered from Canonical at the cost of the media and shipping. Ubuntu and Canonical are trademarks of Canonical Ltd. All other trademarks are the property of their respective owners.

Ubuntu's official documentation is online (https://help.ubuntu.com), and free technical support is available through web forums (www.ubuntuforums.org), mailing lists (www.ubuntu.com/community/lists), and IRC (#ubuntu). Commercial support is also available from Canonical (www.ubuntu.com/support/paid).

Ubuntu is sponsored by Canonical Ltd. For more information, visit www.ubuntu.com and www.canonical.com. To request free Ubuntu CDs, visit https://shipit.ubuntu.com.

The Intel x86 Edition packaged with this book will run on Intel x86–based systems (including Intel Pentium and AMD Athlon). See the section "Version Compatibility" on page 3 for more information. This and all other versions of Ubuntu are available for download at www.ubuntu.com/download.

No Starch Press does not provide support for Ubuntu. However, if the Ubuntu CD packaged with this book is defective, broken, or missing, you may email info@nostarch.com for a replacement.

You are legally entitled and encouraged to copy, share, and redistribute this CD. Share the spirit of Ubuntu!